G. M. A. RICHTER

THE PORTRAITS OF
THE GREEKS

THE PORTRAITS OF
THE GREEKS

WITH 2100 ILLUSTRATIONS

THE PORTRAITS OF
THE GREEKS

BY

GISELA M·A·RICHTER

VOLUME TWO

THE PHAIDON PRESS

NOV 9 1965 Cooper Union Library
TEXT PRINTED BY GEO. GIBBONS LTD · LEICESTER
ILLUSTRATIONS ENGRAVED BY SCHWITTER A. G. · BASLE
AND PRINTED BY V.S.K. PRINTERS · BASLE
BOUND BY A. W. BAIN & CO. LTD · LONDON · ENGLAND

CONTENTS

VOLUME THREE

CHAPTER THREE

A: THE FOURTH AND THIRD CENTURIES B.C.

1. Statesmen and Generals 2. Philosophers 3. Orators 4. Poets
5. Various Others

The portraits of the fourth to the second century B.C. that are treated in this section include some of the best known figures of their time—Xenophon, Plato, Aristotle, Demosthenes, Menander, Epikouros, Chrysippos, Karneades. In their interesting physiognomies one can watch the gradual increase in perception on the part of the artists as they become more and more able to penetrate into the specific individuality of their subject. Always, however, even in the most realistic of these portraits, there remained a tendency to impart the idealizing, spiritualizing quality that was inherited from the past and which remained a salient characteristic of all Greek portraiture with a few possible exceptions among late Hellenistic rulers.

It is also noteworthy that in this period it seems to have become a common practice to erect portraits of the great men of the distant past—to the Seven Wise Men, for instance.

1. STATESMEN AND GENERALS

XENOPHON

c. 430–c. 354 B.C. Historian and soldier. Son of Gryllos, of the Athenian deme of Erchia, and of Diodora.

LIFE

He early became a pupil of Sokrates.

401 B.C. On the invitation of his friend Proxenos, a friend of Cyrus, he went to Sardes 'and became as warmly attached to Cyrus as Proxenos himself', καὶ τοῦ Προξένου φίλος οὐχ ἧττον ἦν αὐτῷ (Diog. Laert. II, 50), and presently joined the expedition of Cyrus against Artaxerxes. After the murder of the generals, he was chosen to lead the army to Trapezus in the famous march of the Ten Thousand (cf. the *Anabasis*).

396 Served under the Spartan king Agesilaos.

394 Accompanied Agesilaos to Greece. Fought at the battle of Koroneia. Banished by the Athenians for siding with Sparta (Diog. Laert. II, 51).

394–371 Settled down on an estate at Skillos, near Olympia, with his wife and his two sons Gryllos and Diodoros. 'Spent his time in hunting, entertaining his friends, and working on his histories', τοὐντεῦθεν διετέλει κυνηγετῶν καὶ τοὺς φίλους ἑστιῶν καὶ τὰς ἱστορίας συγγράφων (Diog. Laert. II, 52).

c. 371 After the Eleans captured Skillos, he went to Corinth, doubtless with occasional visits to Athens, since the decree for his banishment had been rescinded when Athens concluded an alliance with Sparta (Xenoph., *Hell.* VI, 5, 49; 7, 1). His sons served in the Athenian army, and Gryllos died in the battle of Mantineia (Diog. Laert. II, 54).

c. 354 Xenophon died at Corinth (Demetrios Magnes, in Diog. Laert. II, 56).

CHARACTER AND APPEARANCE

Diogenes Laertios sums up Xenophon's character as follows: 'He was a worthy man in general, particularly fond of horses and hunting, an able tactician as is clear from his writings, pious, fond of sacrificing, and an expert in augury from the victims; and he made Sokrates his exact model' (II, 56). In II, 48, Diogenes calls Xenophon a man of rare modesty and extremely handsome, αἰδήμων δὲ καὶ εὐειδέστατος εἰς ὑπερβολήν.

Of his writings the best known are the *Anabasis*, the famous account of the Greek mercenaries in Asia; the *Hellenika*, a history from c. 411 to 362 B.C.; and the *Kyroupaideia*, the education of Cyrus. His attachment to Sokrates is shown in his *Memorabilia*, *Apology*, and *Symposion*. His manual on horsemanship, Περὶ ἱππικῆς, is 'the oldest complete treatise existing on the subject', and his *Oikonomikos* gives a charming account of his life at Skillos and his ideas on estate management.

The high regard in which his writings were held, at least in Roman times, is indicated by Diogenes Laertios' remark (II, 57) that he was named the Attic Muse on account of the sweetness (γλυκύτητι) of his narrative (τῆς ἑρμηνείας). He has been called an amateur historian, an amateur philosopher, an amateur economist, but a master of military tactics, especially of cavalry. As has often been said, he came perhaps nearest among the Greeks to an English country gentleman.

STATUES RECORDED

Pausanias V, 6, 6 gives the only record of a statue erected to Xenophon: 'At a little distance from the sanctuary (of Olympia) was shown a tomb, and upon the grave is a statue of marble from the Pentelic quarry. The neighbours say that it is the tomb of Xenophon', καὶ δὴ καὶ ὀλίγον ἀπωτέρω τοῦ ἱεροῦ μνῆμά τε ἐδείκνυτο καὶ τῆς Πεντελῆσίν ἐστι λιθοτομίας εἰκὼν ἐπὶ τῷ τάφῳ· εἶναι δὲ αὐτὸ Ξενοφῶντος λέγουσιν οἱ προσοικοῦντες.

IDENTIFICATION

With so little to go by for identifying portraits of Xenophon it is not surprising that the most varied suggestions were made; cf. those cited by Bernoulli (II, p. 8) and Studniczka (J.H.S. XLIII, 1923, p. 65), mostly of people who had a mild expression and were clearly not philosophers or poets. Then, in 1949, hypotheses were laid to rest when Adriani published a marble herm, inscribed Ξενοφῶν, which he had discovered in 1940 at the antiquary Abe Mayor, in Cairo, and found there again at the end of the war. Now in the Museum of Alexandria.   FIGS. 882–884
Height 46 cm.
No restorations.
Adriani, Arch. cl. I, 1949, pp. 39ff., pl. XI.

As Adriani says, though there were of course other men named Xenophon, the historian is the only one with sufficient fame in Roman times to come into consideration. For a coin with the head of Xenophon of Kos, a physician of the emperor Claudius, cf. Schefold, B., p. 173, no. 32, and my p. 284.

Only one replica has so far been recognized: Head, mounted on a modern herm, in the Prado, Madrid, inv. 316. From the Azara Collection.   FIGS. 885–887
Height of head 38 cm. (slightly more than life-size).
Restorations: Nose, lower lip, parts of ears and of beard, pieces in the neck and elsewhere.
Hübner, no. 177.
Ricard, no. 110.
Blanco, Cat., no. 100E, pl. L.
Adriani, Arch. cl. I, 1949, p. 40, pl. XLI.

The person represented in these two portraits is after all what one might expect Xenophon to have looked—a man of distinction, of a studious bent, but not original in thought. The style suggests the last decades of the fourth century

B.C. So the original Greek statue was probably erected after Xenophon's death, perhaps from sketches made when he was about 40 years old.

PHOKION

c. 402–318 B.C. Athenian general and statesman. Opponent of Demosthenes in his anti-Macedonian policy. A distinguished orator. Aristocratic in his leanings.
318 B.C. Was arrested for high treason and condemned to drink the hemlock (cf. Lenschau, R.E. XXI, 1 (1941), col. 471).

APPEARANCE

Plutarch (Phokion, 4f.) characterizes him as highly cultured, competent, and austere. His expression is described as severe; and in his dress he is said to have shown a Spartan simplicity.

STATUE RECORDED

According to Plutarch (Phokion, 38): 'After a short time had passed, and when the course of events was teaching them what a patron and guardian of moderation and justice the people had lost, they set up a statue of him in bronze, and gave his bones a public burial', καὶ μέντοι χρόνου βραχέος διαγενομένου . . . ἀνδριάντα μὲν αὐτοῦ χαλκοῦν ἀνέστησαν, ἔθαψαν δὲ δημοσίοις τέλεσι τὰ ὀστᾶ.

ATTEMPTED IDENTIFICATIONS

Visconti (Museo Pio-Clem. II, p. 274, pl. XLIII) identified the statue in the Sala della Biga, Vatican (my figs. 892–893; Helbig, F.³, no. 325; Helbig, F.⁴-Speier, no. 502; Amelung, Vat. Kat. I, pp. 661f., no. 531; Arndt-Br., 281, 282) as Phokion, chiefly on account of the simplicity of the dress. But statue and head have since been shown not to belong together. (On this question cf. Bernoulli II, pp. 57ff.) That the individual portrayed in the head was, however, a prominent general is indicated by the fact that there are two replicas: in the Chiaramonti Museum of the Vatican (Amelung, Vat. Kat. I, pp. 661f., no. 531, pl. 70) and in the Metropolitan Museum (Richter, MMA Sc. Cat., no. 104). The head in the Terme Museum (my fig. 890; Felletti Maj, Ritratti, no. 2) is a 'near replica'.

A possible candidate for Phokion might be—as suggested by V. Poulsen, Port. gr., no. 15—the head in Copenhagen (I.N. 1658, Cat., no. 440) which has at least a severe expression.   FIG. 891

On a modern cameo, once in the possession of Cardinal Al. Albani (Reinach, Pierres gravées, pl. 136, no. 56), is represented the bust of a beardless man inscribed Φωκίωνος, the work of the sixteenth century engraver Al. Cesari (or Ceseti); cf. Bernoulli II, p. 59. Presumably on a supposed similarity to this head, another stone, in the Marlborough Collection (Reinach, op. cit., pl. 110), was identified as Phokion. It too is a work by Al. Cesari; cf. Bernoulli II, p. 59.

Three generals who fought for Athens against Sparta during the first half of the fourth century distinguished themselves sufficiently to have statues erected in their honour: Chabrias, Iphikrates, and Timotheos.

CHABRIAS

Before 400–357 B.C. Son of Ktesippos. From the Attic deme Aixone. Fought for Athens and the rebel kings of Cyprus and Egypt.

378 B.C. Was one of the commanders of the army sent by Athens to aid Thebes against Sparta. He adopted the manoeuvre for which he became famous, that of ordering his soldiers to await the attack of the enemy with spears pointed and shields resting on one knee (cf. Corn. Nepos and Diodoros, quoted below). He thereby turned a probable defeat into a victory.

376 Victory over Sparta at the battle of Naxos.

366 Acquitted of the charge of treachery.

357 Died fighting during the battle of Chios.

STATUES RECORDED

Cornelius Nepos, *Chabrias*, 1, 2–3: Reliquam phalangem loco vetuit cedere, obnixoque genu scuto, projecta hasta impetum excipere hostium docuit.... Hoc usque eo tota Graecia fama celebratum est, ut illo statu Chabrias sibi statuam fieri voluerit, quae publice ei ab Atheniensibus in foro constituta est, 'Chabrias ordered the phalanx not to give ground and instructed them to support their shields on their knees and thrust their spears forward and so receive the attack of the enemy. . . . This feat became so famous throughout Greece that Chabrias expressed a wish that the statue that was set up publicly in his honour by the Athenians in the market place should be made in this posture' (cf. Wycherley, *Testimonia*, no. 694).

The statue was also mentioned by Aristotle, *Rhet.*, 3, 1411b. Diodoros XV, 33, 4, even speaks of several statues in that position having been erected: . . . καὶ τὰς εἰκόνας τὰς ὑπὸ τοῦ δήμου δοθείσας αὐτῷ καθίστανεν, ἐχούσας τοῦτο τὸ σχῆμα. Cf. also Polyainos II, 1, 2.

This achievement was recalled by Aischines (*Ktesiph.*, 243) when Chabrias was attacked: ἐπερώτησον δὴ τοὺς δικαστάς, εἰ ἐγίγνωσκον Χαβρίαν καὶ 'Ιφικράτην καὶ Τιμόθεον, καὶ πυθοῦ παρ' αὐτῶν, διὰ τί τὰς δωρεὰς αὐτοῖς ἔδοσαν καὶ τὰς εἰκόνας ἔστησαν, 'Ask the jury if they know Chabrias, Iphikrates, and Timotheos, and learn from them why they gave rewards and set up statues to them'. Cf. Wycherley, *Testimonia*, no. 693.

PORTRAIT ONCE EXTANT

Headless herm, supposedly in the Vatican, inscribed Χαβρ-(ίας), Κτησ(ίππου), Αἰξων (Αἰξω[νεύς]?) 'Chabrias, the son of Ktesippos, of the deme of Aixone', in three lines. Cf. Visconti, *Mus. Pio-Clementino* I, p. 51, note; *C.I.G.*, 6123;

Bernoulli II, p. 13; Lippold, *Vat. Kat.* III, 1, p. 99.

The herm cannot now be found in the Vatican, in spite of Miss Speier's searchings.

A number of fragments of an inscribed base found in the Athenian agora may have belonged to the statue of Chabrias referred to by Aischines, Cornelius Nepos, and others; cf. Schweigert, *Hesperia* IX, 1940, pp. 314ff., Burnett and Edmondson, *Hesperia* XXX, 1961, pp. 74ff., and especially pp. 89ff. The name of Chabrias is unfortunately missing, but there is much supporting evidence.

For a recent suggestion that Chabrias' statue was not represented crouching but erect, cf. Anderson, *A.J.A.* LXVII, 1963, pp. 411ff.

Though attempts have been made to associate Chabrias' statue with figures represented on gems in a half kneeling position (cf. Cades 33, 158, 162, 159–161) this has not proved successful.

IPHIKRATES

415–353 B.C. Athenian general. Distinguished himself against Sparta during the Corinthian war.

First established the importance of peltasts.

Served also as a mercenary in Thrace. Married a daughter of the Thracian king Kotys.

367–364 Failed to relieve Amphipolis (together with Chabrias and Timotheos). Was impeached and acquitted.

STATUES RECORDED

Statues of Iphikrates, and of the generals Chabrias and Timotheos are mentioned by Aeschines (*Ktesiph.*, 243) and Demosthenes (*Aristokrates*, 198) when their achievements are recalled during their impeachment (cf. *supra*).

Demosthenes (*Aristokrat.* XXIII, 130) refers to the many honours that had been bestowed on Iphikrates, among them also a statue erected for him: ἴστε δήπου τοῦτ', . . . ὅτι χαλκῆς εἰκόνος οὔσης παρ' ὑμῖν 'Ιφικράτει καὶ σιτήσεως ἐν πρυτανείῳ καὶ δωρειῶν καὶ τιμῶν ἄλλων, δι' ἃς εὐδαίμων ἐκεῖνος ἦν.

ATTEMPTED IDENTIFICATION

Mariani (*Bull. com.* XXX, 1902, pp. 3ff.) suggested that the so-called Pastoret head in Copenhagen (cf. p. 101, under Xanthippos) represented Iphikrates.

TIMOTHEOS

Before c. 400–354 B.C. Son of Konon and a Thracian mother (Athen. XIII, 577a). Athenian general. Served also for Persia against Egypt. A friend of Isokrates. Was brought up in Cyprus.

378 B.C. Was elected strategos.

375–374 Distinguished himself in an expedition to Kerkyra (Diodoros XV, 47).

373 Was given the command against Sparta.

363 Raised the siege of Kyzikos (Nepos, *Timoth.*, I, 3.: Cyzicum obsidione liberavit; Diodoros xv, 81, 6: Τιμόθεος . . . Κυζικηνοῖς δὲ πολιορκουμένοις ἐβοήθησε.

STATUES RECORDED

Aischines (*Ktesiph.*, 243) says that Timotheos was honoured with a statue because of his successful cruise to Kerkyra: Τιμοθέῳ δὲ διὰ τὸν περίπλουν τὸν εἰς Κέρκυραν. Cf. *supra*. According to Pausanias (I, 3, 2), there was a statue of Timotheos, together with one of his father Konon (cf. p. 107), and one of Evagoras, king of Cyprus (who had helped Konon to defeat the Spartans off Knidos in 394 B.C.), near the royal stoa, in the Athenian agora: πλησίον δὲ τῆς στοᾶς Κόνων ἕστηκε καὶ Τιμόθεος υἱὸς Κόνωνος καὶ βασιλεὺς Κυπρίων Εὐαγόρας.

Corn. Nep., *Timoth.* II, 3: cuius laudis ut memoria maneret Timotheo publice statuam in foro posuerunt. This must be the same statue as that mentioned by Pausanias.

Pausanias (I, 24, 3) cites a statue of Timotheos, as well as one of his father Konon, on the Athenian Akropolis: ἐνταῦθα καὶ Τιμόθεος ὁ Κόνωνος καὶ αὐτὸς κεῖται Κόνων; and again (VI, 3, 16) he mentions bronze statues of Konon and Timotheos at Samos and Ephesos. See also under Konon.

PORTRAIT ONCE EXTANT

On a base, now lost, once in the Villa Mattei, was an inscription: Τιμόθεος Ἀθην ... Πολυκρ.... Cf. Spon, *Misc.*, p. 135; Visconti, *Ic. gr.* I, p. 203; Loewy, *Inschriften*, no. 482; Kaibel, *I.G.* xiv, 1149; Bernoulli II, p. 14.

The base belongs to the same group as that inscribed 'Dion' (cf. p. 244), and like it evidently is of Roman date, and either supported the actual statue of Timotheos by the sculptor Polykrates (=perhaps the Athenian sculptor mentioned by Pliny, xxxiv, 91), or a copy of it. See under Dion, p. 244.

ATTEMPTED IDENTIFICATION

Six (*Röm. Mitt.* xxvii, 1912, pp. 67ff., pl. I) suggested that the head on a coin of Kyzikos (*B.M.C.*, Mysia, p. 33, no. 103, pl. viii, 9) was intended for Timotheos, since he had raised the siege of Kyzikos in 363 B.C. (see above).   FIG. 897 He, moreover, saw a resemblance to this head in a marble portrait in the Capitoline Museum, no. 46 (Stuart Jones, *Cat.*, p. 242, no. 56; Arndt-Br., 367–368) and so thought that this too might represent Timotheos.

ARCHIDAMOS III

King of Sparta, c. 400–338 B.C. Son of Agesilaos.

After the battle of Leuktra, 371 B.C., he successfully brought back the beaten army to Sparta (Xen., *Hell.* VI, 4, 17f.; 4, 26). Took his father's place in several campaigns, and continued the fighting in Arcadia and against the Thebans after he became king.

Lost his life in southern Italy in an attempt to help the Tarentines against the Lucanians and Messapians (338 B.C.). The fact that Isokrates appealed to him in 356 B.C. to establish peace among the Greeks and to lead them in an expedition against the 'barbarians' shows that he was a leading man of his time.

STATUES RECORDED

1. Pausanias (VI, 4, 9): 'By the side of Sodamas stands Archidamos, son of Agesilaos, king of the Lacedaemonians. Before this Archidamos, no king, as far as I could learn, had his statue set up by the Lacedaemonians, at least outside the boundaries of the country. They sent the statue of Archidamos to Olympia chiefly, in my opinion, on account of his death, because he met his end in a foreign land, and is the only king of Sparta who is known to have missed burial', παρὰ δὲ Σωδάμαν Ἀρχίδαμος ἕστηκεν ὁ Ἀγησιλάου, Λακεδαιμονίων βασιλεύς. πρὸ δὲ τοῦ Ἀρχιδάμου τούτου βασιλέως εἰκόνα οὐδενὸς ἔν γε τῇ ὑπερορίᾳ Λακεδαιμονίους ἀναθέντας εὕρισκον· Ἀρχιδάμου δὲ ἄλλων τε καὶ τῆς τελευτῆς ἐμοὶ δοκεῖν ἕνεκα ἀνδριάντα ἐς Ὀλυμπίαν ἀπέστειλαν ὅτι ἐν βαρβάρῳ* τε ἐπέλαβεν αὐτὸν τὸ χρεὼν καὶ βασιλέων μόνος τῶν ἐν Σπάρτῃ δῆλός ἐστιν ἁμαρτὼν τάφου.

2. A little later (VI, 15, 7) Pausanias seems to mention another statue of Archidamos; at least there is no reference to the one cited before: 'There is also a statue set up of Archidamos, the son of Agesilaos, and of some man or other in the guise of hunter', ἀνάκειται δὲ καὶ Ἀρχίδαμος ὁ Ἀγησιλάου καὶ ἀνὴρ ὅστις δὴ θηρεύοντος παρεχόμενος σχῆμα.

3. Athenaios xiii, 591b mentions 'a statue of Archidamos, king of the Lacedaemonians' as standing at Delphi, near one of Phryne and one of Philip of Macedon. It is not stated whether this was Archidamos III, but since Phryne and Philip both lived in the second half of the fourth century, it seems likely that the later rather than the earlier Archidamos was here represented.

PORTRAIT PERHAPS EXTANT

A herm in the National Museum, Naples, inv. 6156, found at Herculaneum, in the villa of the Pisoni, represents a man wearing a cuirass and baldric. A painted inscription on the right shoulderpiece, in small letters difficult to decipher, was first read Ἀρχιμ[ήδης] (=Archimedes), then, in 1888 by Wolters, Ἀρχίδαμ[ος] (=Archidamos). The cuirass is of course more appropriate for a king and general than for a mathematician. More letters have by now disappeared.

                   FIGS. 888–889

Height 55 cm.; ht. of head 32 cm.

No restorations.

Comparetti and De Petra, *La Villa ercolanese*, p. 276, pl. xxi, 5. Wolters, *Röm. Mitt.* III, 1888, pp. 113ff. pl. iv. Bernoulli I, p. 121, pl. xii.

*Hitzig-Blumner, *Pausanias*, emended [τῇ] βαρβάρων.

Ruesch, *Guida*, no. 1148.

Arndt-Br. 765, 766.

Laurenzi, *Ritr. gr.*, no. 35.

Since there are several Spartan kings named Archidamos, the question arises which of them was here represented. At first Archidamos II (468–427 B.C.)—who had saved Sparta at the time of the insurrection of the helots, who had tried to prevent the Peloponnesian War, and who had subsequently laid Attica waste—was favoured. But Archidamos III, grandson of Archidamos II, is now thought to be the more likely person, first because the style of the head points to the fourth, not the fifth, century B.C., and second, because a number of statues are mentioned by ancient authors as having been erected to him (cf. above, p. 160).

Archidamos III, if it is he, is represented on the Naples herm as a man of about 40, with a flowing beard and long locks, small, deep-set, observant eyes, and a determined mouth. His rather uninteresting personality is in marked contrast to the intellectual Greeks whom one mostly sees portrayed in the fourth century. The style of the head corresponds to the time of Archidamos' death in 338 B.C., when a statue is said to have been erected to him at Olympia (cf. *supra*). One may compare the portrait of Xenophon, for instance.

MAUSSOLOS AND ARTEMISIA

Satrap of Caria under Artaxerxes from 377 to 353 B.C. Son of Hekatomnos. Made himself virtual ruler of Caria. Joined in the revolt against Artaxerxes Mnemon. Conquered much of Lydia and Ionia. Removed the Carian capital from Mylasa to Halikarnassos.

His wife and sister. Ruled after her husband's death, 353–351.

Two colossal statues, found in the Mausoleum of Halikarnassos by Sir Charles Newton in 1856–7, have generally been identified as Maussolos and Artemisia. Now in the British Museum. FIGS. 899–902

Height of Maussolos 2·99 m.; ht. of head 36·7 cm.

Height of Artemisia 2·91 m.; face is missing.

Restorations: in Maussolos, 'the side of the head and such repairs as were necessary for piecing together the fragments' (A. H. Smith, *loc. cit.*); in Artemisia, the right knee and the adjoining drapery.

The two statues were found in many fragments (the Maussolos in 74, cf. Newton, *Röm. Mitt.* I, 1886, p. 188).

Newton, *Travels and Discoveries* II, pp. 114ff., pls. 8–10; *History of Discoveries* II, p. 214.

A. H. Smith, *Cat.* II, pp. 91ff., nos. 1000, 1001, and the references there cited.

Picard, *Manuel* IV, 2, pp. 77ff.

Bieber, *Sc. of the Hell. Age*, pp. 71f.

Riemann, in *R.E.* XXIV, 1963, s.v. Pytheos, cols. 439ff.

According to Pliny (XXXVI, 30), the Mausoleum of Halikarnassos, which ranked in ancient times as one of the seven wonders of the world, was built by Artemisia in memory of her husband, and was voluntarily completed by the

artists after her death. The architects are said to have been Satyros and Pythios, who also wrote a book on the building (Vitruvius, VII, Praef., 12). The frieze that decorated the tomb on the four sides was executed by Skopas, Bryaxis, Timotheos, and Leochares. According to two Byzantine writers, Maussolos himself began the building of the tomb.

The position of the two statues in the building has been much discussed. According to Pliny, loc. cit., 'the colonnade was surmounted by a pyramid equal to the lower structure in height, with a flight of twenty-four steps tapering to a point. On the apex stands a four-horse chariot in marble, the work of Pythis', in summo est quadriga marmorea, quam fecit Pythis. When excavated by Newton, 'the fragments of the horses, of the two colossal figures, and parts of the chariot wheel, together with a large number of steps of the pyramid and fragments of the cornice were found in a confused heap on the outer side of the north wall of the peribolos. The cramps and other fragments of bronze had not been removed, and all seemed to indicate that the contents of the heap had fallen together from the summit of the building and were lying as they fell' (A. H. Smith, *Cat.* II, pp. 89f., who adds, however, that 'some sculptures were found intermixed which did not belong to the chariot group').

After Newton's time the connexion of the statues with the chariot was disputed on the grounds that the horses are too large for the figures, that the Maussolos and Artemisia are not standing as if holding reins, and that the statues were not carved to be seen from such a height; cf. Stark, *Philologus* XXI, 1864, pp. 464ff.; P. Gardner, *J.H.S.* XIII, 1892–93, pp. 188ff., who preferred to think that the two colossal figures were placed inside the cella as cult statues; and this opinion has prevailed with many authorities ever since. One may ask, however, was then the chariot empty? It is true that Pliny mentions no occupants, but this may be explained by the fact that he did not consider it necessary, for an empty chariot would certainly have been an unusual crowning feature of a great monument. And to place in it merely some charioteer also seems meaningless. The many pieces in which it is known that the Maussolos was broken also perhaps point to the statue falling from a height, instead of quietly standing in the cella. And there are two further considerations which seem to point to the statues having been associated with the chariot (both cited by Riemann, loc. cit.): (1) Measurements have shown that the scale of the head of Maussolos concurs with that of the horses' heads; (2) the chiselling away of the projecting folds on the left side of Maussolos' mantle (cf. von Lorentz, 'Maussolos', fig. 1), which suggests contact with another object such as the chariot, and which would not have been necessary in a figure standing in the cella or in the temenos. Cf. von Gerkan, *Gött. Gel. Anz.* CCXIV, p. 6.

The two statues are among the few Greek original portraits that have survived. The type of head of the Maussolos (the face of Artemisia is missing) is somewhat un-Greek (one may note the long hair combined with a short beard, and the full cheeks), but on the whole it follows Greek tradition. It brings before us the dignified figure of the energetic Carian ruler, called by Lucian (*Dial. mort.*, 24) 'goodlooking, tall, and valiant in war', καλὸς ἦν καὶ μέγας καὶ ἐν πολέμοις κρατερός.

Though some doubts of the identity of Maussolos have been raised from time to time, one may ask, as Bernoulli did, who else could he be?

At all events, as a Greek portrait statue definitely datable c. 350 B.C. the Maussolos has become a valuable point of departure for the fourth-century chronology in this field. Six (*Röm. Mitt.* XIV, 1899, p. 81, and G. F. Hill, in *Anatolian Studies presented to Sir W. M. Ramsay* (1923), pp. 207ff.), have thought that there is a similarity between the head of Herakles on some fourth-century coins of Kos (my fig. 898; *British Museum Cat., Caria*, pp. 194f., pl. XXX, nos. 6ff.) and that of Maussolos, who at that time was the ruler of the island. Cf. on this theory also Bernoulli II, p. 42, note 1; Nock, *J.H.S.* XLVIII, 1928, p. 32.

For a suggestion that Satyros was the sculptor of the statues of Maussolos and Artemisia cf. Bieber in *Anthemion, Scritti archeologici e filologici in onore di Carlo Anti* (1954), pp. 3ff.; and for the suggestion that it was Bryaxis cf. Neugebauer, *J.d.I.* LVIII, 1943, pp. 49ff., and Buschor, *Maussolos und Alexander*, 1950, pp. 21ff.; *contra* Picard, *Manuel* IV, 2, pp. 84ff.

A headless, colossal statue (height c. 2m.), found at Kerch and now in the Hermitage, recalls the Maussolos in the rendering of the folds of the mantle, and probably dates from the same period, that is, the middle of the fourth century. This was a period of great prosperity in the Bosphorus (cf. Rostovtzeff, *Iranians and Greeks*, p. 69). Waldhauer (*J.H.S.* XLIV, 1924, p. 51, fig. 5), therefore thought that the figure probably represented a distinguished Bosphorian, perhaps one of the rulers of that time, possibly *Leukon* (389/8–349/8) or *Pairisades I* (349/8–310/9).

OLYMPIODOROS

Athenian archon 294/3 and 293/2, doubtless identical with the general of that name.

LIFE

Led heroic attacks against Macedonians.

c. 301 Delivered Elateia in Phokis from Kassandros of Macedon (Paus. I, 26, 3; X, 18, 7; X, 34, 3).

Succeeded in making a defensive alliance with Aitolia (Paus. I, 26, 3).

294/3 and 293/2 Was archon (Dion. of Halikarnassos).

In a decree, substantial parts of which have been recovered, Olympiodoros is cited as the archon of that year (*I.G.* II–III², 649; Dinsmoor, *The Archons of Athens*, pp. 7ff.; Kirchner, *Gnomon* VIII, 1932, pp. 449ff.; Ferguson, *Athen. tribal cycl.* 22, 62, 69).

288 Delivered Athens from Macedonian occupation by storming the Mouseion (Paus. I, 26, 2; I, 29, 13).

c. 286 Freed the Piraeus and Munychia from Macedonian occupation (Paus. I, 26, 3).

286 'When the Macedonians were raiding Eleusis he collected a force of Eleusinians and defeated the Macedonian invaders' (Paus. I, 26, 3).

Diogenes Laertios (VI, 23) apparently refers to him when he cites an Ὀλυμπιόδωρος ὁ Ἀθηναίων προστατήσας, 'who once served as a magistrate of the Athenians'.

STATUES RECORDED

For his exploits Olympiodoros was held in great esteem, and several portraits are known to have been erected to him:

1. On the Akropolis of Athens (Paus. I, 26, 3; I, 25, 2).
2. In the Prytaneion of Athens (Paus. I, 26, 3).
3. At Eleusis (*ibid.*).
4. A bronze statue at Delphi, dedicated by the grateful Phokians at Elateia (*ibid.*).

'Olympiodoros has not only honours at Athens, both on the Akropolis and in the town hall, but also a painted portrait at Eleusis. The Phocians too of Elateia dedicated at Delphi a bronze statue of Olympiodoros for help in their revolt against Kassandros', Ὀλυμπιοδώρῳ δὲ τοῦτο μὲν ἐν Ἀθήναις εἰσὶν ἔν τε ἀκροπόλει καὶ ἐν πρυτανείῳ τιμαί, τοῦτο δὲ ἐν Ἐλευσῖνι γραφή· καὶ Φωκέων οἱ Ἐλάτειαν ἔχοντες χαλκοῦν Ὀλυμπιόδωρον ἐν Δελφοῖς ἀνέθεσαν, ὅτι καὶ τούτοις ἤμυνεν ἀποστᾶσι Κασσάνδρου.

PORTRAIT EXTANT

A herm inscribed Ὀλυμπιόδωρος was found at Caesarea in Palestine, together with one of Sophokles of about the same dimensions (cf. p. 127, no. 24). It was formerly in the collection of Baron Ustinow at Jaffa and is now in the National Museum, Oslo.   FIGS. 894–896

Height 51 cm.; ht. of head 26·5 cm.

No restorations.

Tiersch, *Zeitschrift des deutschen Palästinavereins*, 1914, pp. 62ff., pl. XIII, 1, 2.

F. Poulsen, *Collection Ustinow*, pp. 21ff., figs. 23–25.

Hekler, *B.b.G.*, p. 33, figs. 28–29; 3rd ed., p. 65, figs. 52, 53.

Katalog over Skulptur, Nasjonalgalleriet, Oslo (1952), no. 4.

No replicas of this head have so far been identified.

The Ustinow head represents an energetic, able man, between 40 and 50 years old, with a domed skull, small eyes placed close together between overhanging brows, sparse strands of hair descending over the forehead, a small mouth, and a close-clipped beard. The serious, commanding expression fits well what little is known of the statesman-general Olympiodoros, and the style of the head should be early in the third century B.C., in the vicinity of that of Demosthenes. There seems to be no doubt, therefore, that, though the name was not uncommon, the portrait represents the greatly honoured general of that period.

Which of the several portraits that were erected for him the extant head reproduces there is no telling. The Roman collector in Palestine may have acquired it in Athens or elsewhere.

DEMETRIOS

Of Phaleron, c. 350–c. 280 B.C. Son of Phanostratos. Peripatetic philosopher, writer, orator, statesman. Not of noble birth (Diog. Laert. v, 75).
Pupil of Theophrastos (Cicero, *de fin.* v, 54, etc.).
In 317 B.C. was made absolute ruler by Kassandros, and governed Athens for 10 peaceful years.
During his tenure he passed the anti-luxury decree against the erection of elaborate tombstones.
307 When Poliorketes took Athens, Demetrios fled first to Boeotia, and then to Egypt, where Ptolemy Soter befriended him. Became librarian of the Museum of Alexandria. During this period he must have composed his many writings (Diog. Laert. v, 80). Also at this time he is said to have lost his eyesight and to have recovered it through Sarapis (Diog. Laert. v, 76).
Fell into disgrace under Ptolemy Philadelphos.
Died from the bite of a poisonous snake.

STATUES RECORDED

In recognition of his services it is said that 360 bronze statues of him were erected, representing him either on horseback, or driving a chariot or a pair of horses: καὶ εἰκόνων ἠξιώθη χαλκῶν ἑξήκοντα πρὸς ταῖς τριακοσίαις ὧν αἱ πλείους ἐφ' ἵππων ἦσαν καὶ ἁρμάτων καὶ συνωρίδων (Diog. Laert. v, 75).
All the statues erected in his honour in Athens were subsequently destroyed, except one, which in the time of Diogenes Laertios stood on the Akropolis (Diog. Laert. v, 77). When Demetrios was told of the destruction of his statues, he is said to have replied: 'That they may do, but the merits which caused them to be erected they cannot destroy', οὗτος ἀκούσας ὅτι τὰς εἰκόνας αὐτοῦ κατέστρεψαν Ἀθηναῖοι, 'ἀλλ' οὐ τὴν ἀρετήν' ἔφη, 'δι' ἣν ἐκείνας ἀνέστησαν'. (Diog. Laert. v, 82).

APPEARANCE

About his appearance we only know that he was good-looking and fond of good things—not enough of a clue for recognizing his portrait.

EXTANT REPRESENTATION

On one of the silver cups from Boscoreale in the Louvre the skeleton of Demetrios is shown opposite to those of the two Cynic philosophers Monimos and Krates (H. de Villefosse, *Mon. Piot* v, 1899, pp. 66f.; Schefold, *B.*, pp. 166f.). Demetrios is represented holding a snake, presumably an allusion to his death. FIG. 1704

ATTEMPTED IDENTIFICATIONS

One of the figures on the exedra at Memphis (with mutilated head) has been interpreted as Demetrios of Phaleron, included in this distinguished assembly by his friend Ptolemy I; cf. Wilcken, *J.d.I.* XXXII, 1917, p. 165; Picard, *Sarapieion*, pp. 69ff.). The fact that he is shown leaning on a support in the form of a herm of Sarapis is thought to recall the tradition that he was cured by Sarapis after the loss of his sight. For the date of this group see, however, Picard, loc. cit.

For the suggestion that one of the figures in the mosaic from Torre Annunziata in Naples—and in its replica in the Villa Albani—represents Demetrios cf. Elderkin, *A.J.A.* XXXIX, 1935, pp. 92ff., and *Röm. Mitt.* LII, 1937, pp. 223ff.; also Picard, loc. cit.

ARTEMIDOROS

Of Perge, Pamphylia. Son of Apollonios. Soldier and prominent citizen. First half and middle of the third century B.C.
Early went to Egypt and entered the service of the Ptolemies.
Went to Thera as a member of the garrison probably during the reign of Ptolemy Philadelphos (284–246 B.C.).
Was 90 years old when he died.
He is known only through inscriptions found at Thera during Hiller von Gaertringen's excavations. One, found in 1899, surrounding a medallion carved in the rock, contains his portrait, in profile, with long, wavy hair, a prominent chin, and wearing a laurel wreath. The inscription, in verse, reads:

Μνημόσυνον Θήραι · καὶ ἕως πόλου ἄστρ' ἐπιτέλλει
γῆς ἐδαφός τε μένει, ὄνομ' οὐ λίπεν· Ἀρτεμίδωρον.

Hiller v. Gaertringen, *Arch. Anz.*, 1899, pp. 187ff., especially cols. 191f.; *Thera* III, pp. 89ff.; *I.G.* XII, 3, Suppl. pp. 294ff., nos. 1333ff.; Wilamowitz, *Glaube der Hellenen* II, pp. 387ff.; Bernoulli II, pp. 144f.

PHAIDROS

Of the deme of Sphettos. Athenian statesman. Joint leader of the moderate, anti-democratic party after Ipsos, 301 B.C.
Served as general under Lachares in 296/5 B.C.
After a chequered career he again came into favour, and was general during the archonship of Xenophon (c. 274 B.C.). A decree in his honour was passed some time after 263 B.C., in which it is stated that a bronze statue of him is to be set up in the agora; cf. *I.G.* II–III², 682, lines 80–81, 86–87, 89):
στῆσαι δὲ αὐτοῦ τὸν δῆμον καὶ εἰκόνα χαλκῆν ἐν ἀγορᾶι.
Wycherley, *Testimonia*, pp. 214f., no. 707.

AUDOLEON

King of the Paionians. Son of Patraos.
Helped the Athenians in an hour of need in 287/6 by sending shipments of grain.
A decree honouring him for his services is preserved in a stele, dated 285/4 B.C., found on the Akropolis; in it is stated that an equestrian statue of him is to be set up in the agora: στῆσ[αι δ]ὲ αὐτοῦ καὶ εἰκόν[α] [χ]αλκῆ[ν] ἐφ' [ἵπ]που ἐν ἀγορᾶι.
I.G. II–III², 654, lines 57f.
Wycherley, *Testimonia*, p. 208, no. 692.

2. PHILOSOPHERS

Academicians

PLATO

c. 427–347 B.C. The philosopher. Son of Ariston and Periktione, both Athenians of prominent families.

LIFE AND CHARACTER

In early youth he studied grammar, music, and gymnastics (Diog. Laert. III, 4).

c. 407 Met Sokrates, and associated with him until Sokrates' death in 399 B.C. Had intended to serve his country as a statesman, since his family was connected with the political life of Athens; but the misdeeds of the Thirty Tyrants and the execution of Sokrates made him abandon this plan and turn to philosophy (Plato, *Letters* VII, 324B–326B).

399 After Sokrates' death he went to Megara with other Sokratics, but soon perhaps returned to Athens.

399–389 Perhaps travelled to Cyrene, Egypt, and other places.

c. 389 Went to south Italy (Plato, *Letters* VII, 326b) and there associated with the Pythagoreans Archytas of Tarentum and Timaios of Lokroi (Cicero, *Rep.* I, 10, 16). Then went to Sicily, perhaps at the invitation of Dionysios I (Cornelius Nepos X, 2; Diod. XV, 7); there met Dion (Plut., *Dion*, IV, 1–2).

388 Returned to Greece. On his way back perhaps was taken prisoner at Aegina, but was soon liberated.

388–347 Resumed writing and teaching. Founded the Academy in 386 B.C., and for forty years taught there.

366–365 Second visit to Sicily (Plut., *Dion*, XIII).

361–360 Third visit to Sicily.

360 Returned to Athens, disillusioned by the conduct of the Sicilian tyrants, and thereafter remained in Greece.

His teachings comprised geometry, arithmetic (including the Pythagorean doctrines), astronomy, geography, natural history, politics.

348–347 Died in his eighty-first year, while writing ('scribens', Cicero, *Cato*, 5, 13), or at a wedding feast (Diog. Laert. III, 2).Was buried in the Academy (Diog. Laert. III, 41). His nephew Pseusippos succeeded him as head of the Academy.

Gk. Anth., XVI, 328: 'Plato, teaching the mind to walk in the aether, utters words concerning things passing comprehension'.

Τὸν νοῦν διδάσκων αἰθερεμβατεῖν Πλάτων.

τοὺς τῶν ὑπὲρ νοῦν ἐξερεύγεται λόγους.

'The richness of Plato's thought, has had—and still has—untold influence upon human thought and therefore upon human history. It traverses the fields of metaphysics, epistemology, ethics and politics, and is written in a style unsurpassed for purity and elegance in the whole domain of Greek prose' (Warrington, *Everyman's Classical Dictionary*, s.v. Plato). 'No other author reveals as Plato does the power, the beauty, and the flexibility of Greek prose' (J. D. Denniston, *Oxford Classical Dictionary*).

And we owe to Plato also the picture of Sokrates' personality—which made so great an impression, not only on his contemporaries, but on all subsequent generations. In the delineation of character it parallels, in the literary field, what was achieved in the sculptured portraits of the time.

APPEARANCE

He is said to have had a broad chest, and on that account to have been called Platon, Πλάτων, whereas his real name was Aristokles (Diog. Laert. III, 4; Seneca. *Epist.* 58, 30; Apuleius, *De Plat. et eius dogm.*, I, 1; Olympiodoros, *Vita* Plat. p. 1, 28, ed. Westermann). But cf. Leisegang, in *R.E.*, s.v. Platon, col. 2343, who points out that Platon was a common enough name.

Plutarch (*De discern. amic. ab adul.*, p. 53C) mentions his 'curved back', 'which was imitated by his followers', Ὥσπερ οἱ τὴν Πλάτωνος ἀπομιμούμενοι κυρτότητα (*Quomodo adol. poetas audire debeat*, p. 26B), καὶ Πλάτωνος ἀπομιμεῖσθαί φασι τοὺς συνήθεις τὸ ἐπίκυρτον. He was 'goodlooking and strong', καλὸς καὶ ἰσχυρός (Epiktetos, *Diss.* I, 8, 13).

Simplicius, *Phys.* IV, 14 (= 772, 29, Diels) mentions the fine shape of his nose, εὔρις, the breadth of his body, πλατὺς τὸ σῶμα, and the beauty of his eyes, εὐόφθαλμος. In his youth his demeanour was so modest and orderly that he never laughed unduly (Herakleides in Diog. Laert. III, 26). His serious and dignified appearance is stressed by the poet Amphis (Diog. Laert. III, 28): 'Oh Plato, all you know is to frown with eyebrows lifted high', Ὦ Πλάτων

ὡς οὐδὲν οἶσθα πλὴν σκυθρωπάζειν μόνον.

Again, Alexis, in Diog. Laert. III, 27: 'I am at my wits' end and walking up and down like Plato, and yet have discovered no wise plan, but only tired my legs'.

ὡς ἔγωγ' ἀπορουμένη

ἄνω κάτω τε περιπατοῦσ' ὥσπερ Πλάτων

σοφὸν οὐδὲν εὕρηκ', ἀλλὰ κοπιῶ τὰ σκέλη.

Ephippos (Athenaios XI, 509 c–d) says that the pupils of Plato 'adorned themselves sumptuously', and describes one of them as having 'well trimmed hair and a long beard'. Εὖ μὲν μαχαίρᾳ ξυστ' ἔχων τριχώματα, εὖ δ' ὑποκαθιεὶς ἄτομα πώγωνος βάθη, which, of course, does not necessarily mean that Plato did so.

STATUES RECORDED

1. Diog. Laert. III, 25, quoting Favorinus' *Memorabilia*, says 'that Mithradates, the Persian, is said to have set up a statue of Plato in the Academy, and to have inscribed upon it these words: "Mithradates, the Persian, the son of Orontobates(?), dedicated to the Muses a statue of Plato, made by Silanion"', φέρεται ὅτι Μιθραδάτης ὁ Πέρσης ἀνδριάντα Πλάτωνος ἀνέθετο εἰς τὴν Ἀκαδήμειαν καὶ ἐπέγραψε· Μιθραδάτης Ὀροντοβάτου(?) Πέρσης Μούσαις εἰκόνα ἀνέθηκε Πλάτωνος, ἣν Σιλανίων ἐποίησε.

This statue can, therefore, be assigned to some time after 386 B.C., the year when the Academy was founded. On this Mithradates cf. p. 169.

2. Cicero, *Brutus* VI, 24, mentions a statue of Plato in his villa at Tusculum: Tum in pratulo propter Platonis statuam consedimus.

3. Christodoros, *Ecphr.* 97 (in *Gk. Anth.* II, 97ff.) cites a statue of Plato in the Zeuxippos of Constantinople.

4. Olympiodoros, *Vita Platonis*, p. 1, 32 (ed. Westermann), mentions that portraits of Plato 'were set up everywhere', πανταχοῦ ἀνακείμεναι.

The only certain reference to a Greek original statue of Plato is, therefore, that by Diogenes Laertios, which is said to have been dedicated to the Muses by Mithradates, and to have been made by Silanion; for those mentioned by Cicero and Christodoros may have been copies of this very statue; and the many portraits of Plato referred to by Olympiodoros may all have been of the same type, and indeed copies of Silanion's work. On the other hand, there may have been other versions that have not survived or that have not yet been identified.

IDENTIFICATION

The identification of Plato's portrait was made possible by the herm inscribed ΠΛΑΤΩΝ, acquired in 1884 by the Berlin Museum (see p. 166, no. 10). It is furthermore confirmed by the herm in the Vatican where the same type of head is combined in a double herm with Sokrates (see below, no. 2). All former hypotheses were thereby eliminated. This applies also to:

a. The small bust, formerly in the Uffizi, Florence, now on deposit in the Palazzo Riccardi, in the Medici section, where it is surrounded by portraits of Lorenzo the Magnificent, to whom it is said to have belonged (but see Mansuelli, loc. cit.). Height 35 cm.; ht. of head 16·5 cm. The former restorations have now been removed. The inscription ΠΛΑΤΩΝ on the bust has been shown to be modern. Cf. p. 168.

Visconti, *Ic. gr.* I, p. 232, pl. XVIII a.
Dütschke III, no. 393.
Kaibel, *I.G.* XIV, 1198.
Mansuelli, *Cat.*, no. 2, fig. 3.

b. The head on a seated statuette inscribed .λάτων, now lost, but extant in plaster casts. Here again the head does not correspond to that of the Berlin head and has been recognized as alien. Cf. p. 167.

PORTRAITS EXTANT AND ONCE EXTANT

1. Herm in Hall of Muses, Vatican, inv. 305. Acquired from a Roman dealer in Naples. On the herm is the modern inscription: Ζήνων. FIGS. 915–917
Height 48 cm.; ht. of head 34–35 cm.
Only the tip of the nose is restored.
Helbig, *J.d.I.* I, 1886, p. 72 (the first to point out that the inscription was not genuine).
Bernoulli II, p. 28, no. 7.
Helbig, *F.*³, no. 261; Helbig, *F.*⁴-Speier, no. 86.
Arndt-Br., 776, 777.
Boehringer, *Platon*, p. 17, no. VI, pls. 23–28.
Lippold, *Vat. Kat.* III, 1, no. 519, pl. 18.
Kaibel, *I.G.* XIV, 1158.

2. Head in a double herm, with Sokrates (cf. p. 112, no. 1), now separated. Until 1909 in the Casino of Pirro Ligorio in the Vatican gardens; then placed at the entrance of the Galleria Geografica; since 1933 in the Ambulacro superiore of the new entrance, inv. 128. FIGS. 909–911
Height 66 cm.; ht. of head 38 cm.
Restorations: The top of the skull. The nose is preserved.
Bernoulli II, p. 27, no. 4.
Helbig, *F.*³, no. 388; Helbig, *F.*⁴-Speier, no. 4.
Boehringer, *Platon*, p. 15, no. III, pls. 11–14.
Lippold, *Vat. Kat.* III, 2, p. 13, no. 3, pl. 8.

3. Head in the Galleria Geografica, Vatican, inv. 2843. Mounted on a modern bust with a painted inscription: Aristoteles. Known at least as early as 1834. FIGS. 912–914
Height of head, as restored, 33 cm.; ht. of ancient part 28 cm.
Restorations: The lower part of the head, comprising part of the back and the end of the beard (which is made rounded instead of pointed). The oblique cut is clearly visible.
Bernoulli II, p. 28, no. 6.
Helbig, *F.*³, no. 404; Helbig, *F.*⁴-Speier, no. 582.
Boehringer, *Platon*, p. 16, no. V, pls. 18–22.
Lippold, *Vat. Kat.* III, 2, p. 489, no. 63, pl. 223.

4. Head in the Terme Museum, Rome, inv. 124480. Found c. 1930 in Rome. Formerly placed in the gardens of the Museum, but after it was recognized as a portrait of Plato (by H. Speier and R. Horn) it was moved inside. FIGS. 926, 933
Height 31 cm.
No restorations, but much damaged.
Boehringer, *Platon*, p. 27, no. XV, pls. 73–77.
Felletti Maj, *Ritratti*, no. 8.

5. Head, mounted on a modern herm, in the Stanza dei Filosofi, Capitoline Museum, no. 47. FIGS. 918–920
Height, with ancient part of beard, 36 cm.
Restorations: Nose, part of neck and end of beard.
Bernoulli II, p. 27, no. 2.
Helbig, *F.*³, no. 828.
Stuart Jones, *Cat.*, p. 242, no. 58, pl. 56.
Boehringer, *Platon*, p. 15, no. II, pls. 6–10.

6. Head, mounted on a modern herm, in the Torlonia Museum, Rome, no. 160. Found at Casalrotondo on the Via Appia. FIGS. 934–935
Height, with neck, 37 cm.; ht. of head 34 cm.
Restorations: Ears and nose.
Visconti, *Cat. Mus. Torl.* (1884), no. 160.
Bernoulli II, p. 27, no. 5.
Boehringer, *Platon*, p. 16, no. IV, pls. 15–17.

7. A head once in the magazzini of the Villa Borghese is now 'lost'.
Kroker, Magazzini di Villa Borghese, *Bull. dell'Inst.* 1884, p. 176.
Helbig, *Bildnisse des Platon, J.d.I.* I, 1886, p. 71: in 'der "stanza dei busti", unmittelbar unter dem Fenster . . . dem Berliner Exemplar nahe verwandt.'
Boehringer, *Platon*, p. 12, no. A.
Bernoulli II, p. 27, no. 3.

Boehringer, loc. cit., quotes the director of the Borghese Gallery as saying (on June 11, 1932): that the government had, at the time of the purchase of the Villa Borghese, taken over only those sculptures and paintings which were included in the 'Fideikommissinventar'; the others were sold between 1884 and 1891 through the antiquaire Giacomini. No portrait of Plato could in Boehringer's time be found in the Villa Borghese. And this was confirmed to me by the present director Signorina Paola della Pergola.

8. A headless herm, inscribed Πλάτων Ἀρίστωνος Ἀθηναῖος, and with two of his famous sayings: αἰτία ἑλομένῳ θεὸς ἀναίτιος and ψυχὴ δὲ πᾶσα ἀθάνατος (taken from the *Rep.* x, 617e, and *Phaedr.*, 245c, with slight changes, viz. ἑλομένῳ for ἑλομένου, and the addition of δέ), was found in 1846 in Tivoli, was first in the Museo Municipale there (Arndt), and is now in the Palazzo Municipale of Tivoli on the stairway (so Mr. Smutny informed me). FIG. 906
Gerhard, *Arch. Ztg.* III, 1846, pp. 342ff.
Viola, *Tivoli nel decennio*, 1848, pp. 289ff.
Bernoulli II, p. 23 (but see *infra*).
Kaibel, *I.G.* XIV, no. 1196.
Mancini, *Inscr. Italiae* I, 1 (1936), pp. 115f., no. 583, and IV (1952), pp. 175f., no. 583, with full bibliography.
Smutny, *Greek and Latin Inscriptions in California* (in preparation).
(The head mentioned by Gerhard and Kaibel, locc. citt., must have been alien, in fact Viola mentions a 'perno', 'pin for fastening'.)

Another headless herm with identical inscriptions (also with ἑλομένῳ instead of ἑλομένου), but with different lettering, is now in the R. H. Lowie Museum of Anthropology of the University of California, inv. 8/4213. Bought c. 1900, in Rome. Unlike the herm found in Tivoli, it has the ends of a taenia on the shoulders, which would seem strange for a portrait of Plato. The herm is apparently ancient, the inscription modern (so Th. Ashby in Mancini, loc. cit., and so M. Guarducci after an examination of a photograph and a squeeze sent me by Mr. Smutny). FIG. 907
Bernoulli II, p. 23, in citing the herm from Tivoli, adds: 'Der Kopf scheint eine Binde getragen zu haben, wie man aus den noch erhaltenen Enden derselben schliessen muss.' This must be due to a confusion with the California herm. Cf. Smutny, loc. cit.

9. Head in the National Museum, Syracuse, 742. FIGS. 921–923
Height 31 cm.
No restorations.
F. Poulsen, *J.H.S.* XL, 1920, p. 191 (the first to mention it).
Boehringer, *Platon*, p. 21, no. X, pls. 49–54.
Libertini, *Museo Archeologico di Siracusa*, p. 148, no. 742.

10. Herm, inscribed Πλάτων, in the Staatliche Museen, Berlin, no. 300. Acquired by Count Tyszkiewicz at an auction of the Castellani Collection in Rome in 1884 and by him donated to the Berlin Museum. FIGS. 903–905, 908
Height 1·42 m.; ht. of head 33·8 cm.; with beard 36·3 cm.
No restorations, but somewhat battered.
Bernoulli II, p. 22, c, pl. IV.
Arndt-Br., 5.
Blümel, *Berichte aus den preussischen Kunstsammlungen* LIV, 1933, p. 66; *Kat.* v, K 192.
Boehringer, *Platon*, p. 14, no. 1, pls. 1–5.

11. Fragmentary head in the Staatliche Museen, Berlin, no. 1854. Said to come from Rome; then in the possession of A. Mahler in Prague; subsequently in that of Stefan von Licht in Vienna; acquired by Berlin in 1932. FIGS. 924–925
Height 35 cm.
No restorations, but much battered.
Blümel, *Ber. aus d. Preuss. Kunstsamml.* LIV, 1933, pp. 66f.; *Kat.* v, K 193.
Boehringer, *Platon*, pp. 25f., no. XIII, pls. 66–69.

12. Head, mounted on a modern herm. In the Louvre, Ma 70. Acquired in Smyrna. FIGS. 930–932
Height 32·5 cm.
Restorations: back of head and neck. The top of the head is abraded (no hair there visible). Face somewhat battered.
Bernoulli II, p. 28, no. 8, pl. VI, b.
S. Reinach, *Rév. arch.* XII, 1888, 2, p. 101; *A.J.A.* IV, 188, pp. 1ff.
Catalogue sommaire, 1922, p. 19, no. 70.
Boehringer, *Platon*, pp. 19f., no. VII, pls. 29–32.

13. Head in a small double herm, with Zenon (q.v.). In the Louvre. Brought from Egypt by the Mission Seymour de Ricci. FIGS. 936–937
Height 11·5 cm.
No restorations. Flattened at top.
Found by Mr. Charbonneaux in the reserve collection of the Louvre and by him published as Plato and Zenon.
Héron de Villefosse and Michon, *Arch. Anz.* 1907, col. 372, no. 14: 'têtes de philosophes barbus (Platon et Zénon)'.
Cat. sommaire (1922), p. 139, no. 3242: 'philosophes barbus'.
Charbonneaux, *A.J.A.* LXVI, 1962, pp. 269ff.

14. Head in the Musée Granet, Aix en Provence, no. 238. Probably found at Aix (Joubin). FIGS. 939–940
Height 35·5 cm.
No restorations.
Gibert, *Le Musée d'Aix*, 1882, p. 171, no. 236 (there thought to represent Macrinus).
Bernoulli II, p. 28, no. 9, pl. VI, a.
Joubin in *E.A.*, 1402–1403.
Espérandieu, *Recueil général* II, p. 451, no. 1692.
Boehringer, p. 20, no. VIII, pls. 33–39.

15. Head, mounted on a modern herm inscribed Lysias, in Holkham Hall. Purchased in Italy in 1753 by the architect Brettingham. FIGS. 927–929
Height 33 cm.
Restorations: End of nose and part of left ear. Surface worn and battered. Right side worked over.
Michaelis, *Anc. Marbl.*, p. 317, no. 48 (there called Lysias).
Bernoulli II, p. 2 (under Lysias).
Kaibel, *I.G.* XIV, 1180 (inscription accepted as ancient).
Huelsen, no. 25.
F. Poulsen, *J.H.S.* XL, 1920, pp. 190f., pl. VIII; *Greek and Roman Portraits in English Country Houses*, no. 5; *Phil. Wochenschrift*, 1938, cols. 1023f. (identified the head as Plato).
Boehringer, *Platon*, p. 22, no. XII, pls. 60–65.

16. Head in the Fitzwilliam Museum, Cambridge, no. 15.
FIGS. 945–947
Height 35·5 cm.
No restorations. The nose almost intact; has only a slight abrasion on left side. It has the same finely curved form as in no. 2.
Wernicke, *J.d.I.* V, 1890, pp. 169ff. (first to recognize it as a portrait of Plato; it was formerly thought to represent Hermarchos).
Bernoulli II, p. 28, no. 10.
Boehringer, *Platon*, p. 20, no. IX, pls. 40–48.

17. Head in the Ny Carlsberg Glyptothek, Copenhagen, I.N. 2553. Acquired in Rome in 1910. Said to have been found in a destroyed villa between the Via Flaminia and the Via Cassia (Helbig), and to have been in the garden of the Countess Cellere at Centocelle (F. Poulsen).
Height 36 cm. FIGS. 948–950
The restored nose was removed in 1951.
F. Poulsen, *Cat.*, no. 415b.
Boehringer, *Platon*, p. 21, no. XI, pls. 55–59.
V. Poulsen, *Portr. gr.*, no. 6.

18. Head in a private collection in Geneva. Said to have come from Athens. FIGS. 942–944
Height 35 cm.
No restorations; a few abrasions. In excellent preservation.
Boehringer, *Platon*, p. 28, no. XVI, pls. 78–92.
Bloesch, *Antike Kunst in der Schweiz* (1943), p. 80, no. 21.
Schefold, *B.*, p. 74, and *Meisterwerke*, no. 332.

19. Head in the Antikenmuseum, Basel. Gift of Robert Käppeli, 1963. Provenance not known. FIGS. 954–956
Height 35·5 cm.
No restorations but somewhat battered.
Berger, *Kunstwerke der Antike aus der Sammlung Robert Käppeli*, no. K10.
Berger, *Die Marmorskulpturen der Sammlung Robert Käppeli*, no. 7.
Richter, A New Portrait of Plato, 3. Beiheft zu *Antike Kunst*, 1965.

20. Head in the Akropolis Museum, Athens. Formerly in the Tower of the Winds. FIGS. 938, 941
Height 24 cm.
No restorations but much battered; back of head and lower part of face with chin and beard missing.

Dohrn, *Ath. Mitt.* 63–64, 1938–1939, pp. 163ff., pls. 65, 66. There dated between Gallienus and Constantine. The variations from the other portraits are explained as due to the sculptor changing the style to conform to that current in his time—a rare procedure in Greek portraits, except in this late period; cf. e.g. the portrait of Menander, fig. 1517. Dohrn nevertheless recognized the head as a Plato when he saw it in the Tower of the Winds. It is indeed fundamentally of the same type as the other portraits, with the same flat face, and with a similar composition of the locks in hair and beard; only the eyes are made larger and more staring.

21. Head in the National Museum, Athens, inv. 3735. From Athens. FIGS. 957–959
Height 16·5–17 cm. About half life-size.
No restorations, but battered; beard mostly missing.
Though reduced, the head is a fairly faithful copy, corresponding also in the expression to the full-size ones. It was, therefore, used by Hekler in his attempted reconstruction of the original statue with a figure, also half life-size. Cf. *infra*.
Hekler, *Praktika tes Akademias Athenon* IX, 1934, pp. 8off.
Boehringer, *Platon*, p. 26, no. XIV, pls. 70–72.

22. Small head in the Museum of Corinth, S1566. 'Found in Corinth on October 6, 1932, in the excavation of Temple E, in a layer of marble chips which contained late Roman coins'. Drapery at back. FIGS. 951–953
Height 11 cm.
No restorations.
To be published by E. Capps Jr.; here illustrated by his kind permission. I owe my knowledge of this piece to E. Harrison, and the photographs of it to Alison Frantz.

23. A small alabaster head in a private collection is soon to be published by H. von Heintze in an article entitled 'Das Platonbildnis des Silanion in spätantiker Umwandlung' in *Röm. Mitt.*, 71, 1964. It is listed in her revision of Hekler, *B.b.G.*³, p. 57, no. 19.

STATUE

The type of statue to which these portraits belonged was recognized by Hekler in a small figure with alien head (height 50 cm.), inscribed ·λάτων, now lost, but preserved in plaster casts in Bonn, Dresden, Strasbourg, Leipzig, Karlruhe (cf. p. 165). He combined this figure with a cast of the head, no. 21, also half life-size, and the result seems eminently satisfactory (my fig. 960). As Hekler says, the two seem to be 'wie aus einem Guss'. An effective composition has thereby been added to our meagre store of Greek portrait statues.
Braun, *Ann. dell' Inst.* XI, 1839, pp. 207ff.; *Mon. dell' Inst.* III, pl. VII.
Bernoulli II, p. 21, b.
Lippold, *Gr. Porträtst.*, p. 55, fig. 7; *Vat. Kat.* III, 1, p. 74: 'wohl identisch mit der 1823 vor Porta Portese gefundenen, Benndorf-Schöne, *Lateran*, zu Nr. 200'.
Hekler, Πρακτικὰ τῆς 'Ακαδημίας 'Αθηνῶν IX, 1934, pp. 8off., pls. I, II; *Forschungen u. Fortschritte* X, 1934, no. 10, pp. 121ff.;

B.b.G. (1940), pp. 22f.; 3rd ed., p. 57.
Schefold, *B.*, p. 210.
Bieber, *Sc. of the Hell. Age*, p. 44, figs. 114, 115.
Dontas, *Eikones*, p. 51, pl. 20, α.

DOUBTFUL EXAMPLES

The identification with Plato is doubtful in the following heads, as recognized by Bernoulli, Boehringer, and others:

1*. Head in the Kunsthistorische Museum, Vienna. Height 15 cm., that is, about half life-size. Cf. Benndorf, *Oest. Jahr.* II, 1899, pp. 250ff., pl. IV, fig. 137.

2*. Head in a small double herm, with an unidentified person, in the National Museum, Athens, 538. Found near the Akropolis. Formerly in the Polytechnikon, Athens. Height 32 cm. Nose was repaired in antiquity. Cf. Benndorf, *Oest. Jahr.* II, 1899, p. 254, fig. 138; Kastriotes, *Glypta*, no. 538.   FIGS. 967–970

3*. Head in a small double herm, with Sokrates (q.v.). In the Staatliche Museen, Berlin. Acquired in 1884 in Chiusi. Lost during the last war (so Frl. Rohde informs me).
                                                        FIGS. 973–975
Height 17.8 cm.
No restorations.
Conze, *Beschreibung*, no. 299.
Helbig, *J.d.I.* I, 1886, pp. 75f.
Bernoulli II, p. 23, f.
Blümel, *Kat.*, K 195.
The type deviates considerably from the full-size representations. One must remember, however, that in a portrait on a reduced scale, and so presumably freely copied, not mechanically, such deviations might occur. Crome's idea (*Bemerkungen*, p. 13) that this portrait represents Xenophon is now contradicted by the discovery of the real Xenophon (cf. p. 158).

4*. Head in the Museum of Sparta, no. 343. Cf. Tod and Wace, *Cat.*, no. 343; Boehringer, *Platon*, p. 13, no. B; Χρυσάνθου Ἀθ. Χρῆστου, Ἀρχαῖα Σπάρτη Ὁδηγός, 1960, p. 122, fig. 40, (there accepted as representing Plato).
Here the head is of an entirely different type from the certified Plato.

5*. The small bust recently found in Hermes Street, Athens (with other small herms, including one of Sokrates, cf. p. 115), which has by some been thought to represent Plato (cf. Frel, *Bulletin de l'association des études classiques* III, 1961, p. 69). The locks, directed from left to right over the forehead, are somewhat similar; but the personality is quite different from that of the accepted Plato. Cf. Daux, *B.C.H.* LXXXV, 1961, p. 613, pl. XXI.   FIG. 965

6*. I should further exclude the head in the Galleria Geografica of the Vatican, which was accepted as a Plato by Lippold, *Vat. Kat.* III, 2, p. 462, no. 22, pl. 199. Though there is some similarity in the design of the hair and beard, the differences in the shape of the head, the setting of the eyes, and the form of the mouth are very marked. The personality, moreover is that of a different, more ordinary, individual.   FIGS. 962–963

7*. The head mentioned by Fuhrmann, *Röm. Mitt.* LV, 1940, p. 90, note 9, as being in Antiquario Comunale seems to be identical with one that has since been stolen (Pietrangeli); in which case, however, it hardly is a Plato.   FIG. 964

8*. The head found at Thasos in 1951 (cf. Deshayes, *B.C.H.* LXXVI, 1952, p. 271, fig. 67 (on p. 266); height 30 cm.) and interpreted as a portrait of Plato by Frel (*Bulletin de l'association des études classiques* III, 1961, p. 69) seems to me also a doubtful one.   FIGS. 971–972

9*. I am also not certain that the fragment in the National Museum, Athens, Karapanos Collection 939, was intended for Plato (cf. Frel, *Bulletin de l'association de philol. class.* V, 1963, fasc. 3, p. 152). Though in some respects the similarity with the certified Plato is considerable, the deviations in the composition of the locks in the beard are very marked.

For a theory that the portraits identified by Studniczka as Aristotle really represent Plato cf. K. Kraft's *Jahrbuch für Numismatik und Geldgeschichte* XIII, 1963, pp. 34ff. (based on the supposition that the inscription on the Vatican herm, my no. 1, is ancient, and that on the Berlin herm, my no. 10, is modern).

10*. The small bust, formerly in the Uffizi, now in the Palazzo Ricardi, with a modern inscription ΠΛάτων. See p. 165, a.   FIG. 966

A number of herms inscribed ΠΛάτων in modern times are listed by Bernoulli II, p. 24, note 2; to which add Kaibel, *I.G.* XIV, 243*, Huelsen, no. 37, inscribed Platon Aristonos Athenaios.

A different type of statue from that listed above is represented in an over life-size figure from the Sarapieion of Memphis, where it was placed with other statues of famous Greeks in an exedra. The ensemble was found in 1850–1853, and has recently been beautifully published by Lauer and Picard, *Les statues ptolémaïques du Sarapieion de Memphis* (1955).   FIG. 961
One of the statues, of which only the lower part has been preserved, has on its plinth the graffito ΠΛάτω (cf. Picard, op. cit., pp. 143ff., figs. 83–84: 'Il n'y a aucune raison de mettre en doute l'appellation suggérée par le visiteur grec ancien'). The statue is represented standing, wrapped in a voluminous himation, and bare-footed. Its present height is 1.24 m. Since, as Picard says, it is a Hellenistic original and not a Roman copy, it would then be a new creation, and not a copy of an earlier type. Its difference from the portrait statuette cited above would thereby be explained. Whether the head reproduced the familiar features cannot of course be determined since no head belonging to the statue has been identified.

That the two mosaics in Naples and in the Villa Albani (cf. p. 82) do not necessarily represent Plato's Academy, as was once thought, has now been recognized. And even if they did, the presumptive Plato would have no value as a portrait, for the likenesses on such mosaics seem to have been mostly fictitious (cf. my *Gr. Portr.* II, p. 27; and p. 12).

There is no reliable portrait of Plato preserved on engraved gems or coins. Here too the former hypothetical identifications had to be abandoned after the discovery of the real portrait; for instance, the head of Dionysiac type grouped with Sokrates (?) on a garnet, once in the Marlborough, then in the Bromilow collection (cf. Reinach, *Pierres gravées*, pl. 113, 3), of which several replicas exist (cf. Bernoulli II, p. 23f.).

A Roman coin with a figure once thought to have been inscribed ΠΛά–των turned out not to be Plato; for the original inscription, Μηλα–σεων had been changed later to Πλάτων (cf. Bürchner, *Ztschr. f. Numism.* IX, 1882, p. 130).

CONCLUSIONS

The life-size heads listed above, nos. 1ff., must all have been reproduced mechanically by the pointing process from the same original; for they correspond with one another in all essentials, in spite of surface variations. A man of commanding personality is represented, with a broad forehead, a domed skull somewhat flat at the top, rather small eyes set close together, protruding lower lip, protruding rounded chin, and finely curved nose (εὔρις cf. p. 164). On the forehead are two horizontal furrows, between the eyebrows two vertical ones. The locks over the forehead are directed from right to left terminating below in a straightish line, and met by others covering the temples; the moustache is long and flowing. A groove separates the lobe of the ear from the skull. The beard is somewhat differently rendered in the various examples, the locks varying in depth; and this is the case also with the locks on the skull, which are sometimes closely adhering, at other times in deeper relief. But the general scheme remains more or less the same in all. A comparison between the different portraits of Plato with one another is indeed instructive regarding the similarities and dissimilarities that could be achieved by the Roman copyists in reproducing the same Greek original by the pointing process (cf. p. 27). How different, for instance, are the expressions in the heads in Geneva (no. 18), in Cambridge (no. 16), and in the Sala delle Muse in the Vatican (no. 1), all conveying the sombre, concentrated thinker, from that in the head in the Galleria Geografica of the Vatican (no. 2) with its bland serenity; and yet this variation is attained merely through a different surface treatment round the eyes, whereas the basic form remains the same.

When the herm now in Berlin first became known as a certain portrait of Plato, many people felt disappointed. Could this cross-looking individual be the idealistic, mystical, poetical Plato? They preferred to think of him as represented in the bronze 'Dionysos' in Naples (inv. 5618; Ruesch, *Guida*, no. 857), which had long passed for Plato. But it has gradually been recognized that in the Berlin portrait and its many replicas, including the reconstructed statue (cf. fig. 960), we have indeed an accurate likeness of the great philosopher. Not only does it correspond to the physical characteristics mentioned by ancient writers—his broad forehead and chest, his bent back, his sombre expression, and his aristocratic bearing—but it embodies what is known of his life and thought. At the time that the portrait was made Plato must have been advanced in years. He had been through many vicissitudes; in his philosophical speculations he had gone beyond the teachings of Sokrates; he had evolved the theory of the existence of Ideas as entities and had come to a belief in a θεὸς ἀναίτιος and in a ψυχή ἀθάνατος, concepts that have made Platonism be regarded as the precursor of Christianity. To evolve such concepts required inward withdrawal. The extant portraits of Plato show such a withdrawn thinker, no longer in his idealistic youth as a follower of Sokrates, but as he became in later life. And in the best examples, for instance in those of the Fitzwilliam Museum (no. 16) and in the private collection in Geneva (no. 18), is conveyed also something of his artistic side, evident in his poetical metaphors and in the matchless quality of his prose.

The question arises: is this remarkable portrait of Plato a reproduction of the one that was erected by the Persian Mithradates in the Academy of Athens and of which it is recorded that it was the work of the sculptor Silanion (cf. p. 165)? Unfortunately this cannot be regarded as certain. Practically nothing is known of Silanion's style—for none of the various works cited by Pliny, Diogenes Laertios, Cicero, and Pausanias (cf. Overbeck, *Schriftquellen*, nos. 1350–1363) has been reliably identified. The information that he wrote on symmetry and proportion (Vitruvius VII, praef. 12) also hardly helps. All that can be said is that the attribution is an attractive possibility, since the extant portraits all go back to one Greek original, presumably a famous one, and that Silanion's dates would approximately fit the style of the portrait; that is, if one supposes that the portrait was commissioned when Silanion was quite young, a quarter of a century or so before his acme. (Pliny XXXIV, 51, dates him in the 113th Olympiad, i.e. 327–324 B.C.)

It has been suggested that the Mithradates who, according to Diogenes Laertios, erected the portrait, was the ruler of Kios on the Propontis who died in 363 B.C., and that this would furnish an *ante quem* date for Plato's statue (cf. Michaelis, in *Historische Aufsätze für E. Curtius*, pp. 107ff.; Schefold, *B.*, p. 205). But this has been questioned by Preuner (*Ath. Mitt.* XXVIII, 1903, pp. 349ff.) on the ground of the age that this Mithradates would have had at the time. Mithradates was after all a common enough Persian name. In Pauly-Wissowa's *R.E.*, s.v. Mithridates, thirty-six persons of that name are listed, and it is well known that Plato's fame brought people from all over the world to Athens and the Academy. The Mithradates responsible for Plato's portrait may, therefore, have been some otherwise unknown, rich Persian admirer of Plato.

Since, therefore, one cannot rely with certainty on Silanion, and much less on a specific Mithradates for supplying a date for our portrait of Plato, we must turn elsewhere, that is, to the style. This points to a period between the portrait of Thucydides (cf. pp. 149f.) and that of the Lysippian Sokrates (cf. p. 116), being more realistic than the former, less so than the latter. Roughly speaking, therefore, it should belong to the middle of the fourth century B.C. To this period also points the style of the drapery in the statuette (cf. fig. 960), with its substantial folds that do not outline the forms of the body. They bring to mind the seated figure on the record relief in Palermo, dated 355–354; the figures of the princes from the Bosphorus, on a record relief dated 346 (cf. Diepolder, *Att. Gr.*, figs. 10, 11, and his apt remarks on p. 45), and the statue of Maussolos (cf. p. 161, fig. 899).

If these premises are correct, one may surmise that the statue was erected either toward the end of Plato's life, or soon after his death.

SPEUSIPPOS

c. 407–339 B.C. Son of Eurymedon and Potone, a sister of Plato. First studied under Isokrates, but joined the Academy on its foundation. Accompanied Plato on his last visit to Sicily in 361.

347 B.C. On Plato's death succeeded him as head of the Academy, and held that position until his death in 339 B.C. Became a close friend of Dion of Syracuse.

Was a prolific author, but little of his writings survives, mostly fragments quoted by Athenaios.

Diogenes Laert. (IV, 3) speaks of his feeble health.

Ursinus (*Imag.*, 54) and Gallaeus-Faber, no. 137, reproduce a headless herm with the modern inscription Σπεύσιππος Εὐρυμέδοντος Ἀθηναῖος (Kaibel, *I.G.* XIV, no. 260)

Peripatetics

ARISTOTLE

384–322 B.C., son of Nikomachos, physician of Amyntas II of Macedon, and of Phaisti(as). For generations the family had been physicians.

LIFE

384 B.C. Born at Stageiros on Chalkidike, and apparently spent his early youth in the North.

c. 367 When 17 years old went to Athens and joined Plato's Academy.

367–347 Remained with Plato, first as a pupil, then as an independent worker, for twenty years. His genius for scientific observation and classification soon became evident.

347 After Plato's death went first to Assos in Mysia to the tyrant Hermias, whose niece he married, then to Mytilene on Lesbos, where he pursued chiefly zoological investigations.

342–341 On the invitation of Philip of Macedon he went to Pella to become the tutor of Alexander (in the archonship of Pythodotos).

335–334 When 50 years old (during the archonship of Euainetos) he returned to Athens, with his family and with Theophrastos, and founded his own school in a grove sacred to Apollo Lykeios and the Muses. The school was later called Peripatetic, either because of the covered court (περίπατος) that was included in the buildings, or because he is said to have walked up and down (περιπατητικός) during his lectures.

With the financial support of Alexander he made collections of manuscripts (the prototypes of the libraries of Alexandria and Pergamon), and of scientific and historical material; for instance, of the constitutions of 158 Greek states (only that of Athens, the Ἀθηναίων Πολιτεία has survived). He organized extensive research by his co-workers in a great variety of fields; e.g., by Theophrastos on botany, mineralogy, and physics; by Eudemos on philosophy; by Aristoxenos on music; by Theodektes on rhetoric; etc.; to which his own early researches on zoology were added.

323 On the death of Alexander and the consequent rise of anti-Macedonian feeling in Athens, the charge of impiety, ἀσέβεια, was brought against him. He fled to Chalkis, leaving the school in Theophrastos' hands.

322 Died in Chalkis.

In his will he made provisions for his relatives, friends, and slaves (cf. Diog. Laert. V, 11–16).

As an Ionian and as a descendant of physicians, Aristotle returned to the scientific research of the pre-Sokratic philosophers, retaining, however, some of Plato's teachings. In his enquiries he entered new fields, and created for the first time a systematic collection of all the available knowledge of his time. For this stupendous work, and for the methodical approach that he initiated his fame has lasted throughout antiquity and to our day.

Gk. Anth. XVI, 330: 'Intellect and the soul of Aristotle, the picture of both is the same'.

Νοῦς καὶ Ἀριστοτέλους ψυχή, τύπος ἀμφοτέρων εἷς.

APPEARANCE

In a Greek epigram in the anonymous *Vita* of Aristotle he is described as small, bald, stuttering, lustful, and with a hanging paunch, σμικρός, φαλακρός, τραυλός, λάγνος, προγάστωρ (cf. Düring, *Aristotle in the ancient biogr. trad.*, p. 349).

Aelian, *Var. hist.* III, 19, also speaks of Aristotle's lisp (τραυλότης). According to Timotheos (in Diog. Laert. V, 1) 'his calves were slender, his eyes small, and he was conspicuous by his attire, his rings, and the cut of his hair', ἰσχνοσκελής, φασίν, ἦν καὶ μικρόμματος ἐσθῆτί τ' ἐπισήμῳ χρώμενος καὶ δακτυλίοις καὶ κουρᾷ.

Aelian (*Var. hist.* III, 19) says that 'he cut his hair and beard short, unlike Plato', ἐκείρετο κουρὰν...ἀήθη Πλάτωνι [κείρω = clip]; 'that he wore many rings'; δακτυλίους δὲ πολλοὺς φορῶν; and that 'he had a mocking expression in his face', μωκία δέ τις ἦν αὐτοῦ περὶ τὸ πρόσωπον.

In the Arabian Mubazsir of the eleventh century, Aristotle is described as white-skinned, a little bald, of fine stature and strong bones, with small eyes, a thick beard, blue-black eyes, an aquiline nose, a small mouth, and a small chest; cf. Jul. Lippert, *Studien zu griech.-arab. Übersetzungs-literatur* I (1894), pp. 19, 33ff.

Part of this description tallies with that of the ancient writers, part is in direct contradiction to it.

From these miscellaneous remarks one may glean a few facts that are important for an identification of Aristotle's portrait: somewhat bald, a short beard, a rather sensual mouth, eyes rather small, a mocking expression, and an aquiline nose.

Small bust of Aristotle, now lost. Drawing in the Vatican Library

STATUES RECORDED BY ANCIENT AUTHORS AND IN INSCRIPTIONS

1. A headless Roman herm, inscribed 'Alexander set up this portrait of the divine Aristotle, the son of Nikomachos, fountain of all wisdom',

[Υἱ]ὸν Νικομάχου σοφίης ἐπίστορα πάσης
    στῆσεν Ἀλέξανδρος θεῖον Ἀριστοτέλην

(the letters are crowded at the end of the lines). Testifies that a statue of Aristotle was erected by Alexander. Found in the Stoa of Attalos, Athens. Now in the Epigraphical Museum, no. 10425.   FIG. 1014
Height as preserved 62 cm., width 31 cm., depth 26·5 cm. Drapery on left shoulder.
Heydemann, *Die antiken Marmorbilder in Athen*, no. 240.
Studniczka, *Aristoteles*, pp. 14f.
I.G. II², 4261.
For other herms inscribed Ἀριστοτέλης, now lost, cf. p. 172.

2. Theophrastos (372–281 B.C.) ordered in his will the replacement of a portrait of Aristotle in the sacred enclosure of the school, presumably after some injury (Diog. Laert. V, 51).

3. Pausanias (VI, 4, 8) in describing the statues that he saw at Olympia, speaks of one that 'bears no inscription, but of which tradition says that it represents Aristotle from Stageira in Thrace, and that it was set up either by a pupil or else by some military man . . .', τὸν δὲ ἕτερον, ὅτῳ μηδέν ἐστιν ἐπίγραμμα, μνημονεύουσιν ὡς Ἀριστοτέλης ἐστὶν ὁ ἐκ τῶν Θρακίων Σταγείρων καὶ αὐτὸν ἤτοι μαθητὴς ἢ καὶ στρατιωτικὸς ἀνέθηκεν ἀνήρ. . . .

4. In his will Aristotle directed that his executors 'see to it that, when the portraits which Gryllion had been commissioned to execute were finished, they be set up', ἐπιμελεῖσθαι δὲ καὶ τῶν ἐκδεδομένων εἰκόνων παρὰ Γρυλλίωνα, ὅπως ἐπιτελεσθεῖσαι ἀνατεθῶσιν (Diog. Laert. V, 15). It is thought probable that a portrait of himself was included among these statues of his relatives.

The statue mentioned by Aelian, *Var. hist.* XIV, 1, as having been erected by Philip of Macedon in Delphi is not otherwise recorded, and presumably is due to a mistake; cf. Bernoulli II, p. 86, note. 7.

5. A bronze statue of Aristotle in the Zeuxippos at Constantinople is described by Christodoros (*Ecphr.*, in *Gk. Anth.*, II, 16ff.): 'Near him [i.e. to the portrait of Aischines] was Aristotle, the prince of Wisdom. He stood with clasped hands, and not even in the voiceless bronze was his mind idle, but he was like one deliberating; his puckered face indicated that he was solving some doubtful problem, while his mobile eyes revealed his collected mind', Ἄγχι δ' ἐκείνου

ἦεν Ἀριστοτέλης, σοφίης πρόμος · ἱστάμενος δὲ
χεῖρε περιπλέγδην συνεέργαθεν, οὐδ' ἐνὶ χαλκῷ
ἀφθόγγῳ φρένας εἶχεν ἀεργέας, ἀλλ' ἔτι βουλὴν
σκεπτομένῳ μὲν ἔϊκτο · συνιστάμεναι δὲ παρειαὶ
ἀνέρος ἀμφιέλισσαν ἐμαντεύοντο μενοινήν
καὶ τροχαλαὶ σήμαινον ἀολλέα μῆτιν ὀπωπαί.

6. In Roman times portraits of Aristotle were common, as indicated by Juvenal, *Sat.* II, 5–6: Nam perfectissimus horum si quis Aristotelem similem vel Pittacon emit, 'No garden is perfect unless it contains a portrait of Aristotle or one of Pittakos.'

7. A portrait of Aristotle is mentioned by Cicero (*Ad Att.* IV, 10) as being in the house of Atticus: Malo in illa tua sedecula quam habes sub imagine Aristotelis sedere, 'I should prefer to sit in the chair that you have placed beneath the portrait of Aristotle'.

8. The followers of the gnostic Karpokrates are mentioned as liking to have portraits of Aristotle (Baronius, *Annal. Ecclesiast.*; Visconti, *Ic. Gr.* I, p. 250).

9. Sidonius Apollinaris (*Epist.* IX, 14) cites the undraped right arm (brachio exserto) as a characteristic of the statues of Aristotle.

The portraits mentioned in 6, 7, 8, and 9, were presumably Roman copies of Greek prototypes (or of the same?). No. 5 may or may not have been a Roman copy. Nos. 1–4 were, it would seem, four different Greek originals.

IDENTIFICATION

For a long time great confusion characterized the attempts to identify the portrait of Aristotle. In the time of F. Ursinus and later in that of Visconti two different types were thought to represent him—a beardless one resembling the head (now recognized as alien) of a statue in the Spada Palace, inscribed ARIST......, (cf. Visconti, *Ic. gr.* I, pp. 255ff., pls. xx, xxa, xxb, xxc, xxd), and a head with a long flowing beard, resembling Leonardo (cf. Ursinus, *Imag.* 57, ill. in next col.). In 1900 Studniczka drew attention to a pencil drawing of a small marble bust, inscribed Ἀριστοτέλης, preserved in the Codex Capponianus 228 in the Vatican. The original of this drawing, by Gallaeus, was described as having been found in Rome, at the foot of the Quirinal hill, in 1592, and as being in the collection of F. Ursinus (cf. also the unpublished manuscript of 1599, by Schoppius, now in the Naples library (Codex Neapolitanus V E17). It was drawn by Rubens, with the note 'apud Ful. Ursinum, in marmore'). It is further described as small (paulo minor media statuarum magnitudine), that is, perhaps about half life-size. The high price paid for the bust—50 gold scudi—speaks for relatively good preservation, and in Faber's commentary the nose is accepted as ancient.

F. Studniczka, *Festblatt zum Winckelmannsfest des arch. Seminars d. Univ. Leipzig*, 1900; *Das Bildnis des Aristoteles*, Leipzig, 1908, pp. 15ff., pl. II, 2 (henceforth cited as Studniczka, *Aristoteles*). See illustration on p. 171.

For a figure of Aristotle, inscribed with his name, in a mosaic found at Baalbek see p. 174.

PORTRAITS EXTANT AND ONCE EXTANT

Through a resemblance to the Vatican drawing, Studniczka was able to identify 11 extant heads as representing Aristotle, and several more have since been added:

Head once thought to represent Aristotle. Ursinus, *Imag.*, 57

1. Head in the National Museum of the Terme, inv. 80702. Gift of Senatore A. Apolloni. Formerly in the possession of the sculptor Apolloni.   FIGS. 982–983
Height of head 28 cm.
Restorations: Back of skull including parts of the ears, end of beard, nose, neck.
Studniczka, *Aristoteles*, p. 24, no. 1.
Felletti Maj, *Ritratti*, no. 15.
Gullini, *Arch. cl.* 1, 1949, p. 140.

2. Head, mounted on a modern alabaster bust, in the National Museum of the Terme, inv. 8575. From the Ludovisi Collection.   FIGS. 979–981
Height, with neck, 34 cm.; ht. of head c. 28 cm.
Restorations: Nose (from c. 2 cm. below the bridge), part of right ear. Surface cleaned and partly scraped (see p. 175).
Schreiber, *Ludovisi*, p. 117, no. 93.
Studniczka, *Aristoteles*, p. 24, H, pl. III, 5, 6.
Bernoulli II, p. 96, no. 2.
Arndt-Br., 365–366.
Helbig, *F.*³, no. 1298.
Felletti Maj, *Ritratti*, no. 14.

3. Head, in a small double herm, with an unidentified portrait (cf. under Straton and Lykon, p. 178), in the Museo delle Terme, inv. 108344. Found in Palestrina, near the Via Prenestina.   FIGS. 1006–1008
Height 23·8 cm.; ht. of head 15·1 cm.
No restorations, but the surface is much corroded.

R. Paribeni, *Not. d. Sc.*, 1926, p. 422, figs. 1, 2 (there thought to be a possible Euripides, as a pendant to a possible Sophokles).
Felletti Maj, *Ritratti*, no. 330 (on p. 166; not illustrated).
Richter, *Gk. Portr.* IV, pp. 33f., figs. 39, 40 (there identified as Aristotle).

4. Head mounted on a modern bust, in the Villa Mattei (now called Villa Celimontana). Now (April 1964) near the orange grove, but I hope soon to be transferred to the Terme Museum, for it is in a precarious condition. The new photographs taken for me by J. Felbermeyer show how much the surface has suffered since the views in *E.A.*, 126-127, were taken.   FIGS. 992–994
Height 31 cm. (larger than life).
Restorations: Nose, moustache with upper lip.
Bernoulli II, p. 96, no. 3.
Studniczka, *Aristoteles*, p. 26, M, pls. II, 6, III, 4.
E.A., 126–127.
Gullini, *Arch. cl.* I, 1949, p. 137, no. 14.

5. Head, mounted on a modern bust, in the Uffizi, Florence, inv. 1914, no. 9. Provenance not known.   FIGS. 989–990
Height of ancient part c. 40 cm.; ht. of head 32 cm.
Restorations: A large part of the forehead with the nose and the left eye and eyebrow.
Studniczka, *Aristoteles*, p. 22, C ('fast bis zur Unkenntlichkeit ergänzt und überarbeitet').
Gullini, p. 137, no. 3.
Mansuelli, *Cat.*, no. 1.

6. Head in the National Museum, Palermo. From Rome.
                                                                          FIGS. 1002–1003
Height 35·5 cm.; ht. of head 25–27 cm. Made for insertion in a statue or herm.
Restorations: Nose, part of upper lip.
Bernoulli II, p. 96, no. 4.
Studniczka, *Aristoteles*, p. 23, F, pl. II, 1.
Gullini, *Arch. cl.*, I, 1949, p. 137, no. 6.

7. Head in the Kunsthistorische Museum, Vienna. Gift of the archbishop V. E. Milde, 1846.   FIGS. 976–978, 985
Height 29 cm.
Restorations: The nose.
R.v.Schneider, *Album der antiken Sammlung.*, Wien, 1895, p. 6, pl. 12.
Studniczka, *Aristoteles*, p. 25, pls. II, 3, III, 1.
Bernoulli II, p. 96, no. 5, pl. XII, a.
F. Poulsen, *From the Collections* I, 1931, p. 49, fig. 39.
Gullini, op cit., p. 37, no. 11.

8. Head in the Ny Carlsberg Glyptothek, Copenhagen, I.N. 2079. Acquired in Rome in 1907.   FIGS. 986–988
Height 29 cm.
The restored nose was removed in 1952. Much weathered. Large part of back with left ear missing.
F. Poulsen, *From the Collections* I, 1931, p. 50, fig. 41; *Cat.*, 415a.
Studniczka, *Aristoteles*, p. 23, D, pl. II, 4.
Gullini, op. cit., p. 137, no. 4.
V. Poulsen, *Portr. gr.*, no. 22.

9. Head in the National Gallery, Oslo, inv. 1232. From the Castellani Collection. Acquired in 1934.   FIGS. 995–997

Height, with neck, 35·1 cm. Worked for insertion in a statue or herm.
Restorations: Nose, small pieces of ears, part of right eyebrow; lips recarved.
Catalogo della raccolta Enrichetta Castellani, no. 199, pl. 24.
Studniczka, *Aristoteles*, p. 25, K.
Hekler, *B.b.G.*, p. 27, fig. 20; 3rd ed., p. 62, no. 2.
Katalog over Skulptur, Nasjonalgalleriet, Oslo (1952), no. 3.

10. Small bust, once in the collection of Mr. Schlens, Berlin. Acquired by a former owner in Italy more than 80 years ago. Now? (Not in the Staatliche Museen, Berlin.)
Height 26·7 cm.; ht. of head 17·5 cm.
Restorations: Nose, a piece in the left cheek, a piece of the left shoulder, and the right edge of the bust.
The head is turned to the (spectator's) left.
Neugebauer, *Antiken in deutschem Privatbesitz*, no. 16, pl. 9.

11. Head in the Louvre, Ma 80 bis. Formerly placed on a statue of Chrysippos (cf. p. 193, no. 17). In the 17th century in the Borghese Collection.   FIGS. 991, 998
Height, with neck, 32·4 cm.; ht. of head 29 cm.
The nose and mouth recut. Top of head worn.
Studniczka, *Aristoteles*, p. 24, G.
Bernoulli II, p. 96, no. 1.
Cat. sommaire, 1922, p. 5, no. 80.
Gullini, op. cit., p. 137, no. 7.

12. Head, mounted on a modern herm, from the Bibliothèque Mazarine, Paris. On loan in the Louvre in 1961.
                                                                          FIGS. 999–1000
Height of ancient part 32 cm.; ht. of head 30 cm.
Restorations: Nose, back of head with a piece of the neck.
Identified by Charbonneaux, who adds: 'La tête a été très retravaillée et sa valeur iconographique est médiocre.'
Richter, *Gk. Portr.* IV, p. 33.

13. Herm in the Musée Grobet-Labadié, Marseilles.
                                                                          FIG. 1001
Height 48 cm.; ht. of head 25 cm.
No restorations, but surface has suffered.
Identified by V. Poulsen.
Richter, *Gk. Portr.* IV, p. 33, fig. 38.

14. For the headless herm, found in the Stoa of Attalos, and now in the Epigraphical Museum, no. 10425, with an inscription recording that Alexander set up a statue to 'the divine Aristotle', cf. p. 171, no. 1.   FIG. 1014

15. Head in the National Museum, Athens, 3291.
                                                                          FIGS. 1012–1013
Height c. 28 cm.
No restorations, but much battered. No nose or neck; back of head mostly missing.
Hekler, *Archäol. Ertesitö* XLIII, 1929, p. 13, fig. 6b; *B.b.G.* p. 47, under note 42, 3rd ed., p. 62, no. 1.

16, 17. Two heads in a double herm in the National Museum, Athens, no. 3772. Both are of the same type. Found during the excavations of the Enneakrounos. Unfinished, like other pieces found in that locality. On the less well preserved head

are traces of a puntello (on left of forehead, above eye); also on other head in same place. The ears are not properly carved. On surface of face are marks of rounded chisel. Final surface evidently not imparted.　　　FIGS. 1004–1005, 1009–1010
Height c. 42 cm.; ht. of head 30 cm.
No restorations. Nose (preserved to 1·5 cm. below the bridge on the better preserved head) shows an initial curve (cf. Richter, loc. cit.).
Studniczka, op. cit., pp. 21f., A, B, pl. III, 2 (from cast), pl. III, 3 (from original).
Bernoulli II, p. 96, no. 6.
Gullini, op. cit., p. 137, nos. 1–2.
Richter, *Gk. Portr.* IV, pp. 31f.
Bernoulli, loc. cit., points out that this is the only double herm known to him in which both portraits are of the same person. I too know of no other, though ideal heads not uncommonly are so combined.

18. Fragmentary head. Only the front, without ears or nose, remains. It is turned slightly to its right. Apparently life-size, and with no restorations. According to Studniczka (*Aristoteles*, p. 23, E), it was then (1908) in the collection of Alden Sampson, who had acquired it in 1905 in Rome. According to Gullini (*Arch. cl.* I, 1949, p. 137, no. 5), it was then (i.e. in 1949) in the Coll. Simpson [*sic*], 'già a Roma, Mercato Antiquario'. But there was never an Alden Sampson Collection in New York. Nor did this piece ever form part of the Alden Sampson Collection, formerly lent to the Smithsonian Institution, Washington, D.C., now in the Art Museum of Princeton University, as a gift from Mr. Edward Sampson. I have not been able to ascertain the present location of this piece, in spite of the kind help of Mr. Edward Sampson, of Miss Frances Jones of the Princeton Museum, and of Mr. D. von Bothmer of the Metropolitan Museum.　　　　　　　　　　　　　　　　FIG. 984
The head is illustrated by Buschor in his *Hellenistische Bildnis*, p. 10, fig. 11, and in *Das Porträt*, p. 116, fig. 77 (as being 'im Kunsthandel').

A herm said to have been found in Rome in 1881 inscribed with the name Aristoteles, and to have passed into the possession of Castellani, is not otherwise known.
Cf. Matz-Duhn I, p. XVIII, Nachtrag zu no. 1174.
Studniczka, *Aristoteles*, p. 15.

The headless herm, said to have been found near Tivoli, inscribed Ἀριστοτέλης Νικομάχου Σταγειρίτης (cf. Kaibel, *I.G.* XIV, 1138; Huelsen, no. 6), seems to be 'lost.' It is not in the Vatican as Bernoulli (II, p. 88, note 1) thought.

For a headless herm with the modern inscription Ἀριστοτέλης ὁ ἄριστος τῶν φιλοσόφων Σταγειρίτης, cf. Kaibel, *I.G.* XIV, 159*; Huelsen, no. 27*; Bernoulli II, p. 88, note 1. And for other such modern inscriptions cf. Huelsen, nos. 26*, 28*, 29*.

For the statue in the Palazzo Spada, with an alien head and an inscription formerly reconstructed to read Aristoteles, see under Aristippos.

ENGRAVED GEMS

Several heads on ancient glass gems resemble Studniczka's Aristotle and evidently represent the same person; cf. e.g. no. 3223 in the British Museum (my fig. 1013a) and no. 1008 of the Arndt Collection in Munich (fig. 1013b) (so identified by K. Kraft in his publication of the glass gems in the Arndt Collection, *Jahb. f. Numismatik u. Weltgeschichte* XIII, 1963, pl. I, figs. 19, 21). Noteworthy characteristics are the prominence of the upper part of the forehead, the short beard, the strongly curving nose with a marked indentation at the bridge, and the somewhat flat contour of the skull—all important for the identification.

MOSAICS AND PAINTINGS

On the mosaic representing the birth of Alexander (cf. p. 253), found in a building at Baalbek is included a bearded man inscribed Ἀριστοτέλης. Only his right side is preserved. It can, however, have little iconographical value, since accuracy in likenesses was not aimed at in such late mosaics (cf. p. 12). Nevertheless, what remains of the head—a bald forehead, with sparse strands descending over it—resembles Studniczka's Aristotle.　　　　　　　　　　FIG. 1011
Cf. Chéhab, *Fasti Archeologici* II, 1947, p. 209, no. 788 (not illustrated); *Bulletin du Musée de Beyrouth* XIV–XV, 1958–59, pp., 48f. pls. XXII–XXVII.

The central figure in the painting of the catacomb in the Via Latina, Rome, has been identified as probably representing Aristotle by P. Boyancé, Mélanges Cardinal Tisserant, vol. IV, 1964, pp. 107ff. The painting had previously been interpreted as a lesson in anatomy (cf. A. Ferrua, *La Catacomba della Via Latina*, p. 70, pl. CVII).

A figure in a painting found in the Criptoportico of Pompeii was thought by Della Corte to represent Aristotle. But only a foot and the seat remain.
Cf. Della Corte, *Röm. Mitt.* LVII, 1942, pp. 55ff.

CONCLUSIONS

The type of head preserved in the marble examples listed above under nos. 1ff., is the same in all, and was evidently derived from the same Greek original. The majority are life-size, presumably executed by the pointing process, the small bust (no. 10) is a reduced version. The man represented appears to be about 60 years old, and has a short beard, a wide mouth, with a full lower lip, and a high, very broad, furrowed, mostly bald forehead, with only a few strands descending over it (the usual way of representing baldness). Perhaps the most distinctive feature is the great prominence of the upper part of the forehead, which recurs in all the copies (and also in the drawing of Ursinus' bust). The expression is one of high intelligence, with exceptional powers of concentrated observation.
The style points to the last quarter of the fourth century B.C. for the Greek prototype, somewhat later than the portraits of Euripides and Sophokles, but before that of Demosthenes. Age, character, and period, therefore, conform to what is known of Aristotle. Moreover, the large number of extant

examples show that a famous man was represented—in all likelihood, therefore, Aristotle.

Whether the sculptor of this portrait of Aristotle was Lysippos, as has often been suggested, is of course not known. If it were certain that the portrait reproduces that set up by Alexander (cf. p. 171, no. 1), the sculptor might well have been Lysippos, since he was often employed by Alexander; but there are of course other possibilities. The only sculptor mentioned by ancient writers in connexion with Aristotle is Gryllion, about whom nothing further is known, and about whom one cannot even be sure that he made a portrait of Aristotle (cf. p. 171, no. 4).

Studniczka's identification of this portrait as representing Aristotle has been more or less accepted—in spite of the clinching evidence of an ancient inscribed name on an extant example being absent—but has recently been questioned by J. H. Jongkees in an article entitled: Fulvio Orsini's Imagines and the portrait of Aristotle, in *Archaeologica Traiectina* IV (1960). He pointed out (1) that in the printed editions of Orsini's drawings by Galle (Th. Gallaeus) of 1598, and by Faber of 1606, the drawing used by Studniczka for his identification was omitted and that there must have been a good reason for this. He surmised the reason to have been that the authenticity of the bust had become suspect. And this surmise he found borne out by the fact that Rubens' drawing differs from that by Galle, whereas Rubens' other drawings of Orsini's portraits correspond closely to those by Galle, the reason for this difference evidently being that Rubens felt he could allow himself some freedom in his rendering, since the portrait in question was not considered to be important; (2) that there are in any case serious discrepancies between the head of the drawings and that of the marble busts, especially in the form of the skull, which is more rounded in the drawings than in the sculptured versions, and in the nose, which is aquiline in the drawings, straight in the marbles (both these objections had already been pointed out by Bernoulli); (3) that the beard and hair, though short, were not short enough to justify the mention of this feature by the ancient writers; that moreover they were not carefully kept, again in contrast to the descriptions in ancient literature; and that Aristotle probably was clean-shaven since he was 'lustful'.

I have tried to answer these objections in my *Gk. Portr.* IV, pp. 30ff., but will briefly recapitulate my arguments here: (1) There is no valid reason to suspect the authenticity of Ursinus' little bust, for it was specifically recorded to have been found in 1592 at the foot of the Quirinal hill, and 'in (Faber's) edition of 1606 as well as in the manuscript of Schottus it is described as the only inscribed authentic portrait of the philosopher' (cf. Jongkees p. 21). It seems, therefore, likely that the later omission of this bust from the published sets of portraits was merely due first to the confusion created by the appearance of other examples supposedly also representing Aristotle (e.g. the Spada statue and the Leonardesque type cf. p. 172), and second to the practical difficulty of publishing so many heads with the expense

involved (cf. Jongkees, pp. 9ff.); in fact Gallaeus insisted that one should limit oneself to publishing only one portrait of each individual. One may also recall how different was Rembrandt's idea of Aristotle's appearance (as shown in the painting now in the Metropolitan Museum of Art) from that in Ursinus' bust.

(2) With regard to the form of the skull, Studniczka's claim that the heads in the Louvre and in Palermo (nos. 11, 6) approach the rounded form of the drawings seems to me well founded. On the other hand, on the glass gems, figs. 1013a, 1013b, the contour of the skull is rather flat, as in the head in Vienna, fig. 997. As for the shape of the nose—which is considered a decisive argument—it is well to remember that in all marble heads above listed the nose is either restored or almost entirely missing. In the Ludovisi head (no. 2) there remains a small part below the bridge, but the surface has evidently been scraped to make it fit the restored portion; in one of the heads in the double herm in Athens (nos. 16, 17) there actually is the beginning of a curve. In the portraits on the glass gems, figs. 1013a and b, the curve of the nose is pronounced.

(3) The beard in the drawings and marble heads is certainly shorter than Plato's, and its length should conform to the expression ἐκείρετο = clipped. Aristotle's adult life was spent mostly in Athens, so he presumably followed Athenian rather than Macedonian fashions. One can hardly take seriously the charge in the epigram that Aristotle was dissolute, for it is contradicted by his life and work.

(4) It is furthermore important to bear in mind that Ursinus' bust was small, and, therefore, a reduced copy, made presumably free hand, and might vary in such details as the composition of the strands of hair over the forehead, etc.

For a theory that the portrait thought by Studniczka to represent Aristotle really represents Plato, cf. K. Kraft, *Jahrbuch für Numismatik und Weltgeschichte* XIII, 1963, pp. 15ff., and my p. 168.

ARISTIPPOS

c. 435–360 B.C., of Cyrene. Philosopher and sophist. Called the father of hedonism, and so the predecessor of Epikouros. Early in life went to Athens and became a pupil of Sokrates.

399 B.C. After the death of Sokrates travelled and then returned to Cyrene, where he founded a school.

c. 361 B.C. Came in contact with Plato in Sicily at the court of Dionysios.

Taught that the chief good in life was pleasure.

Said to have indulged in luxury.

His daughter Arete was his pupil.

Diogenes Laertios (II, 84–85) gives a list of the titles of his writings.

He is said to have been the first of the Sokratics to receive pay for his teachings (Diog. Laert. II, 65).

No statue is recorded in extant ancient literature as having been erected to Aristippos; but the statue in the Palazzo Spada, evidently inscribed with his name (cf. *infra*), shows that there must have been one.

PORTRAIT EXTANT

A statue, with an alien head, in the Palazzo Spada, Rome (height 1·20 m.) is inscribed on the side of the plinth with a name of which the first 5 letters 'Αριστ, and a final sigma are clear, but of the others hardly anything remains. Visconti, *Ic. gr.* I, pp. 251f., pl. xxa, reconstructed Aristoteles, others Aristippos or Aristeides or Ariston Chios. Gullini, op. cit. pp. 130ff., read 'Αριστ(οτέλη)ς. In a recent examination (August 1961) M. Guarducci came to the conclusion that the letter after the tau could only be an iota, and that the space between it and the final sigma allowed for only three further letters, and that Aristippos would seem to be the only possible reconstruction.   FIGS. 1018, 1020

Restorations: Right forearm with the hand, left leg from the thigh down, bits in the drapery.

Mandowsky and Mitchell, *Pirro Ligorio's Roman Antiquities*, p. 123, no. 144 (= Aristides).
Visconti, loc. cit.
Wachsmuth, *Arch. Ztg.*, 1861, cols. 210f (= Aristoteles).
Bernoulli II, pp. 91f.
E. Curtius, *Arch. Zt.*, 1880, p. 107 (the first to point out that the head did not belong to the statue).
Matz-Duhn, no. 1174 (accepted it as Aristotle).
Kaibel, *I.G.* xIV, 1139 (favoured reading of Aristotle).
Studniczka, *Röm. Mitt.* v, 1890, pp. 12ff. (read Aristippos).
Helbig, *F.*³, no. 1819 (favoured reading of Aristippos).
Arndt-Br., 378–380 (cites Studniczka's opinion).
Horn, *Gewandstatuen*, p. 32 (= Aristippos).
Schefold, *B.*, pp. 120f., 3, 210 (suggested Ariston Chios).
Gullini, loc. cit.
Dontas, *Eikones*, pp. 26f., 54f., pl. 21, β, γ ('Aristippos or Aristotle').
Guarducci in my *Gk. Portr.* IV, pp. 32f. (read Aristippos).

ATTEMPTED IDENTIFICATIONS

On a supposed resemblance of this statue to the large bronze statuette (with head preserved) in the British Museum (Walters, *Cat.*, no. 848, and *Select Bronzes*, pl. lxv), K. A. Esdaile identified the latter and its replicas as representing Aristippos (*J.H.S.* xxxiv, 1914, pp. 47ff.). But the Spada statue does not seem to me to be a replica of the British Museum bronze, only somewhat similar in composition. Cf. under my 'Kleanthes', p. 189.

The head on a small double herm in Berlin (Blümel, *Kat.* v, K206), joined to a female head, was by Schefold (*B.*, pp. 78f., no. 4, p. 206) thought to represent Aristippos with his daughter Arete, instead of Krates and Hipparcheia, as Crome (*Arch. Anz.*, 1935, cols. 4ff.) had suggested. As Schefold points out, style and general appearance would fit the attribution to the fourth-century hedonist.   FIGS. 1015–1017

The glass gem in the British Museum (Walters, *Cat.*, no. 3217), with a bearded head in profile to the right and four deities in the corners (Dionysos, Aphrodite, Apollo, Athena), inscribed 'Αριστ—ιππος, must be modern, as Studniczka and Mrs. Esdaile pointed out (cf. Esdaile, op. cit., pp. 58f.), and as I too thought after examining it in the summer of 1961.
                                    FIG. 1019

The inscription 'Αρίστιππος Κυραναῖος on a herm once in the possession of Ligorio, now lost, is considered to be modern; cf. Kaibel, *I.G.* xIV, 157*; Huelsen, no. 24*.

On account of a supposed resemblance to the head on this herm, a male bust carved on a carnelian in the collection of F. Ursinus (Gallaeus-Faber, *Imag.* 32; Bellori, *Imag. phil.*, 5) was interpreted as representing Aristippos; cf. Bernoulli II, p. 9.

THEOPHRASTOS

372/369–288/285 (123rd Olympiad). The philosopher. Son of Melantas, a wealthy fuller. Born at Eresos on Lesbos. His original name was Tyrtamos, but he was renamed Theophrastos by Aristotle, 'on account of his graceful style', διὰ τὸ τῆς φράσεως θεσπέσιον (Diog. Laert. v, 38).
First studied under Alkippos in his native Lesbos.
c. 352 Went to Athens and attended Plato's lectures.
347 After Plato's death probably joined Aristotle in Assos and Mytilene and became his pupil and close friend (cf. p. 170).
Went with him to Macedonia and afterwards to Athens.
323/2 When Aristotle left Athens he became his successor as head of the Peripatetic school (Diog. Laert. v, 36).
322–288 Under him the school was greatly developed. About 2,000 students are said to have attended his lectures (Diog. Laert. v, 37). Among them were Menander and Demetrios of Phaleron. Through the latter's intervention Theophrastos was able to acquire an estate for the school, though he was not a native of Athens. He was highly regarded also by Kassandros and Ptolemy (Diog. Laert. v, 37). He carried on the Aristotelian studies in logic, rhetoric, poetics, ethics, politics, and science, especially on plants and minerals. Diog. Laert. v. 42f. lists over 200 of his works ('comprising 232,808 lines'). Among the few extant ones are his *Characters* and his *Enquiry into Plants*, the latter constituting the first systematic work on botany.
He continued his work until shortly before his death.
286 When he retired he left Strato as head of the school.
285 He died soon afterwards, about 85 years old (Diog. Laert. v, 40).
He was buried in Athens, with a large part of the Athenian populace participating in the funeral (Diog. Laert. v, 41). In his will (preserved in Diog. Laert. v, 51–57) he made elaborate provisions for the estate, his friends, and his nephews (he died unmarried). He was evidently a man of considerable property.

CHARACTER

Diogenes Laertios sums up Theophrastos' character as follows: 'a man of remarkable intelligence and industry', and 'ever ready to do a kindness and enter into discussion', ἀνὴρ συνετώτατος καὶ φιλοπονώτατος . . . ἄλλως τε καὶ εὐεργετικὸς καὶ φιλόλογος.
An indication of his tireless industry is the saying attributed

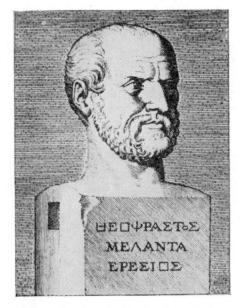  

(a) Engraving from the drawing shown in fig. c.　　　(b) Drawing by Statius.　　　(c) Drawing by Gallaeus. Ursinus, *Imag.*, 57.

HERM OF THEOPHRASTOS IN THE VILLA ALBANI, ROME. Cf. fig. 1022

to him that 'the most expensive item in our expenditure is time'. That he remained alert to his old age is indicated by his saying: 'life ends just when we are beginning to live', ὁπότ' ἀρχόμεθα ζῆν, τότ' ἀποθνήσκομεν (Diog. Laert. v, 41). Though not an original thinker like Plato and Aristotle, he had a critical and sceptical mind, which enabled him to apply, develop, and enlarge the new scientific foundation for philosophy that Aristotle had laid. His works, together with those of Aristotle, represented the Peripatetic school of philosophy throughout the Hellenistic age. And in Roman times writers like Varro, Cicero, and Pliny borrowed freely from his writings. His contributions in the field of botany were considered especially valuable.

STATUES RECORDED

There is no mention by ancient writers of a statue having been erected to Theophrastos, but the inscribed herm in the Villa Albani (see below), evidently copied from such a Greek statue, shows that there must have been one, and this is of course likely, considering his great prestige. Perhaps after his death a statue of him was erected in the sacred precinct of the school.

IDENTIFICATION

The identification of the portrait was made possible by the herm, inscribed with his name, in the Villa Albani (cf. *infra*).

PORTRAITS EXTANT

1. Herm in the Villa Albani, no. 1034, inscribed Θεόφραστος Μελάντα 'Ερέσιος, in letters resembling those on the other herms from near Tivoli (cf. p. 81). Found in the 'villa of Cassius' near Tivoli. Known to F. Ursinus when it was in the palace of the Marchese Massimi; it later went to England

and belonged to Dr. Mead, after whose death it was acquired by Cardinal Albani.　　　　　FIGS. 1022–1023
Height 67 cm.; ht. of head 28 cm.
No restorations except part of the rim of the left ear and a corner of the herm. Herm and head in one piece.
Ursinus, *Imag.*, p. 59; Gallaeus-Faber, 143; Statius. See above.
Visconti, *Ic. gr.* I, pp. 259ff., pl. XXI, nos. 1, 2.
Bernoulli II, pp. 99f., pl. XIII.
Helbig, *F.*³, no. 1881.
Arndt-Br., 231–232.
Kaibel, *I.G.* XIV, 165.
Huelsen, no. 17.

2. Head, mounted on a modern herm, in the Stanza dei Filosofi, Capitoline Museum, no. 74.　　FIGS. 1028–1030
Height of ancient part 28 cm.; ht. of head 26 cm.
Restorations: The nose, edges of ears, lower part of neck, patches on right cheek and eyebrow.
Bottari I, 175.
Bernoulli II, p. 100.
Stuart Jones, *Cat.*, p. 257, no. 97, pl. 60.
Arndt-Br., 233–234.

3. Head, mounted on a modern herm, in the Museo Torlonia, 29. Found on the Via Appia.　　FIG. 1024
Height, with neck, 28 cm.; ht. of head 24 cm.
Restorations: Nose, most of left ear, part of the right ear, most of the left side of the beard, part of back of head.
Visconti, *Museo Torlonia*, no. 29, pl. 8.
Schefold, *B.*, p. 98, no. 3.
L. Curtius, *Röm. Mitt.* LIX, 1944, pp. 17ff., pls. 7, no. 2, pl. 8, no. 2 (the first to recognize it as a portrait of Theophrastos).

4. Head in the Galleria Geografica, Vatican, inv. 2901.　　　　　FIGS. 1025–1027
Height, with herm, 49 cm.; ht. of head 27 cm.

Restorations: Nose, right eyebrow, pieces of the neck; the herm is ancient but alien.

Lippold, *Vat. Kat.* III, 2, p. 450, no. 9, pl. 191.

DOUBTFUL EXAMPLES

The head mounted on a modern herm inscribed Θεόφραστος, in Aranjuez, from the Azara Collection, and said to come from Tivoli, has been considered to be a replica of the Albani by some, not by others. I have not been able to see a reproduction of it.

Height 57 cm. (with modern herm).

Restorations: Nose with moustache and upper lip.

Hübner, p. 105, no. 162: 'Ich fand keine hinreichende Ähnlichkeit mit dem Kopfe Visconti pl. 21.'

Bernoulli II, p. 101: 'An der Azarabüste von Tivoli in Aranjuez, Hübner, 162 ist jedenfalls das Bruststück mit der Namenaufschrift neu, wahrscheinlich aber auch der Kopf'.

Hekler, *B.b.G.*, p. 47, note. 51 (accepts it as an authentic portrait of Theophrastos). Cf. also 3rd ed., revised by H. von Heintze, p. 63, no. 3.

Schefold, *B.*, p. 208, note for p. 98, nos. 3, 4 (includes it as a Theophrastos).

Several spurious portraits of Theophrastos are listed by Bernoulli II, pp. 100f.: an inscribed herm then in the possession of the Dean of Worcester; a head in Turin (Dütschke, IV, no. 161); a head in the Capitoline Museum (Stuart Jones, *Cat.*, p. 227, no. 19).

CONCLUSIONS

In the life-size portraits nos. 1–4, derived from the same Greek original, Theophrastos is represented as a man about 50 years old (that is, at the age when he became head of the Peripatetic school), of sober temperament, great intelligence, a σχολαστικός, as he apparently called himself (Diog. Laert. V, 37), and of a kindly disposition. The physical characteristics are a high, rounded skull; a furrowed brow with two deep vertical grooves rising above the bridge of the nose; two deep grooves descending from the nostrils to the beard; a determined, rather thin-lipped mouth (in the Albani head the lower lip is fuller than in the others); a closely clipped beard; and hair marked by closely adhering, curling strands, going in different directions over the forehead.

The date that has generally been assigned to the original is c. 290–280 B.C.; that is, contemporary with that of Olympiodoros, and shortly before that of Demosthenes. The Roman copies may, therefore, go back to a statue erected to Theophrastos soon after his death, not representing him, however, as a man over 80, but as he was in the prime of life—presumably with the use of a sketch made of him at that time (cf. pp. 18f.).

STRATON

Of Lampsakos. Fl. 286–268 B.C. Son of Arkesilaos.
Succeeded Theophrastos as head of the Peripatetic school, and held that position for over 20 years (Diog. Laert. V, 58ff.).

Was a distinguished physicist, and a writer of many books. Teacher of Ptolemy Philadelphos, from whom he is said to have received 80 talents.

Said to have become so thin at the end of his life that he felt nothing when his end came (Diog. Laert. V, 60).

In his will he said: 'With regard to my monument, it shall be made as Arkesilaos, Olympichos, and Lykon see fit', τὰ δὲ περὶ τὸ μνημεῖον ποιείτωσαν ὡς ἂν δοκῇ 'Αρκεσιλάῳ καὶ 'Ολυμπίχῳ καὶ Λύκωνι (Diog. Laert. V, 64). The word μνημεῖον need not necessarily signify a statue.

As the head in the small double herm, coupled with Aristotle (in the Terme Museum, inv. 108344; height of herm 24·2 cm., ht. of head 16·2 cm.; cf. p. 172) does not represent Plato or some other famous person with whom Aristotle would be appropriately combined, one thinks of a Peripatetic philosopher; and since he is not Theophrastos, Straton would seem to be a possibility. But Diogenes Laertios' remark about Straton's thinness makes one pause, for the individual has a fleshy face—unless one supposes that Straton was corpulent before the end of his life. Cf. my *Gk. Portr.* IV, p. 34.

LYKON

299–225 B.C. Of Troas. Son of Astyanax.

270 B.C. Succeeded Straton as head of the Peripatetic school of philosophy, and held that position for 44 years (Diog. Laert. V, 65ff.).

'He was esteemed beyond all other philosophers by Eumenes and Attalos, who also did him very great service' (Diog. Laert. V, 67).

'He had luxurious tastes' (Athenaios XII, 547d).

225 B.C. Died at the age of seventy-four.

In his will, which is preserved by Diogenes Laertios (V, 69ff.), he gives instructions for the setting up of a statue of himself: καὶ ἀνδριάντα ἡμῶν ἀναθέτω.

He is, therefore, a possible candidate for the companion of Aristotle in the small double herm in the Terme Museum, and perhaps a better one than Straton since, having had luxurious habits, he might have been corpulent (cf. above, and *Gk. Portr.* IV, p. 34). FIGS. 1031–1033

G. Hanfmann has sent me photographs of a head that recently came to the Fogg Museum (1960. 449), through the bequest of David M. Robinson (*A.J.A.* LIX, 1955, p. 28, pl. 21, fig. 48), with the suggestion that it might represent the same person as the Terme head. An attractive possibility. Though the two heads are not replicas, the reduced scale of the head in the Terme Museum may account for the variations. Unfortunately the condition of both heads is very poor, so that details have vanished. FIGS. 1034–1036

XENOKRATES

396–314 B.C. Philosopher. Of Chalkedon. Son of Agathenor. Disciple of Plato; accompanied him on one of his visits to Sicily.

339 B.C. Succeeded Pseusippos as head of the Academy, and held that position until his death.

Was sent by the Athenians on embassies to Philip of Macedon and Antipater.

APPEARANCE

Plutarch, *Marius* II, speaks of Xenokrates' morose disposition. Diog. Laert. (IV, 6) mentions his solemn, graceless mien: σεμνὸς καὶ σκυθρωπὸς ἀεί.

Synesius, *Epistle*, 154, refers to the 'solemn countenance of the portraits of Xenokrates', cf. *Epistolographi Graeci*, ed. Hercher, p. 736. Sidon. Apoll., *Epist.* IX, 4, cites Xenokrates' crure collecto.

PORTRAITS ONCE EXTANT AND SUGGESTED

Ursinus, *Imag.*, 55, and Gallaeus-Faber, no. 149, reproduce a headless herm with a modern inscription Ξενοκράτης Ἀγαθάνορος Καλχαδόνιος Kaibel, *I.G.* XIV, 233*; Huelsen, no. 33; Bernoulli II, p. 57.

In the Glyptothek, Munich, is a head of Chrysippos (cf. p. 192, no. 12), mounted on a modern herm inscribed Ξενοκράτης Χαλκηδόνιος ; cf. Bellori, *Imag.*, 39; Gronov, Thes. II, 91; Kaibel, *I.G.* XIV, 232*; Bernoulli II, p. 57; Furtwängler, *Beschreibung, Glyptothek*, no. 297.

Studniczka, *Neue Jahrb. f. d. klass. Altert.* III, 1900, n. 176, thought of the Capitoline 'Aischylos' (cf. p. 123) as a possible Xenokrates.

ARCHYTAS

c. 428–347 B.C. Of Tarentum. Pythagorean philosopher and general. Son of Mnesagoras or Hestiaios (Diog. Laert. VIII, 79).

Fought successful campaigns as general of the Tarentine army. Met Plato in south Italy and became a close friend of his. Studied chiefly mathematics, physics, and mechanics. Some fragments of his writings on these topics have survived. He contributed to the theories of proportion, music, and acoustics. Propounded the first systematic theory of mechanics. Was much revered by his contemporaries, and was elected strategos 7 times.

Aristotle and Aristoxenos wrote concerning his life and writings (Athen. XII, 545a; Diog. Laert, V, 25); but these works have not survived.

No statue of him is recorded in extant ancient literature, but that there must have been one is indicated by the base of a herm, with feet, inscribed Ἀρχύτας, found in Tivoli with other herms. Now in the Sala delle Muse, Vatican, inv. 316. Cf. Visconti, *Museo Pio Clementino* I, p. 51; Lippold, *Vat. Kat.* III, 1, p. 99; Kaibel, *I.G.* XIV, no. 1141.   FIG. 1021

The head on a Tarentine coin (Bellori, *Imag. phil.*, 4), inscribed ARKI, was once thought by some to represent Archytas, but is now considered to be modern (cf. Bernoulli II, p. 17). As this individual is shown wearing a turban-like headdress, several heads with such a headdress were identified as Archytas; for instance that in the Capitoline Museum (Stuart Jones, *Cat.*, p. 251, no. 80), which, however, was considered by others to be Pythagoras (q.v.). Cf. Bernoulli II, loc. cit.

Cynics

ANTISTHENES

c. 450–370 B.C. (or 444–365). Son of Antisthenes of Athens, and of a Thracian woman (Diog. Laert. VI, 1). Founder of the Cynic school of philosophy. Pupil of Sokrates and teacher of Diogenes.

426 B.C. Fought in the battle of Tanagra, together with Sokrates (Diog. Laert. VI, 1).

At first studied with Gorgias, the rhetorician. Then became a devoted follower of Sokrates (Xen. *Symp.* 8, 4; *Mem.* 3, 11, 17).

399 Soon after Sokrates' death he opened his own school of philosophy in the gymnasium of Kynosarges (Diog. Laert. VI, 13; Suidas)—from which the name 'Cynic' philosophy was by some thought to have been derived.

He is said **not** to have had many pupils, on account of his rough treatment of them (Diog. Laert. VI, 4).

According to Cicero (*De oratore*, III, 62) Antisthenes was chiefly captivated by the teaching of endurance and hardness in the Socratic discourse: qui patientiam et duritiam in Socratico sermone maxime adamarat. His ideal is said to have been αὐτάρκεια, independence.

Xenophon, however, calls him most agreeable in intercourse, and the most temperate in everything else (cf. Diog. Laert. VI, 15). Theopompos said he had consummate skill and could by means of his agreeable discourse win over whomever he pleased (Diog. Laert. VI, 14). Isokrates and Plato attacked him for a certain, not ignoble, joylessness in his nature.

c. 370 The date of his death is computed by his having been alive at the time of the Battle of Leuktra (371 B.C.) (cf. Plut. *Lyk.*, XXX, 6), and apparently not any longer in the 103rd Olympiad (368–365 B.C.); cf. Diodoros XV, 76, 4.

An engaging, yet forceful, personality and a severe simplicity of life were evidently Antisthenes' salient characteristics. He was a realist, and so Herakles was his chief hero, and Plato's doctrine of Ideas did not appeal to him.

Some of the sayings attributed to him mark him out as an enlightened and independent thinker: 'Virtue is an affair of deeds, and does not need a store of words and learning', τήν τε ἀρετὴν τῶν ἔργων, μήτε λόγων πλείστων δεομένην μήτε μαθημάτων; 'Wisdom is a most sure stronghold, which never crumbles away or is betrayed', τεῖχος ἀσφαλέστατον φρόνησις· μήτε γὰρ καταρρεῖν μήτε προδίδοσθαι; 'Virtue is a weapon that cannot be taken away', ἀναφαίρετον ὅπλον ἡ ἀρετή; 'Virtue is the same for women and men', ἀνδρὸς καὶ γυναικὸς ἡ αὐτὴ ἀρετή (Diog. Laert. VI, 11–13). Diogenes Laertios lists his writings 'in ten volumes' (VI, 15ff.). Only a few fragments have survived.

APPEARANCE

He is said to have neglected his appearance and to have let his beard grow, to have worn no chiton, and to have carried a staff and wallet (βάκτρον καὶ πήραν) (Diog. Laert. VI, 13). He was in fact the typical dishevelled philosopher of whom Lucian (*Timon*, 54) has given so vivid a description: 'A halo of beard, eyebrows an inch above their place, superiority in his air, a look that might storm heaven, locks waving in the wind—a very Boreas or Triton from Zeuxis' brush'. Cf. also Lucian, *Fugitivi*, 20.

STATUES RECORDED

No specific mention of a statue of Antisthenes has come down in ancient literature; but that there was one is indicated by the Roman herm inscribed with his name. Moreover, considering his fame and the custom prevalent in the fourth and succeeding centuries of erecting portrait statues to great philosophers, it seems likely that one was set up, after his death, in the Kynosarges where he had taught (cf. p. 179).

IDENTIFICATION

After many erroneous attributions, the identification of Antisthenes' portrait was made possible by the discovery of a herm inscribed with his name (cf. *infra*, no. 1). By the resemblance to this head others could be similarly identified. It is possible that the statuary type is preserved in a terracotta statuette in Naples (cf. p. 181).

PORTRAITS EXTANT

1. Herm in the Sala delle Muse, Vatican, inv. 288. Found 1774 at Tivoli. Inscribed, at the bottom of the herm, Ἀντισθένης. Drapery on both shoulders.   FIGS. 1037–1039
Height 56 cm.; ht. of head 35·5 cm.
Restorations: Nose and pieces on left cheek and hair.
Visconti, *Ic. gr.* I, p. 266, pl. XXII.
Bernoulli II, p. 5, no. 1, pl. II.
Helbig, *F.*³, no. 279; Helbig, *F.*⁴-Speier, no. 67.
F. Poulsen, *From the Collections* I, 1931, p. 54, fig. 43.
Arndt-Br., 441–442.
Lippold, *Vat, Kat.* III, 1, p. 38, no. 507, p. 99, pl. 23.
Kaibel, *I.G.* XIV, 1135.

2. Head, mounted on a modern bust, in the Galleria Geografica, Vatican, inv. 2888. Found in Hadrian's Villa. Acquired in 1777.   FIGS. 1040–1042
Height of head 37 cm.
Restorations: Lower part of nose, the lock on the right above the forehead, ends of hair strands at back, lower part of neck. Some ends of locks are missing.

Bernoulli II, p. 5, no. 2.
Arndt-Br., 443–444.
Helbig, *F.*³, no. 395; Helbig, *F.*⁴-Speier, no. 592.
Lippold, *Vat. Kat.* III, 2, p. 461, no. 21, pl. 200.

3. Head, mounted on a modern herm, in the Stanza dei Filosofi, Capitoline Museum, no. 55. Found in 1744 near the Lateran.   FIGS. 1043–1045
Height of head c. 34 cm.
Restorations: Hair on top of skull, nose, left eyebrow and adjoining parts, some locks.
Bernoulli II, p. 5, no. 3.
Stuart Jones, *Cat.*, p. 248, no. 70, pl. 58.

4. Head, in the Villa Doria Pamphili. After much searching it was found (by Mr. and Mrs. Spencer Corbett), placed high up inside the large archway, not far from the entrance to the garden.   FIG. 1053
Height, with neck, 38·1 cm.
No restorations, but was broken in two and mended.
Matz-Duhn I, no. 1758.
Bernoulli II, p. 5, no. 5.
L. Curtius, *Röm. Mitt.* LIX, 1944, p. 31, fig. 8.

5. Head, mounted on a modern herm, in the National Museum, Naples, inv. 6159. From the Farnese Collection.   FIGS. 1046–1048
Height 33 cm.
Restorations: The nose, some locks of the hair.
Bernoulli II, p. 5, no. 6.
Ruesch, *Guida*, no. 1117.

6. Head, formerly mounted on a modern herm, in the British Museum, 1838. Said to be from the Via Appia. Purchased from Castellani, in Rome, in 1873.   FIGS. 1049–1051
Height of head, with neck, 36·5 cm.; from top lock to end of beard, 35·9 cm. Made for insertion.
No restorations.
Bernoulli II, p. 5, no. 7.
A. H. Smith, *Cat.*, no. 1838, pl. XI.

7. Head, mounted on a modern bust, in Sion House, Chiswick.   FIGS. 1052, 1054–1055
Height of head 37 cm.
Restorations: Nose, lock on right side of forehead.
F. Poulsen, *English Country Houses*, p. 31, no. 4.

8. A head once in the possession of the Cardinal Medici, mounted on an alien herm inscribed Karneades (cf. p. 250, no. 8), is now 'lost'.
Statius, pl. XIV.
Bernoulli II, p. 4.
Perhaps identical with Kaibel, *I.G.* XIV, 1170, and Huelsen, no. 20—there called herma acephalus, Karneades Philokomou Kyrenaios (cf. p. 250, no. 8).

DOUBTFUL EXAMPLES

Four heads by some thought to represent Antisthenes seem to me to be similar, but of a different type, and to represent a different personality (so also L. Curtius for 1*–3* and Lippold for 1*–4*).

1*. Head, mounted on a modern herm, in the Villa Albani, Coffee House, 607.

Height of head 41 cm.

Restorations: Nose, some locks of the hair, part of the neck.

Bernoulli II, p. 5, no. 4.

Arndt-Br., 167–168.

E.A., text, under no. 4038.

Lippold, *Antike Plastik*, p. 227, note 1: 'ähnlicher jüngerer Typus'.

2*. Head, mounted on a modern herm, in the Ny Carlsberg Glyptothek, Copenhagen, I.N. 1284. Acquired in 1895. Said to be from Tusculum.

Height of ancient part 41 cm.

Nose restored. Much of the surface is worked over.

Bernoulli, p. 5, no. 8.

F. Poulsen, *From the Collections* I, 1931, p. 53, fig. 42; *Cat.*, no. 419 (called Antisthenes).

V. Poulsen, *Portr. gr.*, no. 50 (included with a question mark).

Lippold, *Antike Plastik*, p. 227, note 1: 'ähnlicher, jüngerer Typus'.

3*. Head in the Ducal Palace of Mantua. Made for insertion in a herm or statue.

Height 38 cm.

Much corroded. Mouth and chin missing. Formerly mounted on an alien statue.

Dütschke IV, no. 637.

A. Levi, *Sculture greche e romane del Palazzo ducale di Mantova* (1931), p. 39, no. 59.

L. Curtius, *Röm. Mitt.* LIX, 1944, p. 31.

4*. Head in the Museo Civico, Modena.

Height 32·5 cm.

Part of the nose and the under lip are missing.

L. Curtius, *Röm. Mitt.*, LIX, 1944, p. 30, pl. XI, 1.

Lippold, *Vat. Kat.* III, 2, p. 461, under no. 21.

STATUE

The statuary type for the heads listed above under nos. 1–8, may perhaps be preserved, as L. Curtius has suggested, in a large terracotta statuette in the National Museum, Naples (no inv. number). From Pompeii.   FIG. 1056

Height, with seat, 70 cm.

No restorations.

The head is evidently a portrait. It has been variously interpreted: as a physician, perhaps Herophilos (von Rhoden, *Terr. von Pompeii*, pp. 44f., pl. 32); as a tragic actor (Bieber, *Theater*, 1939, p. 152, fig. 206); as a Roman copy of a Greek statue of a philosopher or other noteworthy person (A. Levi, *Le Terracotte del Museo Nazionale di Napoli*, no. 847, pl. XII); and specifically as the philosopher Antisthenes (L. Curtius, *Röm. Mitt.* LIX, 1944, pp. 38ff., pl. 19; cf. also Schefold, *B.*, p. 206, and Dontas, *Eikones*, pp. 64f., pl. 27, α). The fact that the figure is shown seated on a throne indicates that he is an important person, and the style is late Hellenistic. Moreover, the head with its bushy, dishevelled hair and beard and excited expression bears a marked resemblance to the extant Antisthenes type. That he is shown wearing a tunic as well as a mantle, whereas it is specifically recorded that he wore only one garment, doubling it for warmth when

necessary, is a point against the identification, but hardly a weighty one, for, since it was customary to represent both garments in Hellenistic portraits (cf. p. 227), the sculptor might have followed the current fashion. At all events, the statuette is of the Roman period, when Greek statuary types were extensively copied and when Antisthenes was a popular and revered figure. So the statuette may represent Antisthenes, and, if so, being Roman, it would presumably preserve the statuary type of the Greek original; but being of terracotta, it could naturally not have been produced by the pointing process, and would, therefore, be a free copy—a fact which would explain the differences between it and the sculptured type of head (cf. my *Gr. Portr.* III, pp. 33f., fig. 133). For the similar terracotta figure of Pittakos, from Pompeii, of about the same size, shown seated on a similar, backless throne, cf. p. 89, a.

CONCLUSIONS

The life-size heads in the round, above listed (nos. 1–8) all represent the same person, and must have been reproduced mechanically from the same Greek original. They portray a man in advanced years, of commanding personality, but of dishevelled appearance. The same traits recur: the two undulating furrows on the forehead; the strongly arched, contracted eyebrows; the deep-set, not very large eyes; the deep furrows above the bridge of the nose; the nose apparently straight (partly preserved in no. 6, figs. 1049–51); the upper lip covered by the moustache, the lower receding; the beard fairly long and tapering downward; the bushy, unkempt hair. There are also specific renderings that recur and which point to mechanical reproduction, namely, the pronounced curl, directed to the (spectator's) right, over the middle of the forehead ('Muschellocke'), the copious, longish curls placed over the temples, the short curls below the under lip, directed to the right and left centre. In the inscribed Vatican herm a mantle is shown over both shoulders, with no chiton.

The personality closely corresponds to what is known of Antisthenes from literary sources—a self-reliant, hard man, but a visionary. Plato's description of his nature as joyless, but not ignoble seems apt.

The portrait has been variously dated, in the early fourth century (i.e. during Antisthenes' lifetime), in the third, the second, and even the first century B.C. (see bibliography). Stylistically it would seem to me to take its place in the developed Hellenistic style of the second century B.C., contemporary with the Pergamene altar (so also L. Curtius, *Röm. Mitt.* LIX, 1944, pp. 30ff.; Schuchhardt, *Göttingische Gelehrte Anzeigen*, no. 213, 1960, p. 184).

DIOGENES

414–323 B.C. Cynic philosopher. Son of Hikesias of Sinope, on the coast of Pontus.

c. 394 B.C. Left Sinope because his father, who was in charge of the mint of the state, was accused 'of having adulterated the coinage', παραχαράξαντος τὸ νόμισμα (Diog. Laert, VI, 20).

He reached Athens as a penniless refugee, and there came under the influence of Antisthenes (Diog. Laert. VI, 21). 'From that time on, exile as he was, he set out upon a simple life', τοὐντεῦθεν ... ἅτε φυγὰς ὢν ὥρμησεν ἐπὶ τὸν εὐτελῆ βίον (Diog. Laert. VI, 21).

He lived in great poverty as a beggar, believing that happiness consisted in satisfying only one's basic needs and eschewing all else.

On a voyage to Aegina he was captured by pirates and sold as a slave to a Corinthian named Xeniades. The latter took him to Corinth and entrusted him with his household and the education of his children—a task of which Diogenes acquitted himself so well that Xeniades used to go about saying 'A good genius has entered my house', ἀγαθὸς δαίμων εἰς τὴν οἰκίαν μου εἰσελήλυθε (Diog. Laert. VI, 30, 74).

He died in Corinth at the age of nearly ninety (Diog. Laert. VI, 76). By living the simple philosophy that he taught, Diogenes captured the imagination of his contemporaries and of posterity. Countless anecdotes, including the well-known one of his living in a pithos and of his meeting with Alexander, have clustered round this strange personality. Diogenes Laertios (VI, 20–83, passim) gives a long list of them and of his quick repartees.

He was called 'the dog', κύον, hence the word 'Cynic'. Whereas Antisthenes was the founder of the Cynic philosophy (q.v.), Diogenes may be regarded as the initiator of the Cynic way of life.

There are several writings attributed to Diogenes, both dialogues and tragedies (Diog. Laert. VI, 80).

STATUES RECORDED

1. Pausanias (II, 2, 4): 'As one goes up to Corinth are tombs (memorials), and by the gate is buried Diogenes of Sinope, whom the Greeks surname the Dog', Ἀνιοῦσι δὲ ἐς Κόρινθον καὶ ἄλλα ἐστὶ κατὰ τὴν ὁδὸν μνήματα καὶ πρὸς τῇ πύλῃ Διογένης τέθαπται ὁ Σινωπεύς, ὃν κύνα ἐπίκλησιν καλοῦσιν Ἕλληνες.

Diog. Laert. VI, 78: '(Diogenes) was buried beside the gate leading to the Isthmus (of Corinth). Over his grave they set up a pillar and a dog in Parian marble', ἐπέστησάν τ' αὐτῷ κίονα καὶ ἐπ' αὐτῷ λίθου Παρίου κύνα.

2. Diog. Laert. (VI, 78): 'Subsequently his fellow-citizens honoured him with a bronze statue, on which these verses were inscribed: "Time makes even bronze grow old, but thy glory, Diogenes, all eternity will never destroy. Since thou alone didst point out to mortals the lesson of self-sufficingness and the easiest path of life",' Ὕστερον δὲ καὶ οἱ πολῖται αὐτοῦ χαλκαῖς εἰκόσιν ἐτίμησαν αὐτὸν καὶ ἐπέγραψαν οὕτω·

> γηράσκει καὶ χαλκὸς ὑπὸ χρόνου, ἀλλὰ σὸν οὔτι
>   κῦδος ὁ πᾶς αἰών, Διόγενες, καθελεῖ·
> μοῦνος ἐπεὶ βιοτᾶς αὐτάρκεα δόξαν ἔδειξας
>   θνητοῖς καὶ ζωῆς οἶμον ἐλαφροτάτην

(Gk. Anth. XVI, 334).

For the base of a herm inscribed Διογένο(υ)ς, in the Vatican cf. infra.

There are, therefore, records of several memorials having been erected to Diogenes, one in Corinth, consisting of the figure of a dog, and several statues of himself at Sinope. In addition, there may have been others either in Athens or elsewhere, which do not happen to be mentioned in extant literature, for Diogenes was a popular figure.

APPEARANCE

Diogenes walked the streets of Athens as a beggar, with stick and wallet, βακτηρία ... τε καὶ τῇ πήρᾳ (Diog. Laert. VI, 23). When a cottage could not be found for him, 'he took for his abode the pithos in the Metroon', τὸν ἐν τῷ Μητρῴῳ πίθον ἔσχεν οἰκίαν (ibid.). Philostratos, Epist., 18 [22], refers to paintings in which Diogenes and Krates were represented barefoot.

One can imagine that Diogenes did not pay much attention to the cut of his hair and beard, and Sidonius Apollinaris (Epist. XI, 9. 14) specifically mentions the fullness of his beard (barba comante) as a characteristic of his portraits.

IDENTIFICATION

No authentic portrait of Diogenes in the round has as yet been found; only one in a mosaic (cf. infra), which cannot be trusted as a faithful likeness. Nevertheless, it has been possible to identify—provisionally at least—several extant portraits as representing Diogenenes on the evidence of what is known of his life and habits. Thus an unkempt, stooping old man, with such attributes as a wallet, a stick, a dog, and a pithos, has been persuasively named Diogenes.

PORTRAITS EXTANT AND ONCE EXTANT

PORTRAITS IN THE ROUND

1. Base of a herm, with feet, inscribed Διογενος (presumably for Διογένους). Now surmounted by the fragmentary herm of Thales (q.v.). In the Sala delle Muse, Vatican, inv. 16251. Found in 1774, near Tivoli (cf. p. 81).   FIG. 1062
Height 38 cm.; width 47 cm.; thickness 40 cm.
Bernoulli II, p. 47.
Lippold, Vat. Kat. III, 1, no. 490b, pl. 17.
Kaibel, I.G. XIV, 1148.

2. Large statuette in the Villa Albani, 942. For its history see under no 3.   FIG. 1057
Height, as restored, with plinth, 54·6 cm.; without plinth, 49 cm.; height of ancient part 35 cm.; ht. of head 11·2 cm.
Restorations: The nose, both arms from the biceps down, almost the whole left leg, the right leg from the knee down, the feet, the tree trunk, the plinth. The only ancient parts are, therefore, the head and the torso, including the shoulders and the upper right leg (cf. drawings on next page).
Bernoulli II, p. 49, pl. VIII.
Helbig, F.³, no. 1856.
Arndt-Br., 321–322.
Lippold, Gr. Porträtst., pp. 84ff.

Statuette of Diogenes, Villa Albani, Rome. Winckelmann, *Mon. ant. ined.* II, pl. 172

Amelung, *A.J.A.* XXXI, 1927, pp. 287ff.
Richter, *MM. Studies* II, 1929, pp. 31ff.; *MMA. Sc. Cat.*, under no. 191.
Laurenzi, *Ritratti*, no. 81.
Schefold, *B.*, pp. 146f., no. 4.

3. Large statuette, extensively restored, in the Metropolitan Museum, New York, 22.139.1, Rogers Fund, 1922. Purchased in Rome. Once in the possession of Alessandro Albani (cf. Winckelmann, *Mon. ant. ined.* II, (1767), pl. 172). Height, with plinth, 54.1 cm.; without plinth 48.3 cm. The only ancient parts are: the feet, the left side of the left leg, the feet and hindquarters of the dog, the tree trunk (except the piece attached to Diogenes' leg), and the plinth. Missing in the ancient parts are: the big toe of Diogenes' left foot, chips from the plinth. The plinth was broken in two and reattached. FIGS. 1058–1059
It will be observed that the parts missing in the Albani statuette are those preserved in the New York one. Dimensions and marble are moreover the same in both. That the two in fact once formed one statuette is made probable by what is known of the history of the Albani statuette.

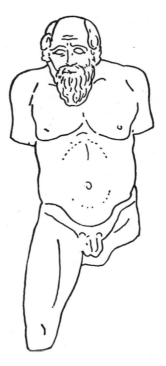

The statuette in the Villa Albani without restorations. Reinach, *Rép.* II, pl. 569, no. 10

In the first edition of the *Indicazione antiquaria per la villa suburbana dell' eccellentissima casa Albani*, 1785, two statuettes are listed as follows: One, no. 593, 'statuetta di Diogene cinico ignudo col cane accanto, e col bastone nella sinistra' (ed. dal Winck. M. I, no. 172, sp. p. 228); another, no. 599, 'statuetta di Diogene simile alla precedente'. Then, in the second edition of 1803, only one such statuette is listed, as no. 564 (ed. dal Winck. M. I, no. 172, sp. p. 228). One may surmise that some time previous to 1767 (for Winckelmann already knew of the two statuettes) the figure now in the Villa Albani was broken, whereupon two statuettes were made from the broken parts, and one subsequently given away. (As noted above, the restored parts in the Albani statuette correspond to those extant in the New York one, and were evidently copied from them.)
The second Albani figure, now in New York, was rediscovered by F. Hauser in the possession of the Duke Braschi at Tivoli. It may be recalled that the Albani and Braschi families were closely connected in the period 1775 to 1799, Pope Pius VI being a member of the Braschi family, and Giovanni Francesco, a cardinal at that time, being a member of the Albani family. That one of two similar statuettes passed from one family to the other would, therefore, be likely.
To make this possibility a certainty one must examine the two pieces together, but this has not yet been achieved.
Winckelmann, *Monumenti antichi inediti*, 1st ed. II, 1767, pl. 172.
Reinach, *Répertoire* II, pl. 569, no. 10 (there shown without restorations, as in a cast in the École des Beaux-Arts, Paris).
Richter, *MMA. Bull.* XXIV, 1929, p. 144; *MM. Studies* II, 1929, pp. 29ff.; *MMA. Sc. Cat.*, no. 191.
Kaschnitz-Weinberg, *Cat. Mag. Vat.*, p. 243, under no. 568.
Eisler, *Rev. arch.* XXXIII, 1931, pp. 1ff.

Schefold, *B.*, pp. 146, 213.
Lippold, *Gr. Pl.*, p. 315, note 1.

4. Fragment in the Magazzini of the Vatican, inv. 3984. Only the lower part of the statuette is preserved; a wallet is substituted for the dog. Recognized by Amelung as part of a statuette of Diogenes in 1921.　　　　　　FIG. 1060
Height 31·5 cm.
No restorations.
Amelung, *A.J.A.* XXXI, 1927, pp. 287ff., fig. 6. His fig. 5 shows this fragment combined with a cast of the Albani statuette; but he recognized that the two could not have belonged together (cf. his p. 289). In fact the marble is different in the two.
Richter, *MM. Studies* II, 1929, p. 39.
Kaschnitz-Weinberg, *Cat. Mag. Vat.*, no. 568.

5. Head, in the Musée Granet, Aix. From a statuette.
　　　　　　　　　　　　　　　　　　FIGS. 1064–1065
Height 10·6 cm.
No restorations.
Bernoulli II, p. 50.
Joubin, in *E.A.*, 1407–1408.
H. Gibert, *Le Musée d'Aix*, I. partie (1882), no. 252.
Richter, *MM. Studies* II, 1929, p. 39.
Espérandieu, *Recueil* III, 1, pp. 354f., 2494.

DOUBTFUL EXAMPLES

Among heads that somewhat resemble the Albani Diogenes and have by some been thought to represent him may be mentioned those in the Capitoline Museum (Stuart Jones, *Cat.*, p. 228, no. 21; Arndt-Br., 325–326)=Hesiod? (q.v.); in the Vatican (Lippold, *Vat. Kat.*, III, 1, p. 7, no. 490a; and in Berlin (*Beschreibung*, no. 320). But the resemblance is not sufficient to warrant an identification. In particular, they lack the sense of suffering from privation that is a distinguishing mark of the Albani and Aix heads.

The inscription Διογένης Ἱκεσίου Σινωπαῖος on a herm published by Statius (*Ill. vir. vult.* XII) and Gronov (*Thes.* II, 88), now in the Conservatori Palace, was recognized as false also by F. Ursinus (praef., p. 6). Cf. Kaibel, *I.G.* XIV,182*; Huelsen, no. 51*; Bernoulli II, p. 47; S. Jones, *Cat.*, p. 55, no. 10.

Likewise modern is the inscription Διογένης on the neck of a bust, once in the Maffei collection (Statius XI). Cf. Kaibel, *I.G.* XIV, 180* and Huelsen, no. 49*.

A small, bearded head, from Herculaneum, in the National Museum, Naples, inv. 6515, has the modern inscription Διογένης. Cf. Bernoulli II, p. 47.

OTHER REPRESENTATIONS
RELIEFS

a. A relief representing Diogenes inside a pithos, confronted by another figure (restored as Alexander) in an architectural setting. In the Villa Albani. Once in the Stosch Collection. Found in 1726 on the Testaccio.　　　　　FIG. 1067
Height, with frame, 78·5 cm.; without frame, 70 cm.; width without frame 78 cm.

Relief of Diogenes, in the Villa Albani, Rome. Drawing by Ghezzi, Vatican Library. Cf. *infra*

Restorations: Of Diogenes: the head, the right forearm, the larger part of the stick; of the dog: the head and a piece of the lower hind thigh; of the second figure only the palm of the right hand is ancient (the fingers are new). There exists an old drawing by Ghezzi of this scene before restoration in the Codex Ottobonus Latinus, 3109, of the Vatican Library; cf. Amelung, op. cit., p. 290, fig. 7, and Schreiber, loc. cit.
Winckelmann, *Mon. ant. ined.*, pl. 174, p. 229.
Schreiber, *Die Hellenistischen Reliefbilder*, pl. 94.
Helbig, *F.*[3], no. 1894.
Lippold, *Gr. Portr.*, p. 84, (suggests that the second figure was Krates).
Amelung, *A.J.A.* XXXI, 1927, pp. 289ff., fig. 7.

b. A relief representing Diogenes inside a pithos in lively conversation with his dog, on the upper part of a cippus. Once in the Museo Borgia, then in the possession of W. Amelung. Present location not known. The lower part of the cippus, with the inscription: P. Egnatius Nicephorus, and a relief representing the death of Archemoros, was once in the Palazzo Barberini (now?). In an old drawing of the cippus the two parts, the upper and the lower, were still combined, cf. Huelsen and Amelung, opp. citt.　　FIG. 1061
No restorations.
Matz-Duhn III, no. 3926.
Altmann, *Grabaltäre*, pp. 102f., no. 84.

Hülsen, *Abh. der Heidelberger Akad.* IV, 1917, p. 65, no. 78a, fig. 51.
E.A., 2940.
Amelung, *A.J.A.* XXXI, 1927, pp. 292f., figs. 8, 9.
A modern copy of this relief is mentioned by Amelung as being in the Grossherzogliche Antiquarium in Mannheim.

STATUETTES AND GEMS

c. Among the bronze and terracotta statuettes there are a number which, instead of being generic philosophers, may have been intended for Diogenes. For instance, the attractive bronze figure in Vienna, 7·4 cm. high, of a bald old man with a long beard carrying a wallet, has by some been thought to represent Diogenes, by others Krates (cf. von Schneider, *Album der Antikensammlung, Wien*, 1895, p. 10, pl. XXV, 4).

d. A carnelian, 10 by 12 mm., in the Thorvaldsen Museum, Copenhagen, is engraved with a representation of Diogenes in his pithos, stick in hand, his dog by his side; he is shown conversing with a disciple, who is seated in front of him, holding an open scroll. The pithos is inscribed M.C.V., presumably the initials of the owner of the seal. Roman period.   FIG. 1068
King, *Antique Gems and Rings*, 1872, vol. II, p. 61, pl. XXXVIII, 2; *Handbook of Engraved Gems*, 2. ed., pl. 78, no. 5.
Furtwängler *A.G.*, pl. XLIII, no. 11.
Lippold, *Gemmen und Kameen*, pl. 67, no. 2.
Fossing, *Catalogue of Engraved Gems and Cameos, Thorvaldsen Museum*, no. 446.

e–g. Similar engravings occur on a carnelian in Leningrad (cf. fig. 1069; Furtwängler, *A.G.*, pl. XLIII, 15), and on two glass gems in Berlin (cf. figs. 1063, 1070; Furtwängler, *Beschreibung*, nos. 1525, 1526). Here too Diogenes is shown emerging from his pithos, in conversation with a disciple or another philosopher.

Visconti (*Ic. gr.* I, p. 272, note 1) mentions a black stone, found on the Esquiline, engraved with a head resembling the Albani statuette and inscribed: Διογ. . . . It was in Ursinus' own collection, but is now lost. If genuine, and really representing the same individual as the Albani figure, we should here have had a welcome confirmation of the identification.

MOSAIC

h. A bust, inscribed Διογένης, is included in the large mosaic from Cologne as the central medallion. In the Römisch-Germanisches Museum, Cologne. He is represented emerging from his pithos, a mantle covering his left shoulder. For the other portraits in this mosaic cf. p. 81. They have no iconographical value. In the case of the Diogenes, however, there is a certain, perhaps fortuitous, resemblance to the Albani statuette.   FIG. 1066
Bernoulli II, pp. 47f., fig. 5.
Schefold, *B.*, pp. 154f.
Parlasca, *Mosaiken*, p. 80, pl. 81, 2.

MENIPPOS

First half of third century B.C. Of Gadara in Phoenicia (Strabo, 759). Cynic philosopher. Probably pupil of Krates. Was of lowly origin, a slave, but later obtained his freedom, and made enough money to acquire Theban citizenship.
On his independence and contempt of wealth, cf. Lucian, *Dial. mort.* 1, 2ff.
According to Diogenes Laertios (VI, 101) he wrote 13 books on Cynic philosophy—all now lost. He wrote in prose, interspersed with verse, and was the originator of the serio-comic style (σπουδογέλοιον), in which philosophical doctrines are put in humorous language. He was popular in Roman times, when his biting wit was much admired. Varro's *Saturae Menippeae* are adaptations from Menippos' writings and Lucian was influenced by him (cf. his *Epistulae Saturnales*).
Schefold, *B.*, pp. 122f., has suggested that we may have a portrait of Menippos in the statue from Civita Lavinia in the Capitoline Museum, Stanza del Gladiatore, no. 9 (Stuart Jones, *Cat.*, p. 347, no. 8, pl. 86; Arndt-Br., 327–329; Helbig, *F.*³, no. 877). It evidently represents a Cynic philosopher, and the date of the Greek original (c. 240 B.C.) would fit; also, as far as one can tell, the physiognomy.   FIGS. 1071, 1074
Height 1·71 m.
Restorations: Nose, most of the right arm, with the hand, the fingers of the left hand, pieces in the drapery, the feet, the plinth. The scrinium is ancient.
There are no replicas, and some have thought that the statue is a Greek original. Related is the statue (with restored head, right arm, plinth, scrinium, etc.) in the Glyptothek, Munich, said to be from Greece, and considered by Furtwängler (*Beschreibung*, no. 288) to be a Greek commemorative statue of the third to second century B.C.: 'Derartige flüchtig, aber geschickt und lebendig ausgeführte Ehren- und Votivstatuen muss es in Griechenland einst zu vielen Hunderten gegeben haben'. Cf. also Arndt-Br., 330.   FIG. 1075
Stylistically related, but not a replica of the head of the Capitoline statue, is a head in the collection of the On. Fiamingo in Rome. As I think it is unknown and unpublished, I take this opportunity of illustrating it. About life-size. No restorations. Provenance not known, but doubtless from Italy. Like the head of Sokrates in the same collection (cf. p. 113), it was perhaps acquired on the advice of Adolfo Venturi.   FIG. 1072
Also stylistically related, it would seem, is the head of another unknown, Louvre Ma 544, and the head in the Metropolitan Museum (Richter, *Sc. Cat.*, no. 187).

KRATES

fl. 328–324 (113th Olympiad, Diog. Laert. VI, 87). Died after 270 B.C. Of Thebes, son of Askondas. Cynic philosopher, pupil of Diogenes and contemporary of Theophrastos. He belonged to a distinguished, wealthy family, but distributed his belongings among his fellow-citizens, went to

Athens, and became a 'sturdy philosopher' (Diog. Laert. VI, 87). Zenon of Kition became his pupil.

Among his most ardent followers was Hipparcheia, a beautiful girl from a rich family, who fell in love with Krates' discourses and way of life, refused her many suitors, and married Krates (Diog. Laert. VI, 96f.).

A number of Krates' witty hexameters and distichs are preserved. Especially popular were the verses: 'Set down for the cook ten minas, for the doctor one drachm, for the flatterer five talents, for counsel smoke, for mercenary beauty a talent, for a philosopher three obols'

τίθει μαγείρῳ μνᾶς δέκ', ἰατρῷ δραχμήν,
κόλακι τάλαντα πέντε, συμβούλῳ καπνόν,
πόρνη τάλαντον, φιλοσόφῳ τριώβολον
(Diog. Laert. VI, 86).

His philosophy of life is well expressed in the saying: 'That much I have which I have learned and thought, the noble lessons taught me by the Muses. But wealth amassed is prey to vanity',

ταῦτ' ἔχω ὅσσ' ἔμαθον καὶ ἐφρόντισα καὶ μετὰ Μουσῶν
σέμν' ἐδάην· τὰ δὲ πολλὰ καὶ ὄλβια τῦφος ἔμαρψεν.

He was called the 'door-opener', θυρεπανοίκτης, from his habit of opening every door and admonishing those within (Diog. Laert. VI, 86).

Of his appearance it is said that he was ugly to look at ἦν δὲ καὶ τὴν ὄψιν αἰσχρός (Diog. Laert. VI, 91), and that he was depicted barefoot in paintings; cf. under Diogenes.

He was everywhere welcome (Julian, Or. 6, p. 201B), as is indicated by the fact that people wrote on their doors Εἴσοδος Κράτητι ἀγαθῷ δαίμονι; and he is said to have brought disputants together again, and to have rebuked, not with bitterness but with charm, οὐ μετὰ πικρίας ἀλλὰ μετὰ χάριτος. Plutarch wrote a life of him, Βίος Κράτητος, now lost.

SUGGESTED IDENTIFICATIONS

A painting from the garden of the Farnesina, now in the National Museum of the Terme, Rome, representing a man (designated as a Cynic philosopher by his stick, animal's skin, and his dishevelled appearance) and a young girl carrying a box on her head (fig. 1079), has been interpreted as Krates and Hipparcheia by Fuhrmann, Röm. Mitt. LV, 1940, pp. 86ff. From a resemblance to the man in this painting, Fuhrmann identified as Krates a head in the National Museum, Naples (inv. 6162; Ruesch, Guida, no. 1136; Arndt-Br., 623-624; Schefold B., pp. 88f., no. 1). No restorations except a piece of the herm on its right side at the back. Height 48 cm.; ht. of head 36 cm. FIG. 1083

That the person represented in the Naples portrait was famous is indicated by the fact that there are replicas: 1. In the Ambulacro of the Vatican, inv. 105, formerly in the Galleria degli Arazzi, cf. figs. 1076-78; Lippold, Vat. Kat. III, 2, p. 5, no. 7, pl. v; nose, bottom of beard, piece on right eyebrow, and herm restored. 2. In the Louvre, from the Campana Collection, Ma 67, Cat. sommaire (1922), p. 16, no. 67 (cf. my fig. 1080); most of left side of face with nose and beard restored. 3. In the Collection Surutschan in Kischinew, cf. Fuhrmann, op. cit., p. 90. Once studio Canova, Matz-Duhn, no. 580, cf. L. Curtius, Röm. Mitt. LIX, 1944, p. 62.

The resemblance to the Farnesina painting seems credible; and the physiognomy is singularly appropriate—kind, intelligent, and full of charm (χάρις), in spite of its 'ugliness'. So that the identification is a possibility; but cf. Lippold, loc. cit.

Stoics

ZENON

333/331-264/261 B.C., of Kition, Cyprus, founder of the Stoic philosophy. Son of Mnaseas (or Demeas).

c. 301 B.C. Was shipwrecked at the Piraeus, whereupon he settled in Athens (Diog. Laert. VII, 2).

c. 300-280 For twenty years studied under Krates and others (Diog. Laert. VII, 2-4).

c. 280 Then he opened his own school in the Stoa Poikile, in the agora of Athens, whence the name Stoic was given to his philosophy (Diog. Laert. VII, 5).

He developed a vast system comprising logic, physics, and ethics, of which Diogenes Laertios gives a lengthy account (VII, 39-160). It was his ethical teaching, however, that most appealed, and through which Stoicism became popular and famous.

When Antigonos Gonatas of Macedon invited Zenon to visit him, he refused on account of his age, but sent younger companions with the promise that if Antigonos associated with them 'he would not fall short of the conditions that lead to happiness', οὐδενὸς καθυστερήσεις τῶν πρὸς τὴν τελείαν εὐδαιμονίαν ἀνηκόντων (Diog. Laert. VII, 9).

The people of Athens held him in high esteem, Ἐτίμων δὴ οὖν Ἀθηναῖοι σφόδρα τὸν Ζήνωνα.

They passed a decree praising him for his teaching of 'virtue and temperance', ἀρετὴν καὶ σωφροσύνην, 'for which his own life served as a pattern', παράδειγμα τὸν ἴδιον βίον ἐκθείς, and honoured him with the building of a tomb in the Kerameikos at public expense, τάφον ἐπὶ τοῦ Κεραμεικοῦ δημοσίᾳ (Diog. Laert. VII, 6, 10-11.).

According to Lucian, Macrob. 19, he died when 98 years old.

APPEARANCE

Diogenes Laertios (VII, 1), quoting various authorities, describes him, in a not very complimentary fashion, as having a twisted neck, being lean, fairly tall, dark-skinned, with thick legs, and

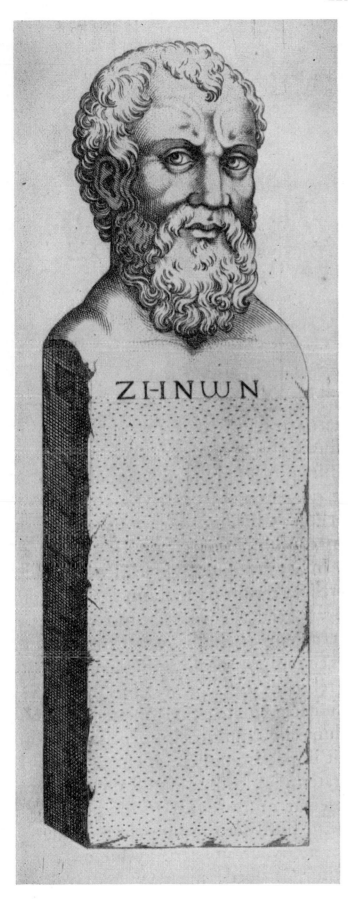

Zenon. National Museum, Naples. Faber, *Imag.*, 151. (Cf. fig. 1089)

flabby and delicate, τὸν τράχηλον ἐπὶ θάτερα νενευκὼς ἦν . . . ἰσχνός, ὑπομήκης, μελάγχρους, . . . παχύκνημός τε καὶ ἀπαγὴς καὶ ἀσθενής.

'He had a morose and bitter expression, and a furrowed face', στυγνόν τ' εἶναι καὶ πικρὸν καὶ τὸ πρόσωπον συνεσπασμένον, and was exceedingly parsimonious (Diog. Laert. VII, 16).

Sidonius Apoll. (*Ep.* IX, 14) refers to 'Zenon fronte contracta'. Krates called him 'a little Phoenician', Φοινικίδιον (Diog. Laert. VII, 3), and this has been thought to indicate that he had some Semitic blood.

RECORDED STATUES

Diogenes Laertios (VII, 6) states that the Athenians honoured Zenon 'with a golden crown and a bronze statue', χρυσῷ στεφάνῳ τιμῆσαι καὶ χαλκῇ εἰκόνι; and that the citizens of his native town did likewise, 'deeming his statue an ornament to their city', κόσμον ἡγουμένους τὴν τἀνδρὸς εἰκόνα; and that 'the people of Kition living in Sidon also laid claim to him, ἀντεποιοῦντο δ' αὐτοῦ καὶ οἱ ἐν Σιδῶνι Κιτιεῖς.

Pliny (XXXIV, 92) says that 'Cato in his expedition to Cyprus sold all the statues found there except one of Zeno'; and 'that it was not the value of the bronze nor the artistic merit that attracted him, but its being the statue of a philosopher', non aere captus nec arte, unam tantum Zenonis statuam Cypria expeditione non vendidit Cato, sed quia philosophi erat.

There were, therefore, a number of statues recorded as having been erected to Zenon, one in Athens, and at least one in Cyprus; and the latter may have been the very one retained by Cato. But all the extant heads are copies of the same Greek original.

IDENTIFICATION

The identification of the portraits of Zenon was made possible by the inscribed name on a small bronze bust from Herculaneum (cf. no. 2), and on a marble herm from the Farnese Collection in Naples (cf. no. 1). In both cases the name Ζήνων is given without further specification, showing that a famous man was represented. There were, therefore, three possibilities: the Eleatic philosopher of southern Italy, born c. 488, pupil of Parmenides; the Stoic philosopher above discussed; and the Epicurean philosopher, a contemporary of Cicero. The first seems excluded, for he is said to have been good-looking (Plato, *Parmenides*, 127B; Apul., *Apologia*, 4), which is hardly an attribute applicable to the Naples heads. The Epicurean Zenon was favoured by some, since the Herculaneum bust was found with portraits of Epikouros, Metrodoros, and Hermarchos (q.v.), and because the owner of the villa, to judge by the papyri found in it, was thought to have had a special interest in Epicureanism; and in such an Epicurean milieu Zenon the Epicurean, though not as famous as the Stoic Zenon, could be designated simply by his name without further specification. But these arguments hardly seemed conclusive. The marble herm in Naples, which is also inscribed only Ζήνων, has no

Epicurean connexion, and, furthermore, the exclusive interest in Epicureanism by the owner of the villa at Herculaneum is by no means certain, as shown by the fact that non-Epicureans like Demosthenes (cf. pp. 217f., nos. 12, 13) and several Hellenistic rulers were found there, and that only a limited number of papyri can be attributed to Epicurean authors. On this subject cf. especially F. Poulsen, *Ik. Misc.*, pp. 16ff. On the other hand, what is known of the Stoic Zenon's appearance—his sombre looks, his almost fanatical temperance, his Phoenician origin—tallies so well with the person represented in the Naples busts, and the style fits so perfectly with the period of his life that the identity seemed assured.

This controversy has now been laid to rest by M. Charbonneaux's rediscovery, in the reserve collection of the Louvre, of a small double herm representing Zenon and Plato (cf. no. 4). The Stoic Zenon is surely the only holder of that name eminent enough to have been coupled with the great Plato.

PORTRAITS EXTANT AND ONCE EXTANT

1. Herm in the National Museum, Naples, inv. 6128. Inscribed Ζήνων on the bottom front of the herm. From the Farnese Collection. Drapery on both shoulders.
                                    FIGS. 1084–1085, 1089
Height 44 cm.; ht. of head 31 cm.
Restorations: Nose, rims of ears.
Visconti, *Ic. gr.*, I, pp. 217ff., pl. XVII, 5, 6.
Bernoulli II, p. 136, no. 1, pl. XVIII.
Arndt-Br., 235–236.
Ruesch, *Guida*, no. 1089.
Schefold, *B.*, pp. 108f., no. 4, p. 209.
Kaibel, *I.G.* XIV, 1156.
Huelsen, no. 11.

2. Small bronze bust in the National Museum, Naples, inv. 5468. Inscribed Ζήνων on the round, ancient base. From the Villa dei Pisoni, Herculaneum. Drapery on left shoulder, and along right one.   FIGS. 1086–1088
Height, with base, 17·5 cm.; ht. of head 9 cm.
No restorations.
Comparetti and De Petra, *Villa ercol.*, p. 263, no. 17, pl. XII, 9.
Bernoulli II, pp. 136f., no. 2.
Ruesch, *Guida*, no. 894.
Schefold, *B.*, pp. 108f., no. 2.

3. Head in the Museum of Lyons. Found at Lyons in 1823 together with the head of a Roman. In 1961 on loan in the Louvre. Both heads are flat at the back, and Mr. Charbonneaux thinks that they may have formed a double herm. However, the heights of the two heads differ, that of Zenon being 42 cm. (including the herm), whereas that of the Roman is 47 cm.   FIGS. 1095–1097
Height of head 33 cm.
No restorations, 'but recut and much cleaned' (Charbonneaux).
Espérandieu, *Recueil* III, 1, p. 23, no. 1768 (for the Roman head see no. 1767). A cast of the head is illustrated by Espérandieu, op. cit., IX, p. 268 (where it is identified as Zenon).
Reinach, *Gaz. des Beaux-Arts* 1912, p. 65.

4. Head in a small double herm, with Plato (q.v.), in the Louvre, Ma 3242. Brought from Egypt by the Mission Seymour de Ricci.   FIGS. 1090–1091
Height 11·5 cm.
No restorations. Flattened at top. Never broken. Surface somewhat weathered.
Héron de Villefosse, *Arch. Anz.* 1907, p, 372, no. 14 (identified as Platon and Zenon).
Cat. somm. (1922), p. 139, no. 3242 (not there identified).
Charbonneaux, *A.J.A.* LXVI, 1962, pp. 269ff. (identified as Platon and Zenon).

5. Head in the Musée Rodin, Paris.   FIGS. 1104–1105
Height 30 cm.
No restorations but surface much weathered, especially on the left side and back.
Charbonneaux: 'La tête comporte comme particularités un agrandissement considérable des yeux et, dans une moindre mesure, de la bouche; on constate donc une idéalisation très nette du type dans le sens classique; mais je ne crois pas que l'on puisse douter qu'il s'agit bien de Zénon—allongement du visage, dessin de la moustache et de la barbe, rides et bourrelet à la racine du nez, bosses du front.'

6. Head in the Musée Granet at Aix-en-Provence. Donation Bourguignon de Fabregoules.   FIGS. 1099–1100
Height 29–32 cm.
Restorations: The nose and the back of the neck.
Espérandieu, *Recueil*, III, 1, p. 353, no. 2489 (ill.).
Bernoulli II, p. 138, no. 3.
Joubin, in *E.A.*, nos. 1405–1406.
H. Gibert, *Le Musée d'Aix*, 1ère partie (1882), no. 237.

7. Head, mounted on a modern herm, in the possession of Miss M. C. Martin, of East Molesey, Surrey. She was given the herm by a Dr. Western of St. Thomas's Hospital, London, who told her that it had once belonged to Lord Elgin. Identified as Zenon by R. Higgins.   FIG. 1098
Life-size.
The nose and the ears are restored. Across the bottom of the modern herm someone has painted the words LYCURGUS (the letters look nineteenth century). I owe my knowledge of the piece, the information regarding it, and the photograph reproduced in fig. 1098 to the kindness of Reynold Higgins.

8. Herm in the Ny Carlsberg Glyptothek, Copenhagen, I.N. 606. Acquired in 1888 from the collection of Count Tyszkiewicz in Rome. Without drapery on shoulders.
                                    FIGS. 1092–1094
Height 47 cm.; ht. of head 29·5 cm.
Restorations: Nose and a little of the moustache.
F. Poulsen, *Ik. Misc.*, p. 18; *Cat.*, no. 418.
Arndt-Br., 237–238.
Bernoulli II, p. 138, no. 4.
V. Poulsen, *Portr. gr.*, no. 40.

9. Head in the National Museum, Athens, 1685.
                                    FIGS. 1101–1103
Height 31 cm.
No restorations, but much battered.

Kastriotes, *Glypta*, no. 1685 (there thought to represent Plato).
Hekler, *B.b.G.*, p. 47, note 56; there said to have been recognized as Zeno by Crome.
Schefold, *B.*, p. 209, note to p. 108, nos. 2, 4.

10. A herm (with head) inscribed Ζήνων is said to have been found in Hadrian's villa, but is now 'lost'.
Lippold, *Gr. Porträtst.*, p. 75, note. 1.
Kaibel, *I.G.* XIV, 1157.
Huelsen, no. 12 ('herma cum capite').

OTHER REPRESENTATIONS

On one of the silver cups from Boscoreale, in the Louvre (height 10·4 cm.), a skeleton inscribed Ζήνων Ἀθηναῖος is shown confronting another skeleton inscribed Ἐπίκουρος Ἀθηναῖος; that is, a great Stoic confronting a great Epicurean (cf. p. 199). Such contrasting juxtapositions were popular in the Roman period (cf. p. 16). Zenon is called an Athenian evidently because he spent most of his life in Athens.   FIG. 1698
H. de Villefosse, *Mon. Piot* v, 1899, p. 61, pl. VIII.
Bernoulli II, p. 139.
Schefold, *B.*, p. 166, no. 2.

Two emblemata of terracotta bowls, found in the Athenian agora (inv. P.15175, and P.22351), have been thought to represent Zenon; but the type is now recognized as being different from the inscribed portraits, and as representing perhaps a Cynic philosopher. A similar, but not identical, emblema was found in Corinth.
Winnefeld, *68. Berl. Winckelmannspr.*, 1908, p. 20, no. 12, pl. III, 3.
H. A. Thompson, *Hesperia* XXI, 1953, p. 56, pl. 17c.
Richter, *Gr. Portr.* III, p. 46, figs. 204, 205.
E. Harrison, *Ancient Portraits from the Athenian Agora*, Picture Book, no. 5, fig. 5.

The marble statue in the Capitoline Museum, once thought to represent Zenon, has long ago been recognized as not a portrait of him (cf. p. 185).
Bernoulli II, pp. 138f.
Helbig, *F.*³, no. 877.
Schefold, *B.*, pp. 122f.

The head in the Terme Museum, inv. 163, also once thought to represent Zenon, is now recognized as an unknown; cf. Felletti Maj, *Ritratti*, no. 37; H. von Heintze, in Hekler, *B.b.G.*³, p. 67, under no. 6.

The inscription Ζήνων on a herm with a portrait of Plato in the Sala delle Muse, Vatican (cf. p. 165, no. 1), has been recognized as modern.

CONCLUSIONS

The physiognomy shown in the portraits in the round above listed (nos. 1ff.) are all so similar that they must represent the same individual, and have been derived from the same Greek original. They show a man with a long, oval face, a long, squarish beard, protruding cheekbones, a receding forehead, a small mouth, and eyes placed rather close together; the brows are contracted, forming deep furrows above the bridge of the nose, and the expression is morose. There is,

moreover, something un-Greek in the general type, recalling Krates' appellation Φοινικίδιον.
The date of the Greek original, to judge by the style of the copies, may be assigned to the third century, perhaps in the third quarter, somewhat after that of Demosthenes (cf. p. 41). As said above, though a number of statues are known to have been erected to Zenon, in Athens and elsewhere (cf. p. 187), the extant portraits all go back to one original.

KLEANTHES

c. 331–c. 231 B.C., of Assos, in the Troad. Son of Phanias. Stoic philosopher, successor of Zenon as head of the Stoa; predecessor and teacher of Chrysippos.
He is said to have been a pugilist before joining Zenon, and to have earned his living while studying by heavy physical work, such as carrying water; so he was evidently of athletic build; in fact he was called a second Herakles (Diog. Laert. VII, 170).
He seems to have been poetically gifted, and more successful as a writer than as a teacher. In his studies he was slow but thorough.
Diogenes Laertios (VII, 170) cites a verse from Timon in which Kleanthes is described as 'a dullard, lover of verse, hailing from Assos, a mass of rock, unventuresome',
μωλύτης ἐπέων φίλος Ἄσσιος ὄλμος ἄτολμος.
Zenon compared him with a wax tablet, difficult to inscribe, but retaining fast what is written.
Diogenes Laertios gives the titles of many of his writings, which he calls κάλλιστα. They include works on physics and ethics.
His hymn to Zeus and other writings have been preserved. He died 99 years-old.

PORTRAITS RECORDED

Juvenal (II, 7) mentions the widespread popularity of his portraits. Sidonius Apollinaris (*Epist.* IX, 14) says that his statues are characterized by digitis corrosis.

ATTEMPTED IDENTIFICATIONS

Schefold (*B.*, pp. 146f., no. 2, 213) suggested that Kleanthes is represented in the large bronze statuette from Brindisi in the British Museum (height 51 cm.; Walters, *Cat. of Bronzes*, no. 848; *Select Bronzes*, pl. LXV), which previously had been thought to be a portrait of Aristippos, on the supposition that the statuette was a replica of the statue in the Palazzo Spada (cf. Esdaile, *J.H.S.* XXXIV, 1914, pp. 47ff., pls. II, III; and my p. 176).   FIG. 1106
There are four or five (?) replicas of the figure, all headless or with alien heads (cf. Lippold, *Gr. Porträtst.*, p. 86, note 3):

1. In the Galleria dei Candelabri, Vatican, inv. no. 2578. Lippold, *Vat. Kat.* III, 2, p. 239, no. 15, pl. 114; Esdaile, op. cit., p. 48, pl. V; Helbig, *F.*⁴-Speier, no. 533. Right forearm, with hand, feet with ankles, and other pieces restored. Height 55·5 cm.   FIG. 1107

2. In the Barracco Museum, Rome. Barracco and Helbig, *Collection Barracco*, pl. 64; Esdaile, op. cit., pl. VI; Pietrangeli, *Guida* (1949), p. 73, no. 161, and (1960), p. 94, no. 161. Height 51·5 cm.   FIG. 1110

3. In the Antikensammlung, Dresden. Herrmann, *Verzeichnis*, p. 48, no. 194; Esdaile, op. cit., p. 48, fig. 1. Feet and plinth restored. Height 56 cm.   FIG. 1109

4. In the Metropolitan Museum, New York. Richter, *A.J.A.* XXIX, 1925, pp. 152ff., fig. 5, *M.M.A. Sc. Cat.*, no. 185, pl. CXXIX. Acc. 24.73. Fletcher Fund, 1924. The head is a cast of that in the British Museum. Height, with head, 54·5 cm.   FIG. 1108

5. In 1911 in the Roman antiquity market (cf. Lippold, *Gr. Porträtst.*, p. 86, note 3; perhaps identical with the one in New York?).

CONCLUSIONS

The observant, calculating expression in the British Museum portrait certainly suggests a philosopher; the number of replicas indicates a famous personality; the style, which points to the third century as the period of the Greek original, would fit Kleanthes, and one may even concede that the physique of the individual shown in the various representations is athletic, though one hardly gets from them the impression of a 'Herakles', or 'dullard'—both appellations, however, that need not be taken literally, since we also hear of Kleanthes' poetic and musical leanings. Kleanthes, therefore, the person may be (so also Bieber, *Sc. of the Hell. Age*, p. 146). But, of course, there are other possibilities— though Lippold's Stoic Zenon is now excluded (cf. p. 188).

CHRYSIPPOS

c. 281/277–208/204 B.C. Of Soloi (Pompeiopolis), in Cilicia. Stoic philosopher. Son of Apollonios (Diog. Laert. VII, 179), or of Apollonides (Suidas), of Tarsos (Strabo XIV, 671).

LIFE

Said to have first been trained as a runner (Diog. Laert. VII, 179).
c. 260 B.C. Went to Athens, and studied with Arkesilaos, head of the Academy, and later with his successor Lakydes (Diog. Laert. VII, 183). Received training in logic. Was converted to Stoicism by Kleanthes.
c. 232 Succeeded Kleanthes as head of the Stoic school.
Elaborated the Stoic system in many written works and defended it against the attacks of the Academy.
He became famous for his dialectics (Diog. Laert. VII, 180; Dionys. of Halikarnassos, Περὶ συνθ. ὀνομ., p. 4, 31), and for the subtleties of his arguments.
He was a prolific writer. According to Diog. Laert. (VII, 180), there were more than 705 scrolls by him; but they contained many quotations from other authors, were repetitious, and deficient in style. The subjects treated were logic, ethics, and physics, λογικόν, ἠθικόν, φυσικόν μέρος. Only fragments now survive.
208–204 He died in the 143rd Olympiad, at the age of 73 (Apollodoros in Diog. Laert. VII, 184).
Chrysippos' reputation in Roman times was great. Cicero (*Academica* II, §24) considered him the chief support of the the Stoic philosophy: Chrysippum qui fulcire putatur porticum stoicorum. He laid the foundation of the spread of Stoicism all over the Graeco-Roman world. During the first two centuries of the Roman empire knowledge of the Stoic philosophy was the concomitant of a cultured man.

APPEARANCE

In appearance Chrysippos is said to have been insignificant (Diog. Laert. VII, 182).

STATUES RECORDED

1. Cicero (*De fin.* I, p. 39) says that 'in Athens there was a statue in the Kerameikos representing Chrysippos seated, with hand extended', Athenis statua est in Ceramico Chrysippi sedentis, porrecta manu.
Diogenes Laertios refers to this statue (VII, 182), saying that 'it shows how insignificant was the bodily appearance of Chrysippos, it being almost hidden by an equestrian statue close by, and this is why Karneades called him Krypsippos (Horse-hidden)', Ἦν δὲ καὶ τὸ σωμάτιον εὐτελής ὡς δῆλον ἐκ τοῦ ἀνδριάντος τοῦ ἐν Κεραμεικῷ, ὃς σχεδόν τι ὑποκέκρυπται τῷ πλησίον ἱππεῖ · ὅθεν αὐτὸν ὁ Καρνεάδης Κρύσιππον ἔλεγεν.

2. Pausanias (I, 17, 2) cites 'a statue of Chrysippos of Soloi in the gymnasium not far from the market place, in the vicinity of the bronze statue of Ptolemy', ἐν δὲ τῷ γυμνασίῳ τῆς ἀγορᾶς, ἀπέχοντι οὐ πολύ . . . εἰκὼν Πτολεμαίου χαλκῆ . . . καὶ . . . κεῖται καὶ Χρύσιππος ὁ Σολεύς.

3. Plutarch (*De stoic. repugn.*, p. 1033E) states that 'Aristokreon, pupil and nephew of Chrysippos, set up a statue of Chrysippos and wrote on it the following elegiac verse: Aristokreon dedicated this youthful Chrysippos, a knife to cut Academic knots', Ἀριστοκρέων γοῦν ὁ Χρυσίππου μαθητὴς καὶ οἰκεῖος, εἰκόνα χαλκῆν ἀναστηλώσας ἐπέγραψε τόδε τὸ ἐλεγεῖον·
Τόνδε νέον (τὸν θεῖον?) Χρύσιππον Ἀριστοκρέων ἀνέθηκε
τῶν Ἀκαδημιακῶν στραγγαλίδων κοπίδα.

4. Sidonius Apollinaris (*Epist.* IX, 14) says that 'for the representations of Chrysippos the fingers contracted for the computation of numbers (?) were a typical feature', Chrysippus digitis propter numerorum indicia constrictis. And Pliny (XXXIV, 88) praises 'a statue by Euboulides represented as counting on his fingers', Eubulidis digitis computans (laudatur). It seems likely that these two statements refer to the same statue, and that, therefore, the statue in the Kerameikos mentioned by Cicero (cf. no. 1), as being 'with hand extended' is that by Euboulides. One must remember,

however, that a seated statue with hand gesticulating is typical of philosophers (cf. Sittl, *Gebärden der Griechen und Römer*, pp. 252ff.; F. Poulsen, *Ik. Misc.*, p. 12; Plautus, *Miles gloriosus*, v, 204).

I may in this connexion illustrate a gem in Corpus Christi, Cambridge, with a presentation of some unknown person, *porrecta manu*, and *digitis constrictis* (cf. fig. 1148).

In Roman times portraits of Chrysippos were exceedingly popular, as was natural considering the popularity of the Stoic philosophy. Juvenal (*Sat.* II, 4–5) speaks of 'the pretence of the unlearned whose houses were crammed with plaster casts of Chrysippos', *Indocti primum, quamquam plena omnia gypso Chrysippi invenias* (cf. on this reference to plaster portraits p. 28).

The statues mentioned by Cicero and Pausanias (nos. 1, 2) were evidently two different portraits, since they were in different localities; and the statue erected by Aristokreon seems not to be identical with either of them, since Chrysippos was there represented as 'youthful' (unless one amends τὸν νέον; cf. Schefold, *B.*, p. 211, and the references there cited).

There were, therefore, perhaps three recorded Greek statues, all in Athens, since the one dedicated by his nephew was presumably also in that city. But we shall see that the many extant portraits executed in Roman times all go back to the same Greek original.

IDENTIFICATION

The identification of the portraits of Chrysippos rests on the following evidence: on bronze coins of Soloi of the Roman period (A.D. 163) two different portrait heads appear on obverse and reverse. Since Aratos and Chrysippos were the two most prominent men whom Soloi has produced, it is natural to think that the portraits represent these two; cf. Galen, *Protrept.* 7: τίς γὰρ ἢ Σταγείρων λόγος, εἰ μὴ δι' Ἀριστοτέλην; τίς δ' αὖ Σόλων, εἰ μὴ δι' Ἄρατόν τε καὶ Χρύσιππον; but as there is no inscription, it was uncertain which head represented whom (cf. p. 239). At first the long-bearded man was thought to be Chrysippos, the short-bearded Aratos, with head raised, looking at the stars, as indicative of an astronomer. The question was settled when von Prott (*Ath. Mitt.* XXVII, 1902, pp. 297ff.) found a headless bust in Athens inscribed Chrysippos (cf. *infra*, no. 16). Though the head is missing, enough of the throat and chest remain to show that the person had a short, not a long beard (no trace of it appears on the chest). Furthermore, of the short-bearded man a large number of portraits exist, a fact that corresponds to the known popularity of Chrysippos, whereas of the long-bearded man only one marble example has so far been identified (cf. p. 240).

It has been argued that the short-bearded man inscribed Ἄρατος, shown standing between two Muses on a Coptic textile, indicates that it is the short-bearded head on the coin of Soloi that represents Aratos, the long-bearded Chrysippos (cf. A. Apostolakis, Εἰκὼν τοῦ Ἀράτου ἐπὶ Ὑφάσματος Μουσεῖον Μπενάκη (1938), and my p. 240, e). It is true that

this head somewhat resembles the portrait in question, especially in the eager, upward look and the arrangement of the drapery which covers both shoulders but leaves the neck and breast bare, and that it is unlike the other head on the coin. But representations of Greek poets and philosophers on late paintings, mosaics, textiles, and mediaeval manuscripts are notoriously untrustworthy from the iconographical viewpoint—witness the Thucydides from Gerasa, the Sokrates from Apamea, and the Sophokles and Sokrates from Cologne (cf. figs. 714, 572; my *Gr. Portr.* II, pp. 26f.). So, in the Benaki textile, a bearded man with an expressive face served its purpose of representing the famous astronomer-poet, regardless of the real physiognomy of the man. At all events, in view of the strong evidence cited above for the identification of Chrysippos, this textile cannot be considered a serious argument against it.

PORTRAITS EXTANT
HEADS IN THE ROUND

1. Head, mounted on a modern herm, in the Galleria Geografica, Vatican, inv. 2897.   FIGS. 1121–1122
Height of ancient part 26 cm.; ht. of head 25·8 cm.
Restorations: Nose, upper lids, upper lip, outer parts of ears, piece at the right of the chin, lower part of neck.
Bernoulli I, p. 167, no. 1, figs. 31, 32 (under Hippokrates).
Helbig, *F.*[3], no. 391; Helbig, *F.*[4]-Speier, no. 586.
Arndt-Br., 933–934.
Lippold, *Vat. Kat.* III, 2, p. 453, no. 13, pl. 194.

2. Herm in the Stanza dei Filosofi, Capitoline Museum, no. 27.   FIGS. 1111–1112
Height 47·3 cm.; ht. of head 25·7 cm. Drapery on left shoulder.
Restorations: The greater part of the nose. The head not broken from the herm.
Bernoulli I, p. 167, no. 2 (under Hippokrates).
Arndt-Br., 939–940.
Stuart Jones, *Cat.*, p. 232, no. 37.

3. Head, mounted on a modern herm, in the Stanza dei Filosofi, Capitoline Museum, no. 26.   FIGS. 1124–1125
Height of ancient part 28·5 cm., ht. of head 25·9 cm.
Restorations: Nose, part of the back of the head, parts of ears, most of the neck.
Stuart Jones, *Cat.*, p. 234, no. 38.

4. Herm in the Villa Albani, no. 631.   FIGS. 1113–1114
Height 47·5 cm.; ht. of head 25 cm.
Restorations: Nose, both eyebrows, right eye, right ear, parts of left ear.
Bernoulli I, p. 168, no. 3 (under Hippokrates).
E.A., nos. 4121–4122.

5. Head, mounted on a modern or alien bust, in the Palazzo Colonna, Rome.
Life-size.
Restorations: Nose and perhaps some other parts. (As it is placed very high up I was only able to see it with my opera glasses.)

Matz-Duhn I, no. 1769 (as Demokritos).

Bernoulli I, p. 168 (under Hippokrates).

?6. Head, mounted on an alien statue, in the Museo Torlonia. Life-size.

Visconti, *Museo Torlonia*, no. 82.

Clarac, pl. 848, no. 2142.

Bernoulli I, p. 168 (as Hippokrates, 'wohl modern').

Dontas, *Eikones*, p. 63, pl. 24, α, β.

Included by Mustilli, *Museo Mussolini*, in his list of replicas, p. 61, no. 8, and by von Heintze in Hekler, *B.b.G.*[3], p. 70, no. 16.

After examining the head in 1964 I feel that it must be modern. Not only, as Bernoulli said, does the intact condition arouse suspicion, but also the fact that, though the head is alien to the statue, it fits the movement perfectly. Moreover, the surface is quite fresh, and a theatrical element has entered into the expression. Copied from the head in Naples (no. 8)?

7. Head, mounted on a modern herm, in the Uffizi, Florence, inv. 1914, no. 398.   FIGS. 1123, 1126

Height with neck 30 cm.; ht. of head 26 cm.

The nose is restored.

Bernoulli I, p. 168, no. 4 (under Hippokrates).

Dütschke III, no. 276.

Amelung, *Führer*, no. 113.

Arndt-Br. 937–938.

Hekler, *Bildniskunst*, pl. 116.

Mansuelli, *Cat.*, no. 14.

8. Bust, on a rounded base, in the National Museum, Naples, inv. 6127. From the Farnese Collection. Drapery on both shoulders.   FIGS. 1115–1117

Height 43 cm.; ht. of head 24 cm.

The nose is restored.

Bernoulli II, p. 149, no. 2 (under Aratos). His figs. 14, 15 by mistake show the head in the British Museum, no. 1846, not that in Naples.

Ruesch, *Guida*, no. 1090.

9. Bust in the British Museum, 1846. Payne Knight Bequest, 1824.   FIGS. 1118–1120

Height 34·5 cm.; ht. of head (to ancient part of beard) 25·9 cm.

Restorations: Nose, upper lip, lower part of beard, most of left ear, drapery at (spectator's) left.

Bernoulli II, p. 150, no. 3 (under Aratos).

Arndt-Br., 931–932.

A. H. Smith, *Cat.*, no. 1846.

10. Head (formerly mounted on a modern bust) in the British Museum, no. 1836. From the Towneley Collection.   FIGS. 1139–1141

Height of ancient part, 26·2 cm.; ht. of head 25·2 cm.

Restorations: Nose, upper part of left ear, neck.

Bernoulli I, p. 168, no. 6 (under Hippokrates).

Arndt-Br., 935–936.

A. H. Smith, *Cat.*, no. 1836.

11. Head, mounted on a modern herm, in the Louvre, Ma 326.   FIGS. 1131–1132

Height of ancient part c. 29·5 cm.; ht. of head c. 26·3 cm.

Restorations: Nose, back of skull, piece in beard at chin.

Visconti, *Ic. gr.* I, p. 384, pl. XXXII, 2, 3 (called Hippokrates).

Piroli, *Monumens du Musée Napoléon* II, pl. 78.

Cat. sommaire (1922), p. 17, no. 326 ('buste dit Hippocrate').

12. Head, mounted on a modern herm, inscribed Xenokrates, in the Glyptothek, Munich. Formerly in the Villa Albani. Acquired in Paris in 1851.   FIGS. 1127–1129

Height, with herm, 55 cm.

Restorations: Nose, lower lip with whole lower part of beard, the upper lids, parts of the eyeballs, left eyebrow, both ears.

Furtwängler, *Beschreibung der Glyptothek* (1910), no. 297.

Bernoulli I, p. 168, no. 7 (under Hippokrates).

13. Head in the Ny Carlsberg Glyptothek, Copenhagen, I.N. 2575. From Rome.   FIGS. 1133–1135

Height 28 cm.

No restorations.

Vaglieri, *Not. d. Sc.* 1908, p. 243 (where it is said to have been found with a head of Alexander the Great, Arndt-Br. 921).

F. Poulsen, *Cat.*, no. 425 a.

V. Poulsen, *Portr. gr.*, no. 46.

14. Head (with neck and part of chest). In the National Museum, Copenhagen, no. 8012. From Steensgaard.
          FIGS. 1136–1138

Height 43 cm.; ht. of head 24 cm. Is turned a little to its right, and slightly raised.

Restorations: Nose, left part of skull and neck with left ear, right ear. Weathered and worked over.

F. Poulsen, *Ik. Misc.*, pp. 7ff., fig. 2, pls. 4, 5.

15. Small head in the Metropolitan Museum, New York, 24.243. Fletcher Fund, 1924. Said to have been found in Rome. Formerly mounted on an alien statuette.   FIG. 1130

Height 14 cm.

No restorations. Broken above the neck. The restored bust has now been removed.

Richter, *A.J.A.* XXIX, 1925, pp. 152ff., figs. 3, 4; *MMA. Sc. Cat.*, no. 188.

Bieber, *Sc. of the Hell. Age*, p. 69, figs. 236, 237.

16. Small headless bust on rounded base in the National Museum, Athens, 3469. Formerly Epigraphical Museum, 3496. Found on the south-east slope of the Akropolis, above the theatre.   FIG. 1146

Height 15 cm.

No restorations. The back is flat, with sides depressed.

On the base of the bust is the inscription: Τὸν Χρ[ύ]σιππον Ἀκρίσιος Μίθρῃ, 'Akrisios (dedicated) the Chrysippos to Mithras'.

I.G. II–III[2], 3794.

von Prott, *Ath. Mitt.* XXVII, 1902, pp. 297ff.

Dontas, *Eikones*, p. 57, note.

On this piece rests the identification of the portrait of Chrysippos (cf. p. 191). As von Prott pointed out, the use of the definite article shows that only the famous Chrysippos could have been intended. The dedication of a portrait of a philosopher to a deity is of course common (cf. p. 3). The cult of Mithras was not widespread in Athens, but, as von Prott says, the dedication to this god may be explained by the fact that the teachings of the Stoa and of Mithraism were alike in some aspects; cf. Cumont, *Textes et monuments* I, p. 237, and *passim*; II, p. 469.

STATUES

17. With the help of the literary evidence (cf. p. 190, no. 1), which records that Chrysippos was represented seated, and with extended hand, it has been possible to recognize the figure which belonged to the portrait heads above listed; cf. Milchhöfer, *Archäologische Studien H. Brunn dargebracht*, 1893, pp. 51ff. M. Charbonneaux has reconstructed a life-size statue of this type in the Louvre, Ma 80, on which an alien head of Aristotle was once mounted (cf. p. 173, no. 1) with a cast of the head of Chrysippos in the British Museum. The folds of the mantle and the direction of the old, wrinkled throat corresponded in head and figure, so that there can be no reasonable doubt that the two types belonged together. Chrysippos is represented sitting on a cushioned folding stool, enveloped in a mantle, the right arm placed on his lap, with palm turned upward.   FIG. 1144
Height with seat and restored head, c. 1·20 m.; ht. of ancient part 1·8 m.; ht. of plinth c. 10·5 cm.
Restorations: 'The left foot with the adjoining part of the leg, the front part of the right foot with three of the toes, pieces in the drapery, the right forearm with the palm of the hand, including probably the thumb and the index finger; it is possible that the three other fingers are ancient; what is certain is that the forearm was nude and placed on the thigh, with the interior part turned upward; so that the restoration has every chance of being correct' (J. Charbonneaux, after a detailed examination in the summer of 1961).
Fea, *Storia delle arti del disegno presso gli antichi di G. Winckelmann*, III, p. 513, pl. XXIII.
Schefold, *B.*, p. 211, note to p. 124, no. 3.
Bieber, *Sc. of the Hell. Age*, pp. 69f., figs. 238–240, 242.
Richter, *Gr. Portr.* I, p. 40, fig. 24.
Dontas, *Eikones*, pp. 56ff., pl. 23, α, β.

18. A replica of this statue has been recognized in a large, headless statuette in the Museo Nuovo dei Conservatori, inv. 1635. Found on the Esquiline. He is shown seated on a throne terminating in front in winged monsters.
Height 51 cm.
Restorations: Upper part of neck with adjoining drapery. The right hand and the right corner of the plinth were worked separately and are missing.   FIGS. 1142–1143
Helbig, *F.*[3], no. 1012.
Mustilli, *Museo Mussolini*, p. 61, no. 1, pl. XLI, 166–167.
Dontas, *Eikones*, p. 57, note.

COINS

a. As we saw, the head on the bronze coins of Soloi-Pompeiopolis in Cilicia of A.D. 163/164 has served as the point of departure for the identification of Chrysippos' portraits (cf. p. 191). It is represented in profile to the right, has a short beard, a bald forehead, and is slightly tilted upward; the mantle that covers the shoulders leaves neck and chest

bare. As in other such cases, the presumption is that the portrait was copied from an existing statue (or relief), erected either in the native city of the philosopher or elsewhere. If made in Roman times it presumably was copied from an already existing Greek original. The close resemblance of the coin type to that of the marble heads makes it likely that both were derived from the same original.   FIG. 1147
Visconti, *Ic. gr.* I, p. 279f., pl. XXIIIA 3 (there thought to be Aratos).
Bürchner, pp. 118, 127, pl. IV, 13 (identity undecided).
Bernoulli II, p. 155, I, Münztafel, pl. II, 11 (= Aratos).
Schefold, *B.*, p. 173, no. 27 (= Chrysippos).

DOUBTFUL EXAMPLES

The head in the Ny Carlsberg Glyptothek, I.N. 2633 (F. Poulsen, *Cat.*, no. 425b; V. Poulsen, *Portr. gr.*, no. 47), though like Chrysippos, cannot be he—as F. Poulsen and V. Poulsen also saw.

The battered head in the National Museum, Athens, cited by Schefold (*B.*, p. 211, note to p. 124, 3) and by von Heintze (in Hekler, *B.b.G.*[3], p. 70, no. 15) as another replica of the Chrysippos type, seems to me a doubtful one. The formation of the eyes, for instance, is quite different from that in the certified portraits.   FIG. 1145

The head of an old man, engraved in profile to the right, on a Roman carnelian in the possession of the family Dümmler, was tentatively identified as Chrysippos by Wolters (*Arch. Anz.*, 1917, col. 117). But the resemblance of the head to the extant portraits of Chrysippos is only superficial.

CONCLUSIONS

In all the portraits in the round above listed the physiognomy is consistently the same—an old man with a lined face, bald on forehead and skull, but with short locks covering the back of the head and the temples, a short beard and moustache, deep-set eyes, and an intelligent, inquisitive, rather sad expression. It has been thought that the extant heads do not all go back to the same Greek original, principally because the inclination varies, sometimes being markedly upward, at other times not. But this variation may be explained by the fact that the head belonged to a stooping, seated statue (cf. fig. 1144), and was turned to its right, and that, therefore, the position had to be changed for use on herms and busts; and this change would not be the same in all cases, sometimes

Chrysippos. Roman bronze coin of Soloi. Ursinus, *Imag.*, 35

corresponding closely to the original, at other times deviating. That, however, all the heads in the round, the life-size ones and some of the reduced ones (cf. no. 15), all go back to one Greek original and were mechanically copied from it, is conclusively shown by the arrangement of the locks, which is practically identical in all: a series of short curls along the right cheek, combed forward but going in varying directions; a different rendering of the locks on the left side, where they are divided into several groups, with some intruding on the cheek (and this occurs also on the right side); the composition of the beard in three tiers, the uppermost starting immediately under the lower lip, the lowest bordered right and left by locks directed toward the centre. It would be difficult to imagine that such an arbitrary composition would recur in more than one original. It is more likely that the slight variations are due to the Roman copyist.

Which Greek original the copies reproduce is of course an open question. The fact that the heads belonged to a seated statue and that the Kerameikos statue was represented seated has been thought to indicate that it is the Kerameikos figure that was the prototype; but the other statues (likewise recorded as being in Athens (cf. p. 190)) may also have been represented seated. As above stated, the close resemblance of the head on the Soloi coin to the extant marble heads suggests that the former was copied from the same original; but where this Greek original stood is not certain, nor whether it was that made by Euboulides—however attractive it may be to associate a popular type with a statue by a known artist. One can only say that this identification seems probable.

It cannot be denied that the representations that have been identified as portraits of Chrysippos correspond to what is known of that philosopher—a serious, argumentative man, whose clear thinking was a decisive factor in the history of Stoicism and ensured for it a large following. The many extant portraits bear out his popularity in Roman times.

ARISTON

Of Chios. Fl. c. 260 B.C. Stoic philosopher. Pupil of Zenon, and teacher of Eratosthenes.

Together with Arkesilaos he became the most influential philosopher of his time.

He declared 'the end of action to be a life of perfect indifference to everything which is neither virtue nor vice', τέλος ἔφησεν εἶναι τὸ ἀδιαφόρως ἔχοντα ζῆν πρὸς τὰ μεταξὺ ἀρετῆς καὶ κακίας (Diog. Laert. VII, 160).

Schefold, B. (pp. 120f., no. 3, p. 210) suggested Ariston as the man represented in the Spada statue (cf. p. 176), reconstructing the inscription Ἀρίστ[ων Χῖο]ς. See also my Gk. Portr. IV, pp. 32f.

Epicureans

EPIKOUROS

342/341–271/270 B.C., the philosopher. Son of Neokles, of the Attic deme of Gargettos, and of Chairestrate. Member of a noble, but apparently impoverished family (Diog. Laert. X, 1).

LIFE

His father had gone to Samos with other colonists in 352/1 and taught there as a schoolmaster, γραμμαδιδάκταλος (Strabo XIV, 638).

Epikouros was probably born in Samos and spent his childhood there. Showed an interest in philosophy when he was fourteen (Diog. Laert. X, 2), or twelve (Diog. Laert, X, 14). Studied with the Platonist Pamphilos in Samos (Diog. Laert. X, 14; Cicero, nat. deor. I, 72), and afterwards perhaps with the Democritean philosopher Nausiphanes in Tenos (Diog. Laert. X, 13–14).

323 Went to Athens when eighteen and afterwards to Kolophon to join his parents, who had left Samos owing to the persecution of Perdikkas (Diog. Laert. X, 1). There studied philosophy by himself (αὐτοδίδακτος).

310 Opened a philosophic school first at Mytilene, then at Lampsakos, gathering round him devoted pupils, of whom Metrodoros (q.v.) was one.

306 Transferred the school to Athens and was followed by a number of his pupils, including Metrodoros.

Kept connexion with the school at Lampsakos, travelling there from Athens two or three times, accompanied by some of his pupils, including Hermarchos (q.v.).

Purchased a house with a garden in Athens, which served as the school, as well as a home for himself and his followers. He was the first to admit women and slaves as pupils.

306–270 Lived there for 36 years, studying and writing, remote from the outside world. He taught that pleasure— which he interpreted as freedom from pain and tranquillity of mind—is the greatest good, τὸ τέλος ἡ ἡδονή; also that virtue is merely necessary for the attainment of such peace, and that the study of nature leads to a better understanding of ourselves.

The devotion of his pupils sometimes amounted almost to worship (cf. under Kolotes).

For the last fourteen years he was practically an invalid.

270 Died in his 72nd year (Diog. Laert. X, 15).

In his will he named Amynomachos and Timokrates his heirs, and left the school and garden to his successors in perpetuity (Diog. Laert. X, 16f.). The library and house at

Melite were left to Hermarchos, who became his successor at the school.

Epikouros' will mentions that a feast should be regularly held on the 20th day of each month in his memory and in that of Metrodoros and Polyaios. Certain slaves who were members of the community were to be freed.

Epikouros' dominant personality impressed itself not only on the circle of his friends but on posterity. The 'Epicurean philosophy' remained potent throughout Hellenistic and Roman times (cf. Lucretius' *De natura rerum*). But since it centred round Epikouros and his doctrines, rather than on research as such, it merely remained a perpetuation of Epikouros' moral precepts. Its great appeal was the promise of happiness in spite of adversities (Cicero, *de fin.* II, p. 96); Compensabatur tamen cum his omnibus (doloribus) animi laetitia (Epikouros, in a letter to Hermarchos).

He wrote about 300 rolls (κύλινδροι), cf. Diog. Laert. x, 26. Of his most important work, 'On Nature', Περὶ φύσεως, fragments have survived.

APPEARANCE

In Cicero, *De fin.* v, 1, 3, Pomponius remarks that 'he could not forget Epikouros even if he wanted; the members of our body not only have pictures of him, but even have his likeness on their drinking cups and rings; nec tamen Epicuri licet oblivisci, si cupiam, cuius imaginem non modo in tabulis nostri familiares sed etiam in poculis et in anulis habent.

In the Priapea XII there is a humorous reference to Epikouros' large nose; cf. Baehrens, *Poetae Latini minores* I, Priapea, p. 62. Sidonius Apollinaris (*Epist.*, IX, 14) speaks of pingitur cute distenta.

The known fact that Epikouros suffered from physical ailments, which he patiently bore, is also perhaps a contributory factor in judging his appearance.

STATUES RECORDED

1. According to Diogenes Laertios (x, 9), Epikouros' native town (i.e. Samos) honoured his memory by the erection of bronze statues, ἥ τε πατρὶς χαλκαῖς εἰκόσι τιμήσασα.

2. In Roman times his portraits were very popular, cf. Cicero (*De fin.* v, 1, 3) cited above.

3. Pliny (XXXV, 5) refers to likenesses of Epikouros being displayed in bedrooms and carried around, Epicuri voltus per cubicula gestant ac circumferunt secum.

4. In Old Paphos, Cyprus, was found a block inscribed Ἐπίκουρος (in letters of the second half of the third century B.C.) which apparently once supported a portrait of the philosopher. Cf. Mitford, *B.S.A.* LVI, 1961, p. 7, no. 10.

IDENTIFICATION

The identification of the many extant portraits of Epikouros was made possible by the discovery at Herculaneum of a small bust inscribed with his name (cf. *infra*, no. 8), and by the double herm in the Capitoline Museum, with heads of Epikouros and Metrodoros, both with names inscribed (cf. *infra*, no. 1). The identification of the type of statue to which the heads belonged has been rendered probable by the evidence of a drawing by Preisler and the discovery of a large headless statuette that once evidently formed a pendant to a statuette of Hermachos (cf. p. 198 no. 2).

PORTRAITS EXTANT AND ONCE EXTANT

1. Head, in a double herm, with Metrodoros (q.v.), in the Stanza dei Filosofi, Capitoline Museum, no. 52, inscribed with the name: Ἐπίκουρος. Found 1742 in the excavations for the building of the portico of S. Maria Maggiore. Presented by Benedict XIV. No drapery on shoulders.

FIGS. 1149–1150, 1153

Height 60 cm.; ht. of head 33cm.
Restorations (on Epikouros): Front of nose, large part of left eyebrow.
Visconti, *Ic. gr.* I, p. 291, pl. xxva.
Bernoulli II, p. 123, no. 1, pls. XVI, XVII.
Arndt-Br. 1081–1083.
Stuart Jones, *Cat.*, p. 244, no. 63, pl. 56.
Kaibel, *I.G.* XIV, 1150.

2. Bust in the Stanza dei Filosofi, Capitoline Museum, 53. Mantle covers left shoulder and passes along right.

FIGS. 1151–1152

Height 48·5 cm.; ht. of head 35·9 cm.
Restorations: End of nose. In fine preservation.
Bernoulli II, p. 123, no. 2.
Arndt-Br., 1084.
Stuart Jones, *Cat.*, p. 244, no. 64, pl. 57

3. Head, mounted on a modern herm, in the Stanza dei Filosofi, Capitoline Museum, no. 13. According to Bottari, found in 1742 in the Piazza S. Maria Maggiore, Rome, and presented by Benedict XIV to the Museum.   FIG. 1160
Height of ancient part 37·3 cm.; ht. of head 32·7 cm.
Restorations: Nose, ears, patch on beard. The head was broken in two pieces.
Bernoulli II, p. 125, no. 20 ('zweifelhaft').
Lippold, *Gr. Porträtst.*, p. 77.
Arndt-Br. 1086–1087.
Stuart Jones, *Cat.*, p. 227, no. 18, pl. 56.

4. Head, mounted on a modern herm, in the Sala delle Muse, Vatican, inv. 301. Found in 1789 in Roma Vecchia, on the Via Appia. Acquired by Pius VI before 1792. No drapery on shoulders. Slight inclination of the head to its right.
Height of ancient part 30 cm.   FIGS. 1157–1159
Restorations: Top and back of head, piece of upper lip, most of nose, piece of left eyebrow, large part of the right ear, left lobe.
Bernoulli II, p. 124, no. 3.
Helbig, *F.*³, no. 283; Helbig, *F.*⁴-Speier, no. 59.
Lippold, *Vat. Kat.* III, 1, p. 21, no. 498, pl. 21.

5. Head, mounted on an alien herm inscribed Solon (q.v.). Formerly in the Museo Chiaramonti, now in the Galleria degli Arazzi, Vatican, inv. 267.

FIGS. 1154–1156

Height of head 30·5 cm.
No restorations, but surface weathered.
Bernoulli I, p. 39.
Amelung, *Vat. Kat.* I, p. 815, no. 734, pl. 87.

6. Head, mounted on a modern herm, in the Villa Albani, no. 29. Only the middle part of the head is ancient.

FIG. 1161

Height of ancient part 18·2 cm.
Restorations: Upper part of head, beard, parts of lower lip and of nose, rims of ears, pieces in the hair.
Bernoulli II, p. 124, no. 4.
E.A., 3269–3270.

7. Head and chest, with tenon for insertion in a statue. In the Barracco Museum. Found near Carsoli in the Abruzzi.

FIG. 1164

Drapery on both shoulders.
Height 42 cm.; ht. of head 32·5 cm.
No restorations. Even the nose is ancient.
Helbig and Barracco, *Coll. Barracco*, pls. 63, 63a.
Helbig, *F.³*, no. 1109.
Pietrangeli, *Guida* (1949), p. 68, no. 155; (1960), p. 86, no. 155.

8. Small bronze bust, inscribed Ἐπίκουρος, in the National Museum, Naples, inv. 5465. Found in 1753 in the villa of the Pisoni, Herculaneum. Drapery on both shoulders.

FIGS. 1175–1177

Height, with base, 20 cm.; ht. of head 12 cm.
No restorations.
Visconti, *Ic. gr.* I, p. 290, pl. xxv.
Comparetti and De Petra, *Villa ercol.*, p. 262, no. 13, pl. XII, 7.
Bernoulli II, p. 124, no. 6, pl. XIX.
Ruesch, *Guida*, no. 902.
Kaibel, *I.G.* XIV, 708.

9. Small bronze head, mounted on a modern bust, in the National Museum, Naples, inv. 5470. Found, like the preceding, in the villa of the Pisoni, Herculaneum.

FIGS. 1180–1182

Height 10 cm.
No restorations.
Comparetti and De Petra, *Villa ercol.*, p. 263, no. 15, pl. XII, 6.
Bernoulli II, p. 124, no. 7.
Ruesch, *Guida*, no. 896.

10. Small bust in the National Museum, Naples, inv. 111392. Found at Pompeii, it is said with a small portrait of Pseudo-Seneca (cf. p. 59, no. 16).   FIGS. 1167–1168, 1171–1172
Height 22 cm.; ht. of head 19 cm.
No restorations; ears unfinished.
Mau, *Bull. dell'Inst.*, 1876, p. 243.
Comparetti and De Petra, *Villa ercol.*, pl. III, 8, p. 34, no. 1 (there thought to be Metrodoros).
Bernoulli II, p. 126, no. 22.
Ruesch, *Guida*, no. 1077 (with wrong inventory number).

11. Small herm in the National Museum, Naples, inv. 110872. Found at Pompeii in 1878.

FIGS. 1169–1170, 1173–1174

Height 32 cm.; ht. of head 23 cm.
Restorations: The right edge of the herm, most of the nose, and other small pieces.
The herm is flattened at the back, but that it was not part of a double herm is shown by the presence of hair at the nape of the neck. It must have been placed against a wall.
Mau, *Bull. dell'Inst.*, 1879, p. 95.
Comparetti and De Petra, *Villa ercol.*, pl. III, 4, p. 34, no. 1.
Bernoulli II, p. 126, no. 23 (doubts identity of Epikouros).
Ruesch, *Guida*, no. 1080 (with wrong inventory number).

12. Bronze head, found in 1752 in Resina. Present whereabouts not known.
Height: almost life-size.
Probably no restorations.
Comparetti and De Petra, *Villa ercol.*, pl. XII, 5, p. 263, no. 14.
Bernoulli II, p. 124, no. 8.

13. Herm in the Museo Nazionale, Ravenna. Found in the Adriatic Sea near Porto Corsini with other herms (cf. p. 95).

FIGS. 1165–1166

Drapery on left shoulder and along right.
Height 49 cm.; ht. of head 34 cm.
No restorations, but several pieces, including the nose, are missing.
Le Arti III, 1940–41, p. 467, figs. 3, 4.
Van Buren, *A.J.A.* XLV, 1941, pp. 465, 467, fig. 15.
Fuhrmann, *Arch. Anz.* 1941, cols. 399ff., fig. 30.
Arias, *J. d. I.* LXVIII, 1953, pp. 114ff., figs. 12–15.

14. Head at a Roman dealer's in 1934. Mentioned by Lippold, *Vat. Kat.* III, 1, p. 21, under no. 498.

FIGS. 1162–1163

15. Another head (or the same?) is mentioned by Adriani, *Annuario* XXIV–VI, 1950, p. 148, note 3, no. 14. And still another one (or the same?) was, I am told, at a Roman dealer's in 1961.

16. Head on a double herm, with Metrodoros, (q.v.), in the Louvre, Ma 88. From the collection of the Duc de Penthièvre in Châteauneuf sur Loire. The two heads were once separated, then joined again. No drapery on shoulders.

FIGS. 1183–1185

Height of head c. 35·3 cm.; ht. with herm c. 61·5 cm.
Restorations: End of nose, part of the moustache, and a few locks of the hair. The herm is ancient, except a piece at the right corner. (These data were given me by M. Charbonneaux after consultation with the marble expert of the Louvre.)
Bernoulli II, p. 124, no. 9.
Cat. sommaire (1922), p. 86, no. 88.

17. Head, mounted on a modern herm, in the Louvre, Ma 363. From the Borghese Collection.   FIGS. 1186–1188
Height of head c. 35·1 cm.
Restorations: Part of nose, pieces under the left eye and in the right ear.

Cat. sommaire (1922), p. 15, no. 363.
Bernoulli II, p. 124, no. 10.

18. Head in the Louvre, Ma 490. In the reserve collection (in 1961). From the Borghese Collection. FIGS. 1189–1191
Height, with neck 34·2 cm.; ht. of head 33·5 cm.
Restorations: Nose, lower part of left ear. Broken in two vertically.
Cat. sommaire (1922), p. 19, no. 490.

19. Head, mounted on a modern herm, in the British Museum, 1843. Purchased in 1873 of Castellani, in Rome. Made for insertion in a statue. FIGS. 1192–1194
Height 37·7 cm.; ht. of head 33·5 cm.
No restorations. Rims of ears mostly missing.
Bernoulli II, p. 125, no. 12.
A. H. Smith, *Cat.*, no. 1843.

20. Herm in the British Museum, 1844. From the Towneley Collection. Purchased in 1873 from Castellani in Rome. Drapery on shoulder. FIGS. 1195–1197
Height 55·5 cm.; ht. of head 32·2 cm.
Restorations: Nose, part of left ear, part of chest with drapery.
Bernoulli II, p. 125, no. 11.
A. H. Smith, *Cat.*, *no.* 1844.

21. Head in the Ny Carlsberg Glyptothek, Copenhagen, I.N. 607. Acquired in 1890 of Martinetti, Rome. Shaped for insertion in a draped herm. A channel passes from the lower part of the face to the mouth. FIGS. 1178–1179
Height 45 cm.
The former restorations (nose, lower lip, top of head) have now been removed.
Bernoulli II, p. 125, no. 17.
Arndt-Br., 38–39.
F. Poulsen, *Acta Arch.* XVI, 1945, pp. 178ff.; *Cat.*, 416.
V. Poulsen, *Portr. gr.*, no. 33.

22. Head, mounted on a modern bust, in the Ny Carlsberg Glyptothek, I.N. 1294. Acquired in Rome in 1895.
FIGS. 1205–1206
Height of ancient part 19 cm.; ht. as restored 47 cm.
Restorations: Neck, lower part of head, including the nose and the moustache.
Bernoulli II, p. 125, no. 18.
E.A., 4628–4629.
F. Poulsen, *Cat.*, no. 417.
V. Poulsen, *Portr. gr.*, no. 34.

23. Head on a small double herm, with Metrodoros, (q.v.), in the Ny Carlsberg Glyptothek, Copenhagen, I.N. 613. Acquired in Rome in 1893. FIG. 1210
Height 24 cm.
The nose is restored. Surface weathered.
F. Poulsen in *E.A.*, 4630–4632: 'Trotz der Zerstörung erkennt man den Epikur an der Form der Stirnhaare, den kränklichen Augen, dem Bau der mageren Wangen, den Linien des Schnurrbarts, und dem zweigeteilten Kinnbart'.
F. Poulsen, *Cat.*, no. 426.
V. Poulsen, *Portr. gr.*, no. 35.
The deviations here from the accepted type are considerable,

even for a reduced copy; but the general scheme is, as F. Poulsen says, essentially the same.

24. Small bust in the Staatliche Museen, Berlin. Probably from the Baireuth Collection. Formerly at Sanssouci. Drapery on both shoulders. FIGS. 1198–1199
Height 25·5 cm.
Restorations: End of nose and two locks in hair.
Conze, *Beschreibung*, no. 306.
Arndt-Br., 40.
Bernoulli II, p. 125, no. 14.

25. Head, mounted on a modern bust, in the Residenz, Munich. FIG. 1204
Height 32·5 cm.
Restorations: Nose, lips. Surface weathered.
Bernoulli II, p. 125, no. 15.
E.A., no. 974.
Bernoulli (II, p. 125, no. 16) cites a second head in the Residenz, Munich, which is, however, not listed in *E.A.*, and seems to be identical with the above.

26. Head in the National Museum, Athens, no. 540. Found in Athens. FIGS. 1224–1225
Height 13 cm.
No restorations, but much battered.
Sybel, p. 119, no. 753.
Kastriotes, *Glypta*, no. 540.

27. Head in the Akropolis Museum, Athens, no. 2186. From old excavations.
Height c. 33 cm.
No restorations, but much battered. The right side of the face is mostly missing, including the nose; but the left side with the eye remains.
To be published by Mr. Dontas.

28. Head, with neck and drapery, in the Metropolitan Museum of Art, New York, 11.90. Rogers Fund, 1911. Purchased in Rome. FIGS. 1200–1203
Height 40·4 cm.
No restorations.
E. Robinson, *MMA Bull.* VI, 1911, pp. 150ff.
Richter, *MMA Bull.* VI, 1911, p. 210; in Arndt-Br. 1124–1125.; *Sc. Cat.*, no. 186.

29. Bust in the Archaeological Museum, Istanbul, inv. 88. Of unknown provenance. Made for insertion in a statue or herm. Drapery on both shoulders. FIGS. 1207–1209
Height 45 cm.; ht. of head, 34 cm.
No restorations.
Mendel, *Cat.* II, no. 616.
H. von Heintze, in Hekler, *B.b.G.*[3], p. 67, no. 26.

DOUBTFUL EXAMPLES

The head in a double herm, with Kolotes(?), in the Prado, Madrid; cf. under Kolotes. The two heads have been differently interpreted. For the old identifications of Epikouros and Metrodoros, there has been substituted 'Kolotes' and some co-pupil of Kolotes (cf. p. 206). But though the

identification with Metrodoros has definitely had to be
abandoned, since the head, though resembling him, is a
portrait that has been recognized in several replicas, that of
'Epikouros' is not otherwise known. Personally I think it
possible that Epikouros was intended, freely worked as is
often the case in double herms, where the portraits are not
really carved in the round (cf. p. 7). Certainly the head has
some of the characteristics that one associates with Epikouros
—especially the long face.   FIG. 1211

I take the head in the Casa del Labrador, Aranjuez (Hübner,
no. 154; Arndt-Br., 1088), not to be Epikouros, as did
Bernoulli (II, p. 125, no. 13), but Metrodoros (cf. p. 201, no. 6).

The head in Stockholm (Brising, *Antik. Konst i. National-
museum, Stockholm*, no. 64), once thought to represent
Epikouros (cf. Wieseler, *Philologus* XXVII, 1886, p. 209) is of
course not he.

The double herm with heads of Epikouros and Metrodoros in
Ramsgate, Kent, was considered to be a modern copy of the
double herm in the Capitoline Museum (p. 195, no. 1) by
Michaelis, *Anc. Marbl.*, pp. 618ff.; cf. Bernoulli II, p. 125,
no. 12a.

STATUES

The type of statue to which these heads belonged has been
identified by Lippold on what seems convincing evidence.
A seated statue with alien head, once in the Ludovisi Collection
(Schreiber, *Ludovisi* (1880) no. 243), now in the garden of
the American embassy in Rome, the former Palazzo
Margherita, evidently is the same as that drawn by Preisler,
Statuae antiquae (1732), pl. 29, called in the index 'Epicurus
philosophus'. And the latter seems to be identical with the
statue of Epikouros cited by Bottari in his *Mus. Capit.* I
(1750), p. 12, as having been seen by Naudeus on the
Ludovisi property: 'Gabriel Naudeus in aedibus Ludovisianis
Romae adservatam fuisse Epicuri statuam adfirmavit'. The
head now on the statue in the garden of the American embassy
is alien and does not correspond to that of Preisler's drawing,
which, though represented bald, might be a free rendering
of an Epikouros head. Lippold suggested that originally the
statue was inscribed with Epikouros' name, and that the
inscription has since disappeared, like that of its companion
piece, a statue of Sokrates (q.v.), also drawn by Preisler.
This ingenious theory is fortified, not only by the fact that
the arrangement of the mantle on the shoulders in the
Ludovisi statue corresponds to that in the majority of the
heads where the mantle is shown, but also by the discovery
of a large headless, marble statuette of the same type as the
Ludovisi statue in a Roman villa, where it evidently acted as
a pendant to a statuette of Hermarchos (both now in the
Museo Archeologico, Florence, cf. *infra*, no. 2 and p. 205,
no. 1).
Five copies of this type of figure, all headless, have been
identified. They are represented seated on a throne, with
rounded back, and terminating in front in the head and leg
of an animal:

Statue of Epikouros now in the garden of the American Embassy in Rome.
Drawing by Preisler, *Statuae antiquae*, pl. 29

1. The statue, above mentioned, in the American embassy
garden in Rome.   FIGS. 1212–1213
Height 1·30 m.
Restorations: Head, neck, right arm with adjoining drapery,
left hand with scroll, front part of right foot, front part
of plinth, lower part of throne with claw foot, patches in
drapery and throne.
Preisler, *Statuae antiquae*, pl. 29.
Schreiber, *Ludovisi*, no. 243.
Lippold, *Gr. Porträtst.*, pp. 78ff., fig. 17; in Arndt-Br., 1126–1127.
E.A., 2092–2093.
Richter, *Gr. Portr.*, I, p. 37, figs. 15–17.
Dontas, *Eikones*, p. 41.

2. Headless statuette in the Museo Archeologico, Florence,
inv. 70990. Found in a Roman villa together with a statuette
of Hermarchos (cf. p. 205, no. 1).   FIGS. 1214–1215
Height 90 cm.; i.e. about half life-size.
No restorations.

Milani, *Il Museo Archeologico di Firenze*, p. 318, no. 89, pl. CLVI, 2.
Lippold, *Gr. Porträtst.*, p. 79, note 2; in Arndt-Br., 1124-1125.
Hekler, *B.b.G.*, p. 48, note 57; 3rd ed., p. 68, no. 3.
Schefold, *B.*, p. 121, 1.
Richter, *Gr. Portr.* I, p. 37, fig. 19.
Dontas, *Eikones*, pp. 41f., pl. 10, β, pl. 11, β.

3. Large statuette in Ince Blundell Hall. Purchased in 1777 from Mr. Jenkins.   FIGS. 1216–1217
Height of ancient part 47 cm.; ht. as restored 57 cm.
Restorations: Head and neck, most of right arm, left hand with scroll, lower part of both legs with drapery, feet, lower part of chair, plinth.
Michaelis, *Anc. Marbl.*, p. 352, no. 44.
Lippold, *Gr. Porträtst.*, p. 79, note 2,
F. Poulsen, *English Country Houses*, p. 43, no. 16; *Ikon. Misc.*, p. 73.
Ashmole, *Cat.*, p. 26, no. 44, pl. 29.
Dontas, *Eikones*, p. 41.

4. Torso of a statuette in the Antiquario Comunale, Rome. Found in April 1876 on the Esquiline. The left hand holds a scroll, the right is missing.
Height 24 cm.
No restorations.
Lippold, *Gr. Porträtst.*, p. 79, note 2.
Hekler, *B.b.G.*, p. 48, note 57; 3rd ed., p. 68, no. 4.
Dontas, *Eikones*, p. 41.

5. Fragmentary statue, headless, found in the Athenian Agora, S826. It formerly decorated the Odeion of the Agora and is now set up in the Gymnasium.
FIGS. 1218–1219
Height c. 1·24 m.
No restorations.
Shear, *Hesperia* VII, 1938, pp. 323f., fig. 7.
H. A. Thompson, *Hesperia* XIX, 1950, p. 124, pl. 78 (identified it as Epikouros).
Dontas, *Eikones*, p. 42.

STATUETTES

For the possibility that the bronze statuette of a bearded, standing figure, mounted on an Ionic column (Metropolitan Museum, *Cat. of Bronzes*, no. 120; Arndt-Br., 1123), once thought to represent Hermarchos, may be a portrait of Epikouros cf. my *Gk. Portr.* IV, pp. 40f. The imposing personality and general type of features would fit the greatest of the Epicurean philosophers. Since the statuette is presumably a Hellenistic original, it may have been a different version of Epikouros from that preserved in the marble copies. One may surmise that the statuette was a prized possession of some Roman admirer of Epikouros. Its total height, including the column, must have been c. 58 cm., and approximately corresponds to that of the statuette of Hippokrates owned by a Roman physician (cf. p. 152). That the New York statuette represents Epikouros, corpulent with protruding paunch, may indicate the later conception of his teachings—advanced by his rivals and enemies—that physical pleasure was the highest good in life.   FIG. 1220
This conception is also apparent in the representation of him on the cup from Boscoreale, where he is shown helping himself to delicacies (cf. *infra*).

A small marble head in the collection of the late Captain Spencer Churchill, Northwick Park, resembles the portraits of Epikouros and may have been intended to represent him. Acquired 'between the two wars'.   FIG. 1223
There are traces of gilding on hair, left ear, and elsewhere. Height with neck 9·5 cm. It was therefore, presumably broken from a statuette about half life-size.

ENGRAVED GEMS ETC.

Portraits of Epikouros occur on several engraved gems of the Roman period, bearing out Cicero's statement that Epikouros' followers wore likenesses of their master on their rings.

a. One of the best is on a red jasper in the British Museum. From the Blacas Collection. He is represented in profile view to the right, with his characteristic large, curved nose, long beard, longish locks, long moustache, deepset eyes, and drapery on shoulder. 14 by 11 mm.   FIG. 1221
Bernoulli II, p. 129.
Furtwängler, *A.G.*, pl. XLIII, 5.
Walters, *Cat. of Gems*, no. 1960, pl. XXV.
Lippold, *Gemmen und Kameen*, pl. 67, no. 6.

b. Another, perhaps also representing him, is on a plasma in the British Museum. Formerly in the Carlisle Collection (1890). Inscribed in modern letters: NEAPKOY. 11 by 8 mm.
FIG. 1222
Walters, *Cat. of Gems*, no. 1961, pl. XXV (with a question mark).

For other examples cf. Bernoulli II, pp. 129f., where also some doubtful ones are listed—including the sardonyx cameo in the National Museum, Naples, no. 25, inscribed Ὅμηρος (cf. p. 129, with note 2, and my p. 56).

c. The skeleton of Epikouros, inscribed with his name (Ἐπίκουρος Ἀθηναῖος) appears on a silver cup (10·4 cm. high) from Boscoreale in the Louvre (*Mon. Piot* V, 1895, pp. 61f., pl. VIII), grouped with the Stoic philosopher Zeno. Epikouros is represented with the stick and wallet of the philosopher, about to help himself to delicacies from a dish. The representation, though iconographically of no value, throws light on the later conception of Epikouros' doctrine as being purely material.   FIG. 1698

d. Della Corte, *Studi Romani* VII, 1959, pp. 129ff., has suggested that a painting in Pompeii, now vanished, but reproduced in a drawing on his p. 132, represents the garden of Epikouros.

CONCLUSIONS

All the life-size portraits of Epikouros in the round above listed are evidently derived from one Greek original. The characteristic traits are: the long, narrow shape of the head; the deeply lined, high, but narrow forehead; the deep-set, rather small eyes with drooping upper lids, pockets beneath the lower lids, crow's feet at the outer corners, and overhanging brows that curve down to the bridge of the nose; the prominent nose with a marked protuberance below the bridge (preserved e.g. in nos. 2, 5, 7, 8, 9); the finely curving, full-lipped mouth, with the upper lip all but hidden by a thick, but rather small moustache (only a triangle of the upper lip is visible); the longish, curling beard, divided into two parts along the middle; and the plentiful hair with locks arranged according to a set pattern, as follows: over the forehead locks forming a single curve, going from (spectator's) left to right, then in the middle changing to locks of double curve with ends directed from right to left; on temples and behind the ears arranged in locks going from right to left; above the neck composed in a series of locks which on the spectator's left go in a horizontal direction, on the right are more variegated.

This set scheme, which constantly recurs in the full-size examples but not in the reduced ones, shows beyond doubt that the former were all mechanically reproduced by the pointing process from the same original. The differences in expression, in age, etc., which have led some authorities to postulate several Greek prototypes (e.g. Bernoulli and Adriani), can all be explained by differences of surface finish. That so arbitrary a scheme in the composition of the hair would not recur in copies from different originals is obvious, and is moreover indicated by the fact that as soon as the copyist worked free-hand (in the reduced copies), he altered the scheme.

Of the statues, evidently only the full-size ones from the Ludovisi Collection and in the Athenian agora faithfully reproduce the Greek original; the reduced copies (cf. pp. 198f., nos. 2, 3) show the usual variations. But here too the basic composition is the same: right leg advanced; left set back; right forearm raised, with hand holding a scroll; left arm inside mantle with only part of forearm protruding and resting on lap; the mantle enveloping the whole figure, except the right arm and the right side of the chest, passing from the left shoulder along the right, with ends hanging down on the left side. The seat is a throne of Hellenistic type, with rounded back and terminating in front in an animal's head and leg.

What is known of the life and character of Epikouros is reflected in his portraits—the imposing appearance, the kindly disposition that enlisted the reverence and love of his followers, the courage in combating adverse fortunes, and the self-satisfied temperament that did not try to reach out to fresh knowledge, but was content with the old atomic theories of Demokritos. That Epikouros' doctrine of happiness did not signify material pleasure is abundantly shown by his idealistic, serious expression. The noble simplicity of his character is conveyed in the seated posture of his statues with the relatively simple arrangement of the folds. The date of the Greek original can, on stylistic grounds, be assigned to the early Hellenistic period; that is, to the first half of the third century, perhaps about 280–270 B.C., not far from the Demosthenes (cf. p. 216). He is portrayed in advanced years, and the fame he enjoyed in his lifetime makes it likely that a statue in his honour was erected either shortly before or immediately after his death. Whether the original was one of the statues that are recorded to have been set up in Samos (cf. p. 195), or some other—perhaps one placed in the Garden—is of course not known.

METRODOROS

Of Lampsakos, 331/330–278/277 B.C. Son of Athenaios (or Timokrates) and Sande (Diog. Laert. x, 22). Pupil and close friend of Epikouros. Was 12 years younger than Epikouros, and died 7 years before him, only 53 years old.

c. 309 Learned to know Epikouros when the latter opened his philosophic school in Lampsakos.

306 Accompanied Epikouros to Athens and remained with him all his life, except for an occasional visit to Lampsakos. The relationship of the two men was exceedingly close. Cicero, *De fin.* II, 92, calls Metrodoros alter Epicurus. Epikouros often mentions Metrodoros in his writings, and dedicated to him his *Eurylochos* and his *Metrodoros*. Metrodoros named one of his sons after Epikouros, and Epikouros made provision for Metrodoros' daughter in his will and requested Idomeneus 'to watch over the children of Metrodoros' (Diog. Laert. x, 22). Epikouros also directed that on the 20th of each month a feast should be held in his and Metrodoros' memory (cf. p. 195).

Diogenes Laertios (x, 23) speaks of Metrodoros' goodness and serenity: γέγονε δὲ ἀγαθὸς πάντα; and of his 'dauntless courage in meeting troubles and death': ἀκατάπληκτος πρός τε τὰς ὀχλήσεις καὶ τὸν θάνατον.

Seneca, *Epist.*, 52, 3–5, states that Metrodoros had not his master's energy and originality of thought, but could attain the truth by the help of others. This estimate is borne out by what remains of Metrodoros' writings. They contain many polemics in defence of Epikouros' teachings.

His chief characteristics, which one may expect to see reflected in his portraits, were, therefore, his serenity, his placid temperament, and his loyalty to Epikouros.

STATUES RECORDED

No mention is made by ancient writers of a statue erected to Metrodoros; but that there must have been one is indicated by the portrait inscribed with his name (cf. *infra*) which evidently reproduces one erected to him in the first half of the third century B.C. One may surmise that Epikouros had a statue set up in his garden after his friend's death. Metrodoros' popularity in Roman times as an eminent Epicurean is attested by the fairly large number of portraits of him that have survived.

IDENTIFICATION

The identification of Metrodoros' portraits was made possible by the head inscribed with his name in the double herm with Epikouros in the Capitoline Museum (cf. *infra*, no. 1). A tentative reconstruction has been made of this type of head with a figure that exists in several examples (cf. p. 202).

PORTRAITS EXTANT AND ONCE EXTANT
HEADS IN THE ROUND

1. Head in a double herm, with Epikouros (q.v.), in the Stanza dei Filosofi, Capitoline Museum no. 52. Inscribed Μητρόδωρος. FIGS. 1230–1232
Height 60 cm.; ht. of head 32 cm.
Restorations: On Metrodoros only the end of the nose, and a piece of the herm. No drapery on shoulders.
Bernoulli II, p. 131, no. 1.
Arndt-Br., 1081–1083.
Stuart Jones, *Cat.*, p. 244, no. 63, pl. 56.
Kaibel, *I.G.* XIV, 1150.

2. Bust in the Stanza dei Filosofi, Capitoline Museum, no. 51. Drapery on both shoulders. FIGS. 1233–1235
Height 47·4 cm.; ht. of head 34·5 cm.
Restorations: Tip of nose, edge of left ear, lower part of bust with name plate.
Bernoulli II, p. 131, no. 2.
Arndt-Br., 1085.
Stuart Jones, *Cat.*, p. 244, no. 62, pl. 56.

3. Head, mounted on a modern herm inscribed Epikouros, in the Galeria Geografica, Vatican, inv. 2836. FIGS. 1227–1229
Height of ancient part 35 cm.; ht. of head 32·6 cm.
Restorations: Nose, upper lip, upper part of right ear, lobe of left ear.
Bernoulli II, p. 131, no. 3.
Lippold, *Vat. Kat.* III, 2, p. 494, no. 69, pl. 226.
Helbig, *F.*⁴-Speier, no. 576.

4. Head, mounted on a modern herm, in the Museo Torlonia, Rome, no. 66. From the Vitali Collection. FIG. 1242
Height 31 cm.
Restorations: Nose, neck, parts of ears.
Visconti, *Museo Torlonia*, p. 45, no. 66, pl. XVII.
Bernoulli II, p. 131, no. 4.

5. Small marble bust in the National Museum, Naples, inv. 119585. Found in Pompeii. Drapery on both shoulders. FIG. 1226
Height 14 cm.; ht. of head 11 cm.
No restorations.
Bernoulli II, p. 132, no. 13.
Ruesch, *Guida*, no. 1082.

6. Head, mounted on a modern herm inscribed Epikouros. In the Casa del Labrador, Aranjuez. Found near Tivoli. Probably from the Azara collection. FIG. 1243
Height, with modern herm, 54 cm.
Restorations: Nose, parts of upper lip and of moustache, patches in ears and beard.
Hübner, no. 154.

Bernoulli II, p. 125, no. 13 (as Epikouros).
Arndt-Br., 1088.

7. Head in a double herm, with Epikouros (q.v.) in the Louvre, Ma 88. FIGS. 1236, 1240–1241
Height of head 34 cm.; ht. with herm c. 59 cm.
Restorations: Nose and herm.
Visconti, *Ic. gr.* I, p. 291, pl. XXVa.
Bernoulli II, p. 132, no. 6.
Hekler, *B.b.G.*, p. 37, fig. 36.
Cat. sommaire (1922), p. 6, no. 88.

8. Head, mounted on a modern herm, in the British Museum, 1845. From the Appian Way, Rome. Bought from Castellani in 1873. FIGS. 1237–1239
Height 44 cm.
The nose was attached in a separate piece, now missing (an ancient repair?).
Bernoulli II, p. 132, no. 7.
A. H. Smith, *Cat.*, no. 1845.

9. Head, mounted on a modern herm inscribed Aristophanes. In Wilton House. FIGS. 1244–1245
Height 33 cm.
Restorations: Nose, patch on forehead, part of moustache on left side.
Michaelis, *Anc. Marbl.*, p. 677, no. 20.
Bernoulli II, p. 132, no. 8.
F. Poulsen, *English Country Houses*, no. 17.

10. Bust in the Staatliche Museen, Berlin. Acquired shortly before 1830. Drapery on left shoulder. FIGS. 1246–1247
Height 41 cm.
Restorations: Nose, pieces of the ears, the right shoulder.
Conze, *Beschreibung*, no. 307 (there called Hermarchos).
Bernoulli II, p. 132, no. 9 (called Metrodoros).
Arndt-Br., 13–14 (called Hermarchos).

11. Head, mounted on an alien or modern bust. In Castle Erbach (called Epikouros). FIGS. 1252–1253
Height of head 33 cm.
Restorations: Nose, lower part of beard, a few patches.
Bernoulli II, p. 132, no. 10: 'Epikur genannt, aber wahrscheinlich Metrodor'.

12. Head, mounted on a modern bust, in the Antiquarium of the Residenz Museum, Munich. FIGS. 1251, 1254
Height 33 cm.
Restorations: Nose and right eyebrow.
Bernoulli II, p. 132, no. 11.
E.A., no. 961.

13. Small bust formerly in the Oberhessische Museum, Giessen, W.G.3713. Destroyed during the second World War. From the Wilhelm Geil Collection. Made for insertion. FIG. 1248
Height 19·5 cm.; ht. of head 14·5 cm.
No restorations.
E.A., nos. 3364–3365.

14. Head in a small double herm, with Epikouros (q.v.), in the Ny Carlsberg Glyptothek, Copenhagen, I.N. 613.

Acquired in Rome, 1893.   FIGS. 1249–1250
Height 24 cm.
Surface much weathered.
F. Poulsen, in *E.A.*, 4630–4632; *Cat.*, no. 426.
V. Poulsen, *Portr. gr.*, no. 35.
von Heintze, in Hekler, *B.b.G.*³, p. 68, no. 16.

15. Head, mounted on a modern herm, once in Rome; cf.
Sale Catalogue, J. Ferroni, Rome, 1909, pl. 70. Now?

16. Bust in the National Museum, Athens, 368. Found in
Athens.   FIGS. 1255–1257
Height c. 59 cm.; ht. of head c. 32 cm. Drapery on shoulder.
No restorations. Base of and back of bust left unfinished.
Nose intact. In excellent preservation.
Wolters, *Arch. Ztg.* XLII, 1884, cols. 153ff. (there called Hermarchos).
Bernoulli II, p. 132, no. 12.
Arndt-Br., 1089–1090.
Kastriotes, *Glypta*, no. 368.

DOUBTFUL EXAMPLES

Bernoulli II, p. 134, lists as doubtful Metrodoroses: a herm
in Palermo, inscribed in modern times Metrodoros, *E.A.*,
559b (cf. my p. 204, under Hermarchos); a herm in Madrid,
inscribed Metrodoros (cf. under Hermarchos, p. 204, no. 17);
a head in a double herm in Madrid (cf. under 'Kolotes', p.
206). To these may be added the double herm with Epikouros and Metrodoros in Ramsgate (cf. under Epikouros,
p. 198).

STATUES

The type of figure that belonged to this portrait was
tentatively identified by Lippold in a slightly over life-size
statue and in two large statuettes, all headless. The evidence
for the identification is that the rendering of the folds of the
mantle on the shoulders (preserved in nos. 2 and 16),
the raised left shoulder, and the prominent clavicles, are the
same in the statues and in the busts and herms.
The following examples are of this type:

1. Statue in the Ny Carlsberg Glyptothek, I.N. 2685.
Found in 1903 with three other headless figures on the
grounds of the Villa Patrizi, on the Via Nomentana, Rome.
Formerly in the Woodyat Collection in Naples. Acquired in
1920.   FIGS. 1258–1260
Height, without restored head, 1·01 m., with head 1·26 m.
On arrival in Copenhagen, the figure was completed with a
plaster cast of the head in Athens (cf. no. 16); and the right
arm (of which much of the forearm and of the hand holding
the scroll remained) was restored. These additions were
removed in 1953.
Gatti, *Not. d. Sc.* 1904, p. 226.
Lippold, *Gr. Porträtst.*, p. 81, fig. 20.
F. Poulsen, *Gaz. des Beaux-Arts* 1937, I, pp. 3ff.; *Ik. Misc.* pp. 73ff.;
Cat., no. 416a.
Adriani, *Annuario* XXIV–XXVI, 1946–1948, pp. 154f.
V. Poulsen, *Portr. gr.*, no. 36.
Dontas, *Eikones*, pp. 37f., pl. 10, α, pl. 11, α.

2. Large statuette, with modern head, in the National
Museum, Naples, inv. 6237. From the Farnese Collection.
Represented seated on a throne of Hellenistic type, wearing
himation and sandals.   FIGS. 1261–1262, 1265
Height 58 cm., with restored head; ht. of ancient part 48 cm.
Restorations: The left hand.
Lippold, *Gr. Porträtst.*, p. 81.
Hekler, *B.b.G.*, p. 48, note 58; 3rd ed., p. 68, no. 1.
Ruesch, *Guida*, no. 1131.
Clarac, pl. 840D, 2143A.
Dontas, *Eikones*, p. 37, note. 1.

3. Large statuette in the collection of Major E. R. F.
Compton, Newby Hall, Yorkshire. Shown seated on a
cushioned chair (klismos of late form).
                                  FIGS. 1263–1264, 1266–1267
Height 53 cm.; with plinth, 59 cm.
Restorations: Head and neck, most of the right arm, half
of the lower left arm (a small piece of the scroll, however,
is ancient), the right foot from the ankle down, three legs of
the chair.
Michaelis, *Anc. Marbl.*, p. 534, no. 35.
Lippold, *Gr. Porträtst.*, p. 81.
E.A., nos. 3128–3131.
Poulsen, *Ik. Misc.*, p. 73.
Hekler, *B.b.G.*, p. 48, note 58, no. 3; 3rd ed., revised by H. von
Heintze, p. 68, no. 2.
Dontas, *Eikones*, p. 37, note 1.

The statuette mentioned by Hekler, *B.b.G.*, p. 48, note 58,
no. 2, as being in Marbury Hall is that in Newby Hall (as
also H. von Heintze saw).

The individual is represented seated, in a relaxed attitude,
the left hand resting on his lap and holding a scroll, the right
arm raised; the action of the arms is, therefore, reversed from
that of Epikouros and Hermarchos. The form of the seat
varies. The reconstruction of this figure with Metrodoros'
head is tempting, both on the evidence presented by Lippold,
and because F. Poulsen's reconstruction appears to make a
harmonious ensemble. But, as Adriani and V. Poulsen have
pointed out, a doubt remains.

CONCLUSIONS

All the heads above listed must reproduce the same Greek
original, the life-size ones mechanically copied, whereas the
small portraits were evidently worked free-hand, and so
show the usual variations. The type often markedly
resembles that of Epikouros, and the two have often been
confused (also with Hermarchos, cf. *infra*). Metrodoros
may be distinguished from Epikouros by his more youthful
aspect, by the less elongated proportions of his head, the less
emaciated cheeks, the smoother forehead (with only the
projection of its lower part forming a horizontal furrow),
the straighter nose, and the more placid expression. The
arrangement of the locks of hair and beard, though similar
in the two types, differ in important particulars. In Metrodoros the locks over the forehead begin, as in Epikouros,
with several single-curved strands directed from (spectator's)

left to right, but then are not followed by several double-curved ones directed from right to left, but by locks going in various directions. Moreover, along the right cheek, there regularly appears a series of short locks going in an oblique direction and terminating at the moustache. The latter is somewhat longer than in Epikouros; and is often a little longer on the right than on the left side; the mouth is often slightly open; the beard is shorter than that of Epikouros, and is not so schematically divided into two separate parts, the direction of the locks being more variegated.

The stylistic date of the Greek original must be in the first half of the third century B.C.

HERMARCHOS

Of Mytilene, c. 340–after 270 B.C. Epicurean philosopher. Son of Agemortos.

LIFE

He came of a poor family, and at first studied rhetoric (Diog. Laert. x, 24).

c. 310 B.C. Must have met Epikouros when the latter opened his school at Mytilene (cf. p. 194). Became his pupil and follower.

306 Followed Epikouros to Lampsakos, and thence to Athens, and remained his close friend for about 40 years. Accompanied Epikouros on one of his journeys to Lampsakos (Usener, *Epicurea*, frgt. 176).

270 When Epikouros died, Hermarchos became his successor as head of the school, as directed in Epikouros' will. He was then an old man, for he was about the same age as Epikouros, who speaks of him as τοῦ συγκαταγεγηρακότος ἡμῖν ἐν φιλοσοφίᾳ (Usener, *Epicurea*, p. 167, frgt. 217, 20).

Epikouros' regard for Hermarchos is also shown by other provisions in his will, and by the bequest of his library (cf. pp. 194f.).

In Seneca, *Epist.*, 52, 4, Epikouros classes Hermarchos among those who do not struggle for the truth out of their own initiative, but reach it with the help of others: non duce tantum opus sit, sed adiutore et, uti ita dicam, coactore. Some of the titles of Hermarchos' writings are cited by Diogenes Laertios (x, 24–25) and called excellent; βιβλία κάλλιστα: Πρὸς Πλάτωνα, Πρὸς Ἀριστοτέλην, Ἐπιστολικὰ περὶ Ἐμπεδοκλέους, Περὶ τῶν μαθημάτων.

They suggest polemical works directed against the other philosophical schools.

STATUES RECORDED

No statues of Hermarchos are recorded in ancient literature, but that at least one statue was erected to him is indicated by the extant portraits of him that go back to a Greek original of the third century B.C. As a friend of Epikouros, and his successor as head of the school, he was naturally revered by the Epicureans.

IDENTIFICATION

The identification of Hermarchos' portrait was made possible by a small bronze bust from Herculaneum inscribed Ἕρμαρχος (cf. *infra*, no. 10). And from the similarity of this head to that of a small marble statue (cf. p. 205, no. 1), the type of portrait statue has been recognized (cf. p. 205).

EXTANT PORTRAITS

HEADS IN THE ROUND

1. Head, mounted on a modern herm, in the Sala delle Muse, Vatican, inv. 286. Acquired under Pius VI, before 1792. Provenance not known. FIGS. 1268–1270
Height of head 32 cm.
Restorations: Nose, most of the beard on the right cheek, parts of both ears, upper eyelids. The restored eyelids and the hollow irises somewhat change the expression from that in the other copies.
Bernoulli II, p. 140, no. 1, pl. 20.
Helbig, *F.*³, no. 278; Helbig, *F.*⁴-Speier, no. 69.
Lippold, *Vat. Kat.*, III, 1, no. 509, pl. 23.
Adriani, *Annuario* XXIV–XXVI, 1946–1948, p. 152, note 3, no. 1.

2. Bust, mounted on a modern herm, in the Galleria Geografica, Vatican, inv. 2845. Provenance not known. Turns a little to his left. FIGS. 1276, 1279
Height of ancient part 41 cm.; ht. of head 31·2 cm.
Restorations: Most of nose, right ear, rim of left ear, lower lip, edge of bust at left with part of drapery.
Bernoulli II, p. 140, no. 2.
Lippold, *Gr. Portr.*, p. 82, note 2; *Vat. Kat.* III, 2, p. 488, no. 61, pl. 221.
Adriani, loc. cit. no. 2.
Helbig, *F.*⁴-Speier, no. 584.

3. Head, mounted on a modern herm, in the Stanza dei Filosofi, Capitoline Museum, no. 35. Inv. Albani, B75.
FIGS. 1271–1273
Height of head 31·2 cm.
Restorations: Nose, edges of ears.
Bernoulli II, p. 140, no. 3.
Stuart Jones, *Cat.*, p. 254, no. 87, pl. 60.
Arndt-Br., 1091–1092.
Adriani, loc. cit., no. 3.

4. Head in the Museo Nazionale delle Terme, Rome, inv. 125567. Once in the possession of the antiquary Fanfani, and acquired by the Museum in 1947. FIGS. 1274–1275
Height with neck 33 cm.; ht. of head 26 cm.
No restorations.
Adriani, op. cit., p. 162.
Felletti Maj, *Ritratti*, no. 36.

5. Head, mounted on a modern herm, in the Villa Albani, no. 736. FIGS. 1277–1278
Height of ancient part 35; ht. of head 31 cm.
Restorations: Nose, neck.
Bernoulli II, 140, no. 4.
Lippold, in *E.A.*, nos. 4352–4353.
Adriani, loc. cit., no. 4.

6. Head in the court of the Palazzo Gaetani, Rome.

FIGS. 1285–1287

Height c. 38 cm.; ht. of head c. 28 cm. Trimmed for insertion in a herm or statue.

No restorations.

Mentioned by Adriani, op. cit., p. 162.

Richter, *Gr. Portr.* IV, p. 41, figs. 58–59.

7. Head in the American Academy, Rome. FIGS. 1288–1290

Height 34 cm.; ht. of head 27·5 cm.

No restorations.

Mentioned by Adriani, op. cit., p. 162.

8. Head formerly in the Lateran Museum, now transferred to the Vatican, inv. 10166.   FIGS. 1280–1281

Height, with neck and part of chest, 36 cm.; ht. of head 30 cm.

Restorations: Nose, pieces of the ears, back of head on right side. Worked for insertion in a herm or statue.

Benndorf and Schöne, *Die antiken Bildwerke des Lateranischen Museums*, no. 221, pl. IV, 2.

Bernoulli II, p. 140.

Arndt-Br., 1093–1094.

Adriani, op. cit., p. 152, note 3, no. 6.

9. Head once in the collection of Cardinale di Carpi. Now 'lost'.

Statius, p. XXXVIII.

Lippold, *Gr. Porträtst.*, p. 67.

Adriani, op. cit., p. 162.

10. Small bronze bust, inscribed Ἕρμαρχος, in the National Museum, Naples, inv. 5466. Drapery on both shoulders. Found in the Villa dei Pisoni, Herculaneum.

FIGS. 1291–1293

Height, with ancient base, 20 cm.; ht. of head 12 cm.

No restorations.

Comparetti and De Petra, *Villa ercol.*, p. 263, no. 16, pl. XII, 8.

Visconti, *Ic. gr.* I, pp. 293f., pl. XXVI, 1, 2.

Bernoulli II, p. 139, pl. XIX.

Ruesch, *Guida*, no. 900.

Adriani, op. cit., p. 152, note 3, no. 5.

Kaibel, *I.G.* XIV, no. 709.

11. Head in the National Museum, Naples, inv. 150238.

FIGS. 1282–1284

Height 34·5 cm.; ht. of head 28 cm.

No restorations.

Adriani, op. cit., p. 162, pl. XVIb.

12. Small bronze bust in the National Museum, Naples, inv. 5471. From the villa of the Pisoni, Herculaneum.

FIGS. 1294–1296

Height, without modern base, 13 cm.; ht. of head 10 cm.

No restorations.

Comparetti and De Petra, *Villa ercol.*, p. 263, no. 18, pl. XII, 2.

Bernoulli II, p. 131, no. 5 (as Metrodoros).

Ruesch, *Guida*, no. 895 (as Metrodoros).

von Heintze, in Hekler, *B.b.G.*[3], p. 69, no. 9 (as Hermarchos).

After some hesitation, I have decided in favour of Hermarchos

instead of Metrodoros for this head. The design of hair and beard seem to me to point to Hermarchos. Note especially the hair above the forehead, which is brushed from left to right in the manner invariably occurring in his portraits. This being a reduced head, one must expect some variations from the life-size ones.

13. Head, mounted on a modern herm, in the National Museum, Palermo, inv. 735.   FIGS. 1297–1299

Height 25–27 cm.

Restorations: Nose, neck, and part of the left side of the face with a large part of the back of the head.

Bernoulli II, p. 134 (as a doubtful Metrodoros).

E.A., no. 559, b (as Metrodoros).

Adriani, op. cit., p. 162.

For the bronze bust in the Museo Archeologico, Florence, inv. 1647, by some thought to represent Hermarchos cf. p. 242 (under Apollonios Rhodios).

14. Head in the Ny Carlsberg Glyptothek, Copenhagen, I.N. 2689. Said to be from Naples. Acquired in Rome in 1923.   FIGS. 1300–1302

Height 32 cm.

In good preservation, with intact nose.

F. Poulsen, *B.C.H.* XLVIII, 1924, pp. 377ff., pls. XIV, XV; *Gaz. des Beaux-Arts*, 1937, I, p. 11, figs. 8–10; *Cat.*, no. 417a.

Adriani, op. cit., p. 152, note 3, no. 9.

V. Poulsen, *Portr. gr.*, no. 37, pl. XXVII.

15. Head, mounted on a modern herm, in the British Museum, no. 1854. Bought from Castellani, 1873. Said to have been found on the Appian Way, Rome. FIGS. 1303–1305

Height, with neck, 36·3 cm.; ht. of head 27·3 cm.

No restorations.

A. H. Smith, *Cat.*, no. 1854, pl. XIX.

Adriani, op. cit., p. 162 (was the first to recognize it as Hermarchos).

16. Bust in the Museum of Art, Budapest, inv. 4999. Said to be from a Roman villa in Asia Minor. Formerly owned by Pollak. One of the best specimens known.

FIGS. 1306–1309

Height 52 cm.

No restorations. Nose ancient.

Hekler, *Die Sammlung antiker Skulpturen, Budapest*, 1929, p. 54, no. 46; *B.b.G.*, p. 37, fig. 37.

Adriani, op. cit., p. 152, note 3, no. 8.

Bieber, *Sc. of the Hell. Age*, p. 57, figs. 177, 178.

17. Head, mounted on a modern herm inscribed Metrodoros. In the Prado, Madrid. Found in the excavations of Azara at Tivoli in 1779.   FIGS. 1310–1312

Height 57 cm.; ht. of head 32·5 cm.

Restorations: Nose, upper lip with left part of moustache.

Bernoulli II, p. 126, no. 25 (as a doubtful Epikouros).

Hübner, no. 167.

Ricard, no. 101, pl. LV.

Blanco, *Cat.*, no. 19E, pl. IV (as Hermarchos).

The head in a double herm in the Prado, Madrid, is not Hermarchos, as has been thought by some, but of the so-called Kolotes type (q.v.).

18. Head in the Museum of Alexandria, 3356.

FIGS. 1313–1315

Height 28 cm.

No restorations.

Graindor, *Bustes et statues portraits d'Égypte romaine*, no. 30, pl. XXVIIa (Callimaque?).

Lippold, *Gr. Porträtst.*, p. 67, fig. 12 (Kallimachos).

Adriani, op. cit., p. 162 (first to recognize it as Hermarchos).

19. From Prof. Jucker I learn that there is a marble bust of Hermarchos in the Archaeological Museum, Jerusalem (Jordan), no. 35.3449, which he hopes to publish soon. Life-size. Said to be from Sebaste.

20. A bust was in 1938 in the Roman antiquity market (Jandolo) = Adriani, op. cit., p. 152, note 1, no. 10?, and F. Poulsen, *B.C.H.* XLVIII, 1924, p. 377? To judge by the photographs it is in excellent condition, only the nose being missing.

FIGS. 1316–1318

21. A headless herm inscribed Ἑρμάρχου, found in 1780 in 'the villa of Cassius', Tivoli, is now 'lost'. It is not in the Vatican or the Lateran, according to Miss Speier, who has made a thorough search for it.

Visconti, *Ic. gr.* I, p. 294; *Museo Pio-Clementino* I, pl. VIII, p. 51.

Benndorf and Schöne, *Lateran*, p. 85.

Bernoulli II, p. 140, note 2.

Kaibel, *I.G.* XIV, 1151.

STATUES

In addition to these heads, two seated figures have been recognized as representing Hermarchos:

1. A small statue in the Museo Archeologico, Florence, inv. 70989. Found in a Roman villa in Tuscany, belonging to the family Gilli. Acquired in 1878. Recognized as Hermarchos from the likeness of the head to his portraits.

FIGS. 1319–1320

Height 1·07 m.; ht. of head 25 cm.

No restorations, except at the join of head and neck.

Milani, *Museo Archeologico di Firenze* I, p. 318, no. 88, pl. 156, I (there called Sophokles).

Lippold, *Gr. Porträtst.*, pp. 79, 82.

Schefold, *B.*, p. 120, no. 2, p. 210.

Richter, *Gr. Portr.* (I) p. 38, fig. 20.

2. Headless large statuette in the Museum of Ostia, 1135.

FIGS. 1322–1324

Height 31 cm.

No restorations.

Vaglieri, *Not. d. Sc.*, 1913, p. 298, fig. 4.

Hekler, *B.b.G.*, p. 48, note 57 (there called Epikouros).

Schefold, *B.*, p. 210 (recognized as Hermarchos).

Richter, *Gr. Portr.*, p. 38, figs. 21, 22.

von Heintze, in Hekler, *B.b.G.*[3], p. 69, no. 2 (as Hermarchos).

In both figures Hermarchos is shown seated, in a similar attitude to that of Epikouros (cf. p. 198), that is, with his right forearm raised, the left placed on his lap, the right leg put forward, the left set back. However, the folds of the enveloping mantle show variations, being, for instance,

differently composed in the region of the left knee, and lacking the descending end that occurs in the Epikouros. In the Florence copy Hermarchos is shown seated on a backless throne of rectangular shape, whereas in the little statuette in Ostia he sits on a throne with rounded back, ending in front in an animal's head, similar to that in Epikouros' statue. Such differences in the rendering of seats in portrait statues are not unusual.

The date of the Greek original can hardly be far removed from that of Epikouros, i.e. circa 270 B.C. One may surmise that the three seated statues of Epikouros, Metrodoros, and Hermarchos once occupied prominent places in the garden of Epikouros, as an inspiration to the later Epicureans.

STATUETTE

For the suggestion that the silver statuette in the Bibliothèque Nationale (published by Chabouillet, *Catalogue des camées . . .*, no. 2870, as a possible Sophokles) may represent Hermarchos cf. my *Gk. Portr.* IV, p. 41, figs. 56, 57. Height with base 13 cm. Found at Bordeaux in 1813. Acquired in 1837. It is true that the pose and the rendering of the drapery differ from those in the marble figures, nos. 1, 2; but the divergencies may be due to the fact that the statuette in Paris reproduces a Hellenistic original different from that preserved in the copies in Florence and Ostia. That in Roman times statuettes of eminent Greeks were prized possessions is well known; cf. Lucian, *Philopseudes*, 21, and my *Gk. Portr.* II, p. 23, III, pp. 33ff.

FIG. 1321

For a bronze statuette once tentatively identified as Hermarchos, now as a possible Epikouros cf. p. 199.

CONCLUSIONS

The portraits of Hermarchos have often been confused with those of Metrodoros, or even identified with other persons. Adriani clarified the problem by his convincing exposition that several heads once thought to represent Kallimachos, etc. really represented Hermarchos. He postulated two different types, created at two different periods. In my opinion, however, all the portraits above listed go back to the same Greek original, and the divergencies are due—as in other cases (cf. e.g. pp. 223, 235)—to the nature of the ancient pointing process used by the Roman copyists (cf. p. 27). Though the expression somewhat changes from one example to another, the basic composition is always the same. Thus, the hair over the forehead is regularly arranged in a series of tufts forming a single curve and directed from left to right along an almost horizontal line, and is then carved in thicker, double-curved locks along the temples as far as the ears. The rendering of the moustache is also more or less constant; it is long, and its downward direction starts almost from beneath the nose, so that the design is that of a triangle truncated at the top. The beard is about as short as that of Metrodoros; below the lower lip it is rendered in a series of oblique, only slightly curving tufts, and below these come again thick curls. The eyes are placed close together; the nose is long and straight; the skull only slightly rounded;

the forehead slightly receding, with only one horizontal furrow running across it; the mouth is small with a full lower lip, and with lips parted.

The physiognomy in all the portraits is the same—of a man of about 40 years of age with a bland expression—not a great personality like Epikouros, and not as serene as Metrodoros, but intelligent and inquisitive. An excellent portrayal, in fact, of the man as we know him from what is said of him by ancient authors.

The date of the Greek original may be assigned to c. 270 B.C.

KOLOTES

Fourth to third century B.C. Epicurean philosopher. Of Lampsakos. Pupil of Epikouros.

His unbounded admiration for Epikouros is indicated by the incident (recorded in an extant letter by Epikouros to Kolotes) of Kolotes falling at the feet of Epikouros, after one of the latter's discourses, as if to a deity. It is also known that he was vehement in his attacks on other philosophers, especially on Plato.

Our information concerning Kolotes comes chiefly from fragments that have been preserved of letters by Epikouros to Kolotes (cf. Usener, *Epicurea*, frgt. 141, p. 145), and from some references in Plutarch's writings.

Nothing is known of his appearance, and no statue to him is recorded in extant ancient literature, so the identification of a possible portrait of him among the many unknowns is difficult. Nevertheless, Schefold (*B.*, pp. 116f. nos. 3, 4, p. 209) has made an attractive suggestion, namely that he is represented in a portrait existing in several examples which in style would fit the time of Kolotes (the rendering of the hair recalls that of Menander), and which evidently represents an Epicurean philosopher, since he markedly resembles both Metrodoros and Hermarchos. Lippold, *E.A.* 1634–1645, and Hekler, *Arch. Anz.*, 1938, cols. 233f, listed a number of examples of this type; to which more can now be added:

1. Herm in the Capitoline Museum, no. 67. Formerly in the Cesi Collection. FIGS. 1325–1326
Height 59·5; ht. of head 30 cm. Over life-size.
Restorations: End of nose, rims of ears, part of neck, edge on left side of herm.
Bottari I, 49.
Bernoulli I, p. 44 (mentioned as resembling Periander).
Stuart Jones, *Cat.*, p. 252, no. 81.
Hekler, *Arch. Anz.*, 1938, col. 233.

2. Head, mounted on an alien or modern bust, in the court-yard of Via Giulia, 4, Rome, placed high up on a support against the wall (1962). FIG. 1336
Life-size.
The neck is restored and the surface has suffered from exposure. Recognized as being of this type by E. Berger.
German Institute photograph 61.77.

3. Herm in the Museo Civico, Venice, inv. 34. Gift of Giovanni Grimani, 1586. Once in the Cesi Collection, at which time it was published by Statius (pl. 33).
FIGS. 1327–1329
Height 47 cm.; ht. of head 33 cm.
Restorations: Nose, rim of ear.
Arndt-Br., 967–968.
Anti, *Guida, Museo Archeologico nel Palazzo Reale di Venezia*, 1930, p. 77, no. 16.
Hekler, *Arch. Anz.*, 1938, cols. 233f., fig. 1.

4. Head, in a double herm, in the Prado, Madrid. Of unknown provenance. FIGS. 1331–1332
Height 53 cm.
Restorations: Nose and lower part of herm.
Hübner, no. 147 ('Epikur und Metrodor?').
Ricard, no. 100.
Blanco, no. 103 E, pl. XLIX (only profiles) 'dos filosofos epicureos'.
Bernoulli II, p. 126, no. 26: 'Die Köpfe sind sich ausserordentlich ähnlich, entbehren aber der für Epikur und Metrodor charakteristische Züge'. But see my pp. 197f., under Epikouros.
E.A., 1643–1645.
Hekler, *Arch. Anz.*, 1938, col. 233.
Schefold, *B.*, p. 209.

5. Head in the Museum of Kassel. Said to have been found on the Aventine. Made for insertion in a statue.
FIGS. 1333–1335
Height 46 cm.; ht. of head 32·5 cm.
No restorations.
Bedeutende Kunstwerke aus dem Nachlass Dr. Jacob Hirsch, Auktion Hess, Lucerne, Dec. 1957 (E. Langlotz).
E. Berger, *Kunst in Hessen und am Mittelrhein*, Beiheft to vol. 1–2, 1962, p. 59 (there thought perhaps to represent Aristippos).
Hafner, *Geschichte der griechischen Kunst*, p. 242, fig. 244 (there thought perhaps to represent Alkibiades).
Schefold, *Festschrift Hahnloser* (1961), p. 9, note 14.

6. Head once in a private collection in Munich. Now?
FIG. 1339
Height 30 cm.
No restorations, but fragmentary.
Antike und byzantinische Kleinkunst, Auktion Helbing, München, October 28–30, 1913, no. 13, pl. I.
Hekler, *Arch. Anz.* 1938, col. 233.

7. Head, mounted on a modern bust, in the Residenz, Munich. FIGS. 1337–1338
Height of face 36 cm.
Restorations: Neck, nose, and upper lip.
E.A., 963.
Hekler, *Arch. Anz.*, 1938, col. 233.

8. Herm found in recent excavations at Apollonia, Albania.
FIG. 1330
Life-size.
No restorations.
Illustrated London News, July 1, 1961, p. 21, fig. 5 (there interpreted as Thucydides).
J. Frel, *Eunomia*, Prague, 1960, p. 44ff.
A. Kahn, *Archaeology*, 1961, p. 164.

CONCLUSIONS

Against Schefold's identification of these heads as Kolotes it has been argued that the style points to a period around 300 B.C., that is, somewhat early for Kolotes; and Aristippos has, therefore, been proposed. However, one does not know the age of Kolotes; that he was a pupil of Epikouros does not necessarily mean that he was younger (Hermarchos was the same age as Epikouros). One may also think that the rather phlegmatical physiognomy of the portrait in question seems inappropriate for the impetuous temperament of Kolotes, as indicated at least by the incident recorded of his falling at the feet of Epikouros during one of the latter's discourses as well as by his attacks against Plato and other philosophers; but such impressions are often misleading. If, as seems at least possible, the companion in the double herm in Madrid was intended for Epikouros (cf. p. 198)—worked free-hand, not mechanically, for the heads are so to speak in relief—then this would be another argument in favour of Schefold's proposal. For Kolotes seems to be the only Epicurean besides Metrodoros and Hermarchos to have had a special relation to Epikouros, and therefore to have been appropriately associated with him in a double herm. The alternative is to think of Polyainos or Idomeneus, as Schefold did, both known to have been, like Kolotes, from Lampsakos, and both pupils of Epikouros. We then, however, enter still further into the realm of hypotheses.

3. ORATORS

LYSIAS

c. 458–380 B.C. Orator. Born in Syracuse (or Athens, Cic., *Brutus*, 63), son of Kephalos, a native of Syracuse and a man of substance, who went to Athens in the time of Perikles (Lysias, 12, 4; Dion. Hal., *Lysias*, 452).

443 B.C. At the age of fifteen he joined other Athenians who went as colonists to Thourion, in Italy, and settled there. Studied under the orators Teisias and Nikias (Ps.-Plut., *Vit. X Orat.*, Lys., p. 835D; Dion. Hal. 452f.).

413 After the collapse of the Athenian army at Syracuse, he returned to Athens with his elder brother Polemarchos, and devoted himself to oratory, probably the teaching of it. Also studied with Sokrates (cf. Lucian, *De domo*, 4).

404 His property was confiscated by the Thirty Tyrants, and his brother Polemarchos was executed (Ps.-Plut., *Vit. X Orat.*, Lys., p. 835Eff.). He fled to Megara.

403 There he became a logographos, a writer of orations for others, his earliest being against Eratosthenes, who had been responsible for the death of Polemarchos.

Helped Thrasyboulos to overthrow the Thirty Tyrants. Thrasyboulos' attempt to confer on him Athenian citizenship was not successful.

Soon after 380. Died at an advanced age (at 76 or 80 or 83; cf. Ps.-Plut. *Vit. X Orat.*, Lys. 836A). He was considered the foremost orator of his time, his style being distinguished for clarity, simplicity, and grace.

Many of his orations are extant (cf. Loeb ed.).

STATUES RECORDED

No statue of Lysias is mentioned by ancient writers. The passage in Ailios Aristeides ἹΙερῶν λόγων (ed. Keil ɪ, pp. 440f.; ed. Dindorf §520): Ἔκαμνον γὰρ τριταίῳ οἵῳ βαρυτάτῳ καὶ ὁρῶ Λυσίαν τὸν ῥήτορα, νεανίσκον οὐκ ἄχαριν, which has by some been thought to refer to a statue of young Lysias, 'is—as seen by the context—merely a vision' (A. D. Nock).

EXTANT PORTRAITS

1. Head, with bust, in the National Museum, Naples, inv. 6130. Inscribed Λυσίας at the bottom of the bust. From the Farnese Collection. Known to F. Ursinus. Made for insertion in a statue. Drapery on both shoulders.

FIGS. 1340–1342

Height 36 cm.; ht. of head 29 cm.

Lysias. National Museum, Naples. Ursinus, *Imag.*, 75

Restorations: Nose, upper lip, moustache, right eyebrow.
The surface a little worked over in parts (cf. *infra*).
F. Ursinus, *Imag.*, 75; Faber, *Imag.*, no. 85; Bellori, *Imag.*, 84.
Visconti, *Ic. gr.* I, p. 337, pl. XXVIII.
Bernoulli II, pp. 1f., pl. 1.
Arndt-Br., 131–132.
Ruesch, *Guida*, no. 1116.
Kaibel, *I.G.* XIV, no. 1179.
Huelsen, no. 24.

2. Head, mounted on a modern herm inscribed Lysias, in
the Stanza dei Filosofi, Capitoline Museum, 73. From the
Albani Collection.   FIGS. 1343–1345
Height of ancient part 30 cm.; ht. of head 29 cm.
Restorations: End of nose, most of the rims of both ears,
and part of the lobe of the left ear.
Bernoulli II, p. 2.
Arndt-Br., 133–134.
Stuart Jones, *Cat.*, p. 257, no. 96, pl. 60.

The head, mounted on a modern herm inscribed Lysias,
in Holkham Hall, which was thought by Conze and
Michaelis (*Anc. Marbl.*, p. 317, no. 48) to be a replica of the
Capitoline and Naples portraits, is the now well known
Plato, as F. Poulsen saw (cf. p. 167, no. 15).

For a head at Stratfield Saye somewhat resembling Lysias
(which I have not seen) cf. Vermeule and von Bothmer,
A.J.A. LX, 1956, p. 332, pl. 108, no. 15 *bis*; von Heintze, in
Hekler, *Bild. b. Gr.*³, p. 55, top, no. 3.

CONCLUSIONS

Though the two heads 1 and 2 vary in the renderings of
hair, beard and the region round the eyes (in no. 2
simplified and linear, in no. 1 more modelled) the basic
forms are identical in both; note especially the curious
formation of the skull and the composition of the locks.
Both must, therefore, have been copied from the same
original. 'The complete reworking of the surface', claimed
by Studniczka (*Menander*, p. 7) does not seem likely. Prof.
Maiuri after a recent re-examination of the head thought
this out of the question: 'only a few non-essential details
(in hair, on cheeks, and the furrows on the forehead) might
have been reworked'. This is what I also thought when I
examined the head in 1959. There are rootmarks on the
beard, the hair and left cheek, i.e. the regions which differ
from those in the Capitoline head (no. 2), and which cannot,
therefore, have been extensively reworked. Cf. my *Gr. Portr.*
II, p. 10, note 1.

In Ursinus' *Imag.*, p. 75, is illustrated another inscribed
portrait of Lysias. But this seems to have disappeared, as
already noted by Bernoulli II, p. 3.

The inscription Lysias on still another headless herm was
considered modern by Kaibel, XIV, 224*.

The heads in the Stanza dei Filosofi of the Capitoline
Museum (Stuart Jones, *Cat.*, pp. 225f., nos. 13, 14, 15, pl. 55)
by some once thought to represent Lysias have long ago

Lysias. National Museum, Naples. Drawing by Gallaeus. Cf. fig. 1341

been excluded; for these and other former claimants cf.
Bernoulli II, pp. 2f.

CONCLUSIONS

The two heads 1, 2, are, therefore, the only extant heads of
Lysias. In them is represented a middle-aged, bald, bearded
man with a broad, furrowed forehead, a flat skull, and small
eyes, placed horizontally. The style points to the first
quarter of the fourth century B.C. as the date of the prototype.
The original Greek portrait may have been erected soon
before or after Lysias' death—in recognition of his political
services and his distinction as an orator.

ISOKRATES

436–338 B.C. The orator. Son of Theodoros, of the Attic
deme of Erchia, and of Hedyto. His father was a manufac-
turer of flutes and well-to-do.

LIFE

He had a careful education. Said to have studied under
Prodikos and Protagoras, to have visited Gorgias in Sicily.
403–392 After the loss of his father's fortune in the Peloponnesian war, he first became a λογογράφος, that is, a writer of
speeches for others, not appearing in court himself, on
account of nervousness and the poorness of his voice (cf.
Pliny the Younger, *Ep.*, VI, 29; Lucian, *Parasitus*, 42).
399 Appeared in mourning after Sokrates' death.
c. 390 Opened a school of rhetoric in Athens and continued
his teachings with great success for 40 years. Cicero (*Brutus*,

32) called him 'a great orator and ideal teacher', 'whose house became a veritable training school or studio of eloquence open to all Greece'; magnus orator et perfectus magister, Isocrates cuius domus cunctae Graeciae quasi ludus quidam patuit, atque officina dicendi.

380 Composed the *Panegyrikos* for recitation at the Olympic festival.

c. 360 His friend and admirer the Athenian general Timotheos (411–354) erected a statue of him at Eleusis (see below). (For a laudatory estimate of Timotheos by Isokrates cf. Isokr., XV, 101–139.)

c. 350–338 The last years of his life were spent chiefly in writing, his faculties remaining unimpaired to the end; in fact, some of his best works were written when he was ninety, e.g. the *Philippos* and the *Panathenaikos*.

338 He died shortly after the battle of Chaironeia (cf. Lucian, *Macrob.*, 23). His last composition is said to have been a letter addressed to Philip, congratulating him on his victory. In contrast to Demosthenes, he saw the salvation of Greece in her union under one man who could lead her in a national war against Persia and spread Hellenism throughout the world. He has been called the 'geistiger Wegbereiter Alexanders des Grossen' (Schefold, *B.*, p. 160).

Over 20 of his orations have survived. They are distinguished for their lofty tone and the grace and elaboration of their style.

STATUES RECORDED

1. Heliodoros in Ps.-Plutarch, *Vit. X orat.* 839C, refers to an equestrian statue of Isokrates on the Akropolis which represented him as a boy, evidently as a victor in a race (κελητίζων).

2. Ps.-Plut., *Vit. X orat.*, Isokrates 838D, records that a bronze statue of him was set up at Eleusis by Timotheos, the son of Konon, with the following inscription: "Timotheos dedicated this statue of Isokrates to the goddesses, as a sign of his affection and his admiration for his friend. It is the work of Leochares',

Τιμόθεος, φιλίας τε χάριν, ξύνεσίν τε προτιμῶν,
'Ισοκράτους εἰκὼ τήνδε ἀνέθηκε θεαῖς.
Λεωχάρους ἔργον.

As Timotheos was banished in 356 B.C. and Leochares began his career c. 370, the statue must date between these years, when Isokrates was 66 to 80 years old.

3. After Isokrates' death his adopted son Aphareus set up a bronze statue of Isokrates, mounted on a column, in the Olympieion of Athens where it was still seen by Pausanias (I, 18, 8; Ps.-Plut., *Vit. X orat.*, Isokr. 839B): καὶ εἰκόνα αὐτοῦ χαλκῆν ἀνέθηκε πρὸς τῷ 'Ολυμπιείῳ, ἐπὶ κίονος καὶ ἐπέγραψεν·

'Ισοκράτους 'Αφαρεὺς πατρὸς εἰκόνα τήνδ' ἀνέθηκε
Ζηνί, θεούς τε σέβων καὶ γονέων ἀρετήν.

4. Christodoros, *Ecphr.* in *Gk. Anth.* II, 256ff., mentions a bronze statue of Isokrates in the Zeuxippos at Constantinople:

Χαῖρε φάος ῥήτρης 'Ισόκρατες, ὅττι σὺ χαλκῷ
κόσμον ἄγεις· δοκέεις γὰρ ἐπίφρονα μήδεα φαίνειν,
εἰ καὶ ἀφωνήτῳ σε πόνῳ χαλκεύσατο τέχνη.

5. A painted portrait of Isokrates in the Pompeion in Athens is mentioned by Ps.-Plutarch, *Vit. X orat.*, Isokr., 839C: γραπτὴ εἰκών.

Three different statues of Isokrates are, therefore, recorded in extant ancient literature as having been set up in Greek times—two in Athens (on the Akropolis and in the Olympieion), and one at Eleusis; in addition, there was a painted portrait in the Pompeion. The statue cited by Christodoros may have been a Roman copy.

IDENTIFICATION

The identification of the portrait of Isokrates was made possible by the bust in the Villa Albani inscribed with his name (cf. *infra*).

PORTRAITS EXTANT AND ONCE EXTANT

1. Small bust in the Villa Albani, no. 951, inscribed Εἰσοκράτη(s), let into a modern herm to act as a pendant to one of Q. Hortensius. Found in 1767 and set up in the villa in 1785. FIGS. 1346–1347

Height 28·5 cm.; ht. of head 16·2 cm.

Restorations: Tip of nose and patches on shoulder.

Visconti, *Ic. gr.* I, p. 345, pl. 28a, nos. 3, 4.
Arndt-Br., 135.
Bernoulli II, p. 15.
Helbig, *F.³*, no. 1853.
Schefold, *B.*, pp. 160f., no. 3.
Kaibel, *I.G.* XIV, 1169.

2. Head, mounted on a modern bust, in the Staatliche Museen, Berlin. Acquired in 1766 from the Natali collection in Rome. Formerly in Sanssouci Castle. FIGS. 1348–1349

Height of head, with beard, 25·8 cm.

Restorations: Nose, under lip, part of left ear, a piece of the hair at the top of the skull, the left end of the beard, part of the neck.

Conze, *Beschreibung* (1891), no. 301 (there accepted as Isokrates).
Kekule, *Gr. Sk.³*, p. 290 (accepted as Isokrates).
Bernoulli II, pp. 15f. (identification doubted).
Blümel, *Kat.* v, K199, pl. 12 (identification of Isokrates doubted).
von Heintze, in Hekler, *B.b.G.³*, p. 61 ('sehr wahrscheinlich').

3. In Statius' *Imag.*, χ, a herm is illustrated inscribed 'Ισοκράτης Θεοδώρου 'Αθηναῖος and said to be in hortis Cardinalis de Medicis. It had an alien head, as Ursinus in his preface noted (1870); nevertheless it is cited by Faber, *Imag.*, 76, and Bellori, 82, as a portrait of Isokrates. The herm itself is 'lost.'

Kaibel, *I.G.* XIV, 1168; Huelsen, no. 19.

The inscription 'Ισοκρά(της) on a herm with a bearded, bald head, in the Prado, Madrid, is modern, as Hübner saw (no. 165). Kaibel, *I.G.* XIV, 211*; Bernoulli II, p. 16.

CONCLUSIONS

The head in Berlin certainly shows considerable variations from the inscribed portrait in the Villa Albani. But in comparing the two one must remember that the Albani bust is small, and, therefore, probably worked free-hand; and so divergencies would be natural. It seems to me, therefore, possible that the two represent the same person—a man of about 35–40 years old, with an almost abnormally high forehead, protruding markedly in its upper portion, curling hair and beard, and a small mouth.

The expression has been called mild and uninteresting, but the portrait after all shows the characteristics associated with Isokrates—the shyness and sensitiveness that made it difficult for him to speak in public (but enabled him to write distinguished Attic prose) and the visionary outlook that prevented him from appraising current events as did Demosthenes.

Whether the Albani portrait goes back to the statue by Leochares (cf. p. 209) or some other, one cannot of course tell. The style of the bust suggests a date not earlier than the last third of the fourth century, and so it might well reproduce either the statue set up by Timotheos or that by Aphareus. Since Isokrates is represented as relatively young, whereas he lived to be over 90, the original sketch must have been executed fairly early during his life, and somewhat reworked in a later style for the official statue. Also to-day it is customary, when representing a man who lived to an advanced age, to utilize sketches or photographs made of him earlier in life.

HYPEREIDES

c. 390–322 B.C. Attic orator. Born of a well-to-do family. Son of Glaukippos of the Attic deme of Kollytos.

LIFE

Studied under Plato (Diog. Laert. III, 46; Ps.-Plut., *Vit. X orat.*, Hyper., 848d; Suidas) and Isokrates (Athen. VIII, 342c; *Vit. X orat.*, Isokr., 837d).

Said to have been an epicure (ὀψοφάγος) and a bon vivant (Athen. VIII, 341e–f, XIII, 590c–d).

Was at first a professional speech writer, later a successful prosecutor in public trials.

Took an active part in the Lamian war (*Vit. X orat.*, Hyper., 849f; Plut. *Phokion*, 23). Staunch supporter of Demosthenes in his opposition to Macedon, and showed much courage in that connexion. Spoke, for instance, against the request by Alexander to hand over the orators who had sided against Macedon (though he himself was not involved), and against the delivery of ships for Alexander's Asian campaigns.

Among the people he defended in his trials was the hetaira Phryne (see below).

324–323 Opposed Demosthenes in the Harpalos bribery trials (cf. p. 215).

322 After the battle of Krannon his surrender was demanded by Antipater, and he was condemned to death (Plut. *Demosth.*, 28; Suidas, s.v. ᾽Αντίπατρος). He fled from Athens, was seized in Aegina, and was executed, perhaps in Macedonia.

His speeches became famous for their trenchant wit and for the naturalness and grace (χάρις) of the language. He was by some considered even greater than Demosthenes (cf. Ps.-Plut., *Vit. X orat.*, Hyper., 849d).

STATUES RECORDED

A papyrus from Oxyrhynchus, Egypt, states that after the Athenians had once more recovered their freedom (i.e. in 307 B.C.), they honoured him (Hypereides) with . . . statues, ᾽Αθηναῖοι δὲ πά[λ]ιν τὴν ἐλευθερίαν ἀνακομισάμενοι κα[λλίστοις?] αὐ[τ]ὸν ἀνδριάσιν ἐ[τίμησαν]. Grenfell and Hunt, *The Oxyrhynchus Papyri* XV (1922), no. 1800, fragment 8, lines 30–33.

This information supplies a definite date for portraits erected for Hypereides, that is, after 307 B.C., when Athens was freed of Macedonian domination by Demetrios of Phaleron.

PORTRAIT ONCE EXTANT

On the base, evidently of a statue, once in the Villa Mattei, now lost, is the inscription: 'Hypereides, the orator, Zeuxiades made it', Ὑπερίδες ῥήτωρ (Ζ)ευ(ξ)ιά(δ)ης ἐποίει. Zeuxiades was a pupil of Silanion (Pliny XXXIV, 51).

Spon, *Miscell.*, p. 137.
Visconti, *Ic. gr.* I, p. 378.
Bernoulli II, p. 59.
Kaibel, *I.G.* XIV, 1149, 3.
Loewy, *Inschr.*, no. 483.

The base is of Roman date and belongs to a group, each with an egg moulding, and all once in the Villa Mattei (cf. pp. 160, 244, and Loewy, *Inschriften*, nos. 481–484). On them presumably were mounted either copies of Greek portraits, with the names of the Greek sculptors added, or the original Greek statues, carried off from Greece without their bases, and then mounted on new ones.

IDENTIFICATION

Though there is no extant inscribed portrait of Hypereides, an identification has been made probable by F. Poulsen's suggestion that the two people in a double herm in Compiègne (see below) represent Hypereides and the famous hetaira Phryne (q.v.), whom he defended on the charge of godlessness, ἀσέβεια, and whose portrait was carved by Praxiteles (Paus. IX, 27, 5; X, 15, 1). There are a number of replicas of the male head in this herm, showing that the individual must have been prominent and popular also in Roman times, which would fit Hypereides; and the style of the head points to the end of the fourth century, when portraits of Hypereides are said to have been erected (cf. *supra*). It is also known that the speech he made in defence of Phryne was much admired in Roman times (cf. Quintilian X, 5, 2).

F. Poulsen's suggestion has, therefore, met with general approval, though there have also been dissenters, for instance Crome (*Arch. Anz.*, 1935, cols. 1ff.), and Gullini (*Arch. cl.* I, 2, p. 133, note 5), who thought that in the Compiègne herm, instead of Hypereides and Phryne, the philosopher Aristippos (q.v.) and his daughter Arete, a teacher of philosophy, could be represented. On the other hand, it has been pointed out that these two are more plausibly identified in another double herm now in Berlin; cf. E. Schmidt, *Arch. Anz.*, 1935, col. 384, and my p. 176.

At all events, since Poulsen's identification of Hypereides is based on sound, though of course not clinching, evidence, the extant examples are listed herewith.

1. Herm in the Museo Torlonia. Said to have come from Ostia. FIGS. 1350–1351

Height 43·5 cm.; ht. of head 27 cm.

No restorations, but the surface must have been extensively reworked (note the hard transitions in the beard and nose).

P. E. Visconti, *Museo Torlonia*, no. 30, pl. VIII (there called Lysias). In the French edition (by C. L. Visconti) the head is said to have come from the Giustiniani Collection; but the reference given to the *Galleria Giustiniani* (II, 34) is to a different head and no portrait of Hypereides is included in that publication. It is likely, therefore, that C. L. Visconti made a mistake and that the provenance of Porto d'Ostia given by P. E. Visconti (who excavated at Ostia in 1880) is the correct one. The head will be published by R. Calza in her forthcoming *Ritratti d'Ostia*.

2. Bust in the Museo Archeologico, Florence, inv. 89041. Gift of Count G. Conestabile della Spaffa di Perugia, in 1927. Drapery on both shoulders; head is inclined forward.
FIGS. 1352–1354

Height 41 cm.; ht. of head 32 cm.

No restorations. The nose is missing; it was once attached with two rivets.

Crome, *Arch. Anz.*, 1935, cols. 1ff.
E. Schmidt, *Arch. Anz.*, 1935, cols. 377ff.

3. Head in a double herm in the Musée Vivenel, Compiègne.
FIGS. 1355–1357

Height 33 cm.; ht. of head 29 cm.

No restorations except for lower parts of necks. The female head is only partly preserved, but included is the hair with a knot at the top (which, according to E. Schmidt, loc. cit., is more suitable to Phryne than to a teacher of philosophy).

Espérandieu, *Recueil* v, p. 144, no. 3892.
F. Poulsen, *Mon. Piot* XXI, 1913, pp, 48f., figs. 2, 3.
E. Schmidt, *Arch. Anz.*, 1935, col. 384.

4. Head in the Ny Carlsberg Glyptothek, Copenhagen, I.N. 1967. Said to have been found at Parma. Acquired in 1903. FIGS. 1358–1359

Height 27 cm. Perhaps once part of a double herm (F. Poulsen); but not that with Demosthenes (cf. p. 219, no. 33). The restored nose and neck were removed in 1952. Top of head and back missing, and surface weathered.

F. Poulsen, *Ik. Misc.*, p. 4; *Cat.*, no. 422; *Mon. Piot* XXI, 1913, pp. 47ff., pl. III.
V. Poulsen, *Portr. gr.*, no. 21.

5. Head with neck, in the National Museum, Copenhagen, inv. 8011. Formerly in the Castle Steengaard. Acquired in Italy in 1780. FIGS. 1362–1364

Height 34·5 cm.; ht. of head 27 cm.

Restorations: End of nose, part of the right ear. The modern herm has now been removed. It was made for insertion in a statue; a piece of the himation is preserved at the back, and of the chiton below the right shoulder.

F. Poulsen, *Ikon. Misc.*, pp. 4ff., fig. 1, pls. 1–3.
E. Schmidt, *J.d.I.* XLVII, 1932, p. 298, fig. 47.
Guide to the Danish National Museum, Dept. of Oriental and Classical Antiquities, p. 83, no. 8.

6. Small head in the Kunsthistorisches Museum, Vienna. Found in Athens. FIGS. 1360–1361

Height 15 cm.; that is, about half life-size.

No restorations.

Benndorf, *Oest. Jahr.* II, 1899, pp. 250ff, pl. IV, fig. 137 (there thought to represent Plato).
F. Poulsen, *Ik. Misc.*, p. 4.

STATUE?

The type of statue belonging to this portrait has been tentatively identified in a headless figure in the National Museum, Naples (no inv. number). Height 1·85 m. Found in the Via Pendino, near S. Agostino la Zecca, in Naples. It is shown standing, holding a scroll in its left hand, wearing a chiton and mantle, somewhat in the same attitude as that of Aischines (cf. p. 213, no. 6). It is likely, therefore, that an orator was here also represented. FIG. 1368

Sogliano, *Not. d. Sc.* 1893, p. 264, II.
Ruesch, *Guida*, no. 1113, fig. 65.
E. Schmidt, *J.d.I.* XLVII, 1932, pp. 296ff.; *Arch. Anz.* 1935, cols. 377ff.
Gullini, *Arch. cl.* I, 2, p. 133, note. 5.
Amelung, *E.A.*, no. 766.

That the statue in the Sala della Biga, Vatican (Helbig, *F.*[3], no. 328; Helbig, *F.*[4]-Speier, no. 502; inv. 2347) is not, as Amelung thought, a replica, has been pointed out by Herrmann, *E.A.*, Serie IV, p. 67, Nachtrag zu no. 766. The same applies to the similar statue in Marbury Hall, *E.A.*, 3105.

CONCLUSIONS

The six heads above listed must all have been reproduced from the same Greek original—the life-size ones, nos. 1, 2, 4, 5, evidently mechanically by the pointing process, the small head in Vienna and the double herm in Compiègne perhaps free-hand, since they show considerable variations in the composition of the locks in hair and beard, though they too are fairly faithful copies in essentials. A middle-aged man is represented, with a long, oval face; protruding cheekbones; a high, rounded skull; a furrowed, bald forehead; short, closely adhering locks in hair and beard; a straight, wide mouth; a moustache descending at right angles; deep, curving furrows travelling from the nostrils along the cheeks; rather narrow eyes; bushy, arching eyebrows; and an intelligent, calculating expression. Not the likeness of a poet, but of a practical, studious, gifted man, such as we know Hypereides to have been.

LYKOURGOS

c. 390–324 B.C. The Attic orator. Son of Lykophron, and member of the aristocratic family of the Eteoboutadai.

In charge of Athenian finances from 338 to 326 B.C., when he distinguished himself for his ability and honesty. Supporter of Demosthenes.

Built the Panathenaic stadium, completed the theatre of Dionysos, and dedicated there the three statues of Aischylos, Sophokles, and Euripides (q.v.).

Of the 15 speeches by him known in antiquity only one is now extant *Against Leokrates*, which is said to show him more interested in his subject than in style.

STATUES RECORDED

Though no portrait of Lykourgos has as yet been identified, there are records of several statues having been erected to him:

Ps.-Plutarch (*Vit. X orat.*, Lycurg., 843e–f) mentions wooden statues of Lykourgos and his sons by Timarchos and Kephisodotos, the sons of Praxiteles (location not stated): καὶ εἰκόνες ξύλιναι τοῦ τε Λυκούργου καὶ τῶν υἱῶν αὐτοῦ Ἅβρωνος, Λυκούργου, Λυκόφρονος ἃς εἰργάσαντο Τίμαρχος καὶ Κηφισόδοτος οἱ Πραξιτέλους υἱεῖς.

Ps.-Plut. (*Vit. X orat.*, Lycurg., 843c, e) mentions a bronze statue of him in the Kerameikos, and wooden statues of him and his sons in the Erechtheion: ἐστεφανώθη δὲ ὑπὸ τοῦ δήμου πολλάκις καὶ εἰκόνων ἔτυχεν· ἀνάκειται δ' αὐτοῦ χαλκῆ εἰκὼν ἐν Κεραμεικῷ κατὰ ψήφισμα, ἐπ' Ἀναξικράτους ἄρχοντος (= Ol. 118, 2); ἐν Ἐρεχθείῳ . . . εἰκόνες ξύλιναι τοῦ τε Λυκούργου καὶ τῶν υἱῶν αὐτοῦ.

Ps.-Plut. (*Vit. X orat.*, Demosthenes, 847D) mentions a statue of him in the agora of Athens, erected in the first year of the 125th Olympiad: καὶ αὐτῷ τετελευτηκότι τὴν εἰκόνα ἀνέθεσαν ἐν ἀγορᾷ ἐπὶ Γοργίου ἄρχοντος.

Plutarch, *Psephism.* (III, 852e) refers to this same statue as erected by the people to Lykourgos 'for his probity and justice': δεδόχθαι τῷ δήμῳ ἐπαινέσαι μὲν Λυκοῦργον Λυκόφρονος Βουτάδην ἀρετῆς ἕνεκα καὶ δικαιοσύνης καὶ στῆσαι αὐτοῦ τὸν δῆμον χαλκῆν εἰκόνα ἐν ἀγορᾷ. . . .

Pausanias I, 8, 2, also refers to this statue and specifies that it stood in the agora, after the statue of the Eponymoi: ἐνταῦθα Λυκοῦργός τε κεῖται χαλκοῦς ὁ Λυκόφρονος.

PORTRAITS ONCE EXTANT

The fragment of the base of a statue was found in the Athenian agora, inscribed 'Lykourgos, son of Lykophron, of the family of the Boutadai', [Λυκοῦργος Λυκ]όφρονος Βο[υτάδης], in letters of the end of the fourth century B.C.
FIG. 1365

In the Epigraphical Museum, no. 10607. *I.G.* II–III², 3776. Surface preserved at bottom and in front; broken on both sides and at back.

Width, as preserved, c. 64 cm.; ht. 21 cm.; thickness 34 cm. As the style of the letters points to the time when statues were being erected to Lykourgos, and as the fragment is said to have been found in the agora, it should belong to the base of the statue set up to Lykourgos by the people of Athens (cf. *supra*).

Hitzig, *Pausanias* I, pp. 159f.

Wycherley, *Testimonia*, p. 214, no. 705.

A headless herm inscribed with his name, that of his father, and the place of his birth, probably from Tivoli, is recorded by Kaibel, *I.G.* XIX, no. 1178: Λυκοῦργος Λυκόφρονος Ἀθηναῖος. Now lost. Cf. Bernoulli II, p. 60.

A marble base of a statue, inscribed Λυκοῦργος [ὁ ῥ]ήτωρ, is in the Epigraphical Museum, no. 10606; cf. *I.G.* II–III², 4259: 'Initio principatus'. Found near the church of Panagia Pyrgiotissa.
FIG. 1366

Height 25 cm.; width 75 cm.; thickness 42 cm.

Wycherley, *Testimonia*, p. 214, no. 705.

SUGGESTED IDENTIFICATION

C. Torr, *Rev. arch.* LXX, 1895, pp. 160ff., suggested that a figure on a Panathenaic amphora in the Louvre, on one of the two columns right and left of Athena, was intended for Lykourgos, on account of his connexion with the Panathenaic stadium. The figure is shown standing, wearing a himation, the right arm raised, a Nike in the left. The date of the amphora is 313 B.C. (archonship of Theophrastos).
FIG. 1367

AISCHINES

c. 390/389–after 314 B.C. The orator. Son of a schoolmaster named Atrometos, and Glaukothea of Athens.

LIFE

His father had lost his fortune in the Peloponnesian war, and Aischines had early to earn his living. We hear of him as a soldier, a schoolmaster, a scribe, and as an actor (he took the part, for instance, of Kreon in Sophokles' *Antigone*).

357 B.C. Obtained political employment under Euboulos. Finally turned to oratory, for which he had natural gifts, having a fine voice and the ability to speak extemporaneously.

348 Was a member of the embassy sent to negotiate a peace with Philip of Macedon after the fall of Olynthos. Came back a staunch supporter of Philip, which he remained throughout his life, in strong opposition to Demosthenes.

346 Was a member of a second embassy to Philip. On his return he was charged by Timarchos with having accepted a bribe to promote Philip's ends.

345 Speech against Timarchos.

343 Accused by Demosthenes of treachery. Aischines replied with the speech 'On the Embassy'.

338 The decisive victory of Philip at Chaironeia showed the Athenians that Demosthenes' fears were only too justified.

337 Ktesiphon proposed to confer a golden crown on Demosthenes at the Great Dionysia in the Athenian theatre. Aischines declared this proposal illegal.

330 The case was finally heard. Both Aischines' speech against Ktesiphon, in which he violently attacked Demosthenes, and Demosthenes' celebrated reply, *De Corona*, are extant. Aischines failed to obtain the necessary one-fifth of the votes, and was fined 1,000 drachmas. He went into voluntary exile first to Ephesos, then to Rhodes, where he is said to have founded a school of rhetoric (Ps.-Plut., *Vit. X orat.*, Aischines, p. 840d), and finally to Samos.

c. 314 Died in Samos, about 75 years old.

As a self-made man of many parts but apparently without high principles, he has gone down to posterity as a distinguished orator, the political enemy of Demosthenes, and the friend of Macedon.

STATUES RECORDED

Christodoros (*Ecphr.* in *Gr. Anth.* II, 13ff.) describes a bronze statue of Aischines in the Zeuxippos at Constantinople as 'seeming to contract his bearded cheeks as if about to take up the fight in the bustling assembly',

>   ... Λασίης δὲ συνείρυε κύκλα παρειῆς,
>   οἶα πολυτροχάλοισιν ἀεθλεύων ἀγορῆσιν.

This is the only statue of Aischines mentioned in ancient literature. From where it was taken to Constantinople is not known. The fact that the herm in the British Museum (no. 7 below) was found in Macedonia has been thought to indicate that a statue was erected to him there in recognition of his services to the Macedonian cause. But as the herm is of Roman date, it cannot definitely be said where the original from which it was copied stood in Greek times.

IDENTIFICATION

The identification of the portraits of Aischines is based on the two herms inscribed with his name, in the Vatican and in the British Museum (see below, nos. 1 and 7). From their resemblance to these heads a number of others, a statue, and two medallions have been identified; also, tentatively, the emblema of a terracotta bowl.

Since no other individual named Aischines was famous enough to have his name inscribed without further particulars, it may be taken for granted that the Aischines in the inscribed herms is the orator; cf. also *infra*, nos. 3, 4.

PORTRAITS EXTANT AND ONCE EXTANT

1. Herm in the Sala delle Muse, Vatican, inv. 297. Found 1780 in the 'villa of Cassius', near Tivoli. Inscribed Αἰσχίνης at the bottom of the herm.   FIGS. 1372–1374
Height 45 cm.; ht. of head 29.8 cm. Drapery on left shoulder.
Restorations: Nose and left temple with the adjoining parts of the forehead, and of the cheek (including part of the eyebrow and several locks of the hair). The surface has been cleaned.
Visconti, *Ic. gr.* I, pp. 363ff., pl. xxIxb.
Bernoulli II, p. 61, no. 1, pl. IX.
Helbig, *F.*³, no. 281; Helbig, *F.*⁴-Speier, no. 62.

Arndt-Br., 641–642.
Lippold, *Vat. Kat.* III, 1, p. 26, no. 502, pl. XXII.
Kaibel, *I.G.* XIV, 1129.

2. Head, mounted on a mostly modern herm, in the Stanza dei Filosofi, Capitoline Museum, no. 50.   FIG. 1384
Height of ancient part 32 cm.; ht. of head 26 cm.
Restorations: Nose, lower part of herm.
Visconti, *Museo Pio-Clementino* VI, p. 175, note 4. Visconti was the first to recognize the head as a replica of that in the Vatican; previously it was held to be Thucydides.
Bernoulli II, p. 62, no. 3.
Arndt-Br., 119–120.
Stuart Jones, *Cat.*, pp. 243f., no. 61, pl. 56.

3. Part of a head in a small double herm, with Demosthenes (q.v.), in the Terme Museum, Rome, inv. 125840. Found at Fianello, near Rieti.   FIGS. 1380–1381
Height 24.7 cm.
No restorations.
Faccenna, *Not. d. Sc.*, 1951, pp. 69f., fig. 15.
Felletti Maj, *Ritratti*, p. 19 (mentioned in her list of portraits of Demosthenes, under no. 7).
Richter, *Gk. Portr.* IV, pp. 37f. (there identified as Aischines by the characteristic long lock behind the left ear, and the general design of the beard).

4. Visconti (*Ic. gr.* I, p. 364) reported that he saw in the Barberini Palace in Rome two perfectly similar herms, evidently found in the same excavation, one representing Demosthenes (q.v., p. 217), the other Aischines. Both are now lost.

Incidentally the combination of the two heads of Aischines and Demosthenes, in a double herm in no. 3, and as pendants in no. 4—and perhaps also in the medallion cited below—definitely shows that the Aischines in the inscribed herms is the orator, not some other Aischines.

5. A herm inscribed Αἰσχίνης Ἀτρομήτου Ἀθηναῖος appears in Ursinus, *Imag.*, p. 79, and Gallaeus-Faber, no. 2, with an alien, beardless head. It was said to have been in the possession of the Duke of Tuscany, but could not be located either by Visconti (*Ic. gr.* I, pp. 362f.) or by Bernoulli (II, p. 63). Cf. Kaibel, *I.G.* XIV, 1128; Huelsen, no. 1.

6. Statue in the National Museum, Naples, inv. 6018. Found in the theatre of Herculaneum. Represented wearing chiton, himation, and sandals.   FIGS. 1369–1371
Height 2.10 m.
Broken in a number of pieces and put together with missing parts restored (especially in the drapery). On the head are restored: the left eyebrow, the upper lip, half of the lower lip. The head, though broken from the body, undoubtedly belongs. (It was kindly re-examined for me by A. de Franciscis some years ago.)
Comparetti and De Petra, *Villa ercol.*, p. 277, no. 83, pl. XXVII, 1, 2.
Bernoulli II, p. 62, no. 4.
Arndt-Br., nos. 116–118.
Ruesch, *Guida*, no. 1139.
Lippold, *Gr. Portr.*, pp. 95ff.

7. Herm in the British Museum, no. 1839. Found in Bitolia, Macedonia, early in the 19th century. Presented by Col. W. M. Leake in 1839. Inscribed Αἰσχίνης.

FIGS. 1375, 1378–1379

Height 79 cm.; ht. of head 31·6 cm.

No restorations, 'but much worked over'.

Bernoulli II, pp. 61f., no. 2.

A. H. Smith, *Cat.* III, no. 1839.

8. Herm in the Ny Carlsberg Glyptothek, Copenhagen, I.N. 1734. Acquired in Rome in 1899.   FIGS. 1385–1387

Height 44 cm.

No restorations, but surface cleaned.

Bernoulli II, p. 63, no. 6.

Arndt-Br., 643–644.

F. Poulsen, *Cat.*, no. 437.

V. Poulsen, *Portr. gr.*, no. 25.

9. Relief of a bust in profile to the right on a marble medallion. In the Hermitage, Leningrad, inv. 64. Found in 1756 in the harbour of Baiai, near Naples.   FIG. 1376

Diam. 65 cm.; head life-size. In the background is shown a bundle of scrolls.

Restorations: Several pieces in the bust; surface cleaned. Otherwise in excellent condition.

Bernoulli II, p. 63, no. 7.

Kieseritzky, *Cat.* (1901), with illustration.

Waldhauer, *Anc. Sc.* (1923), no. 362 (in Russian); *Studies in the History of Ancient Portraits* (1938), pp. 90f., pl. 23.

Considering that this is a work in relief, the deviations from the heads carved in the round are not considerable. It was evidently copied with care.

10. Head in the University of Mississippi. From the collection of D. M. Robinson, and bequeathed by him to Mississippi.   FIGS. 1388–1390

The dimensions and the details regarding the condition were given me by Dr. Lucy Turnbull of the University of Mississippi.

Total height 36·5 cm.; ht. of head 33·1 cm.

The nose is restored. Missing are several locks of hair, and the rim and lobe of the left ear. The surface is considerably abraded.

Richter, *Gk. Portr.* IV, p. 39, figs. 48, 49.

DOUBTFUL AND MODERN EXAMPLES

Bust in front view on a medallion in the Villa Doria Pamphili. Inserted high up in the outside wall of a building, as a pendant to the Demosthenes medallion (q.v.). Diam. 50 cm.

FIGS. 1382–1383

Restorations (as seen on photograph): Nose and perhaps part of the background. Since the photograph was taken the relief has much suffered.

Visconti, *Ic. gr.* I, p. 364, pl. XXX, 1.

Matz-Duhn, no. 3610.

Bernoulli II, p. 63, no. 10 ('zweifelhaft').

E.A., nos. 2353, 2354.

Richter, *Gr. Portr.* II, p. 18, fig. 19.

The dimensions are about the same as those of the medallion

with Demosthenes, also in the Villa Doria Pamphili (cf. p. 217, no. 9); the two were, therefore, thought to have been made as pendants (cf. Visconti). The extensive variations from the extant heads in the round have led to considerable doubt as to whether Aischines was here represented; but these differences may perhaps be explained by the fact that the medallion was a free, not a mechanical copy. The Demosthenes in the medallion, inscribed with his name, is also markedly different from the full-size heads in the round, and so is the Sokrates in the medallion in the Villa Albani (cf. p. 113, no. 8) different from the Sokrateses carved full size and in the round.

The head, mounted on a modern herm, in the Louvre, Ma 250, from the Borghese Collection, is similar to the portraits of Aischines, but the expression is quite different (not so bland) and the composition of the locks shows many divergencies. I, therefore, hesitate to accept it as an Aischines.

FIGS. 1391–1393

Height, with neck, 38·5 cm.; ht. of head 32 cm.

Most of the nose is restored.

Cat. sommaire, 1922, p. 19, no. 250 (there called Pittakos).

Another head of Aischines in the Louvre, Ma 73, from the Campana Collection, is modern—as M. Charbonneaux pointed out to me.   FIGS. 1394–1396

Bernoulli II, p. 62, no. 5 ('von verdächtig guter Erhaltung').

Hekler, *B.b.G.*, p. 47, note 41 (there listed among the genuine examples, as also in the 3rd edition, p. 62, no. 5).

Cat. sommaire, 1922, p. 20, no. 73.

A herm in the Palazzo Colonna, Rome (at that time 'placed on top of the window and, therefore, difficult to examine') was mentioned by Bernoulli (II, p. 63, no. 8) as 'zweifelhaft'. It is not listed by Matz-Duhn. In 1962 it was still placed high up, and as far as I could make out with my opera glasses, it not only looks modern but is in one piece with a herm which is not of an ancient shape.

The resemblance to Aischines of a figure in high relief, placing one hand on a herm, in Catania, must, as Bernoulli said, be fortuitous.

40 by 30 cm.

Hauser, in *E.A.*, 764.

Bernoulli II, p. 66.

A bust serving as the emblema of a terracotta bowl was tentatively identified as Aischines by Winnefeld (*68. Berl. Winckelmannsprogramm*, p. 18, no. 2; p. 23, fig. 3), and it indeed bears a marked resemblance to the extant heads (it even has the pendant lock behind the ear). It was once in the Rhousopoulos collection in Athens, then went to the Loeb Collection in Munich, and at present is 'lost'. (On enquiry, I was informed that it was not in the Museums of Munich or Amsterdam where most of the objects from the Loeb Collection went.) As a Demosthenes has been tentatively identified in a similar emblema (cf. my *Gr. Portr.* III, p. 46, fig. 202), an Aischines as a counterpart is not excluded, for the mutual enmity of these two men joined them for ever in the thoughts of posterity (cf. p. 213).   FIG. 1377

H. Speier, in the *Röm. Mitt.* XLVII, 1932, pp. 64, 72, pl. 25, 1, 2, pointed out the marked resemblance of the radiating folds in the statue of Aischines with those in a figure on a Panathenaic amphora in the Louvre, datable to 313/312 by the name of the archon Theophrastos (second tenure). Cf. also Süsserot, *Griechische Plastik des 4. Jahrh.*, p. 86, pl. 8, 2.

CONCLUSIONS

All the life-size heads in the round above listed under nos. 1–10, in spite of occasional superficial variations, must have been reproduced mechanically from the same Greek original. The composition of the strands of hair sufficiently attest this. Significant in this connexion is the different rendering on the restored part of the hair in the Vatican herm (cf. no. 1), and in the doubtful and modern example in the Louvre (cf. *supra*).

We are especially fortunate in the case of Aischines to have not only two herms inscribed with his name, but a full-size statue showing him in a characteristic pose. The personality brought before us is of a man with a fine presence, but not of outstanding intelligence. His placid expression is in marked contrast to the nervous, unhappy countenance of Demosthenes; and, one might add, the fussy rendering of the drapery in the statue suggests a more commonplace character than that in the statue of Demosthenes with its simpler, beautifully composed folds, conveying the nobility of the man.

The relatively few portraits of Aischines, who played so prominent a role in the fortunes of Athens, are also in strong contrast to the large number of extant portraits of Demosthenes, and may be said to reflect the ultimate judgement of posterity.

The style of the heads of Aischines, and of the drapery in the statue no. 6, suggest a date in the last quarter of the fourth century B.C., somewhere between the portraits of the three tragedians (cf. p. 35) and that of Demosthenes (cf. p. 216, no. 2); perhaps around 320–310. This assignment is borne out also by the fact that in the statue a chiton is represented beneath the mantle, for this addition, as far as is known, does not occur before the end of the fourth century (cf. p. 36).

DEMOSTHENES

c. 384–322 B.C. The orator. Of the Attic deme of Paianeia. Son of Demosthenes and of Kleoboule.

LIFE

He lost his father when he was 7 years old. His guardians mismanaged the considerable estate, and Demosthenes found himself with practically no resources when he came of age (Plut., *Dem.* IV).

In spite of physical disabilities he determined to become an orator. Said to have studied the works of Thucydides, Plato, and Isokrates to improve his style.

His first case was against his guardians. Then acted as a logographos, i.e. writer of speeches for others, and thereby obtained a wide experience.

355–352 Became assistant to official prosecutors.

351 Started his political career. He early recognized the danger of Philip of Macedon's rising power to the independence of Greece, and he spent the rest of his life in combating it. Cf. his three Philippic (351, 344, 341 B.C.) and the Olynthiac orations (349, 348 B.C.).

In his anti-Macedonian policy he was opposed by Aischines and others.

343 He impeached Aischines for his part in concluding a dishonourable peace with Macedon (cf. *De falsa legatione*), but Aischines was acquitted.

Through Demosthenes' influence Athens made an alliance with her old enemy Thebes.

338 Battle of Chaironeia. Demosthenes was chosen to make the funerary oration for those who had fallen in the battle.

335 Death of Philip and accession of Alexander.

330 Aischines accused Ktesiphon of illegality in proposing that a golden crown be awarded to Demosthenes, and heaped accusations against him (cf. pp. 212f.). Demosthenes answered in his famous speech *De Corona*. The verdict went against Aischines, who left the country.

325–324 Demosthenes was accused of having received bribes from Harpalos, governor of Babylon. He vigorously denied the accusation, but was brought to trial and condemned to pay 50 talents, whereupon he left Athens (Plut., *Dem.* xxvff.; Paus. II, 33, 3ff. who cites evidence indicating Demosthenes' innocence).

323 Death of Alexander. Demosthenes tried to organize a joint effort with the Peloponnesians against Macedon. Recalled from exile to Athens.

Victory of Antipater at Krannon. Athens received a Macedonian garrison. Demades carried a decree for the execution of Demosthenes and Hypereides (q.v.).

322 Demosthenes escaped and took refuge on the island of Kalaureia, in the temple of Poseidon. To avoid capture he took poison.

Herewith ended a turbulent life, marked by public and private enmities, by courage and perseverance. As one of the noblest patriots of Greece, and her greatest orator, his reputation lasted through antiquity and has persisted to our day.

About sixty of Demosthenes' orations have been preserved.

APPEARANCE

Plutarch, in his *Comparison between Demosthenes and Cicero*, I, 3, 6, refers to the lack of lightness and gayness in Demosthenes' character, and to the seriousness and severity of his expression; he was considered as having a bitter and harsh disposition: ἔξω παντὸς ὡραϊσμοῦ καὶ παιδιᾶς εἰς δεινότητα καὶ σπουδὴν συνηγμένος. On this account his enemies called him morose and ill-mannered, ὅθεν καὶ δύσκολον αὐτὸν οἱ ἐχθροὶ καὶ δύστροπον . . . ἀπεκάλουν.

IDENTIFICATION

The identification of the many extant portraits of Demosthenes was rendered possible by the finding in 1753, at Herculaneum, of a small bronze bust, inscribed with his name. Previously several quite different types had been thought to represent Demosthenes, in spite of the real type so exactly corresponding to what is known of his life and character.

On other inscribed portraits since discovered cf. *infra* and my *Gk. Portr.* IV, pp. 36f.

STATUES RECORDED

1. Pausanias (II, 33, 2–3) mentions a monument of Demosthenes in the enclosure of the sanctuary of Poseidon in the island of Kalaureia: ἔστι δ' οὖν Ποσειδῶνος ἱερὸν ἐνταῦθα ἅγιον. . . . τοῦ περιβόλου δὲ ἐντὸς καὶ τὸ Δημοσθένους μνῆμά ἐστι.

Whether this μνῆμα was a statue or some other form of memorial is uncertain.

2. In Ps.-Plut., *Vit. X orat.*, Demosth., 847a, is mentioned a statue of Demosthenes, erected by the Athenians, on the order of his nephew Demochares, 42 years after the death of Demosthenes (that is, in 280 B.C.), in the agora of Athens, not far from the altar of the Twelve Gods, the work of the sculptor Polyeuktos: κεῖται δὲ ἡ εἰκὼν πλησίον τοῦ περισχανίσματος καὶ τοῦ βωμοῦ τῶν Δώδεκα Θεῶν, ὑπὸ Πολυεύκτου πεποιημένη. On it was written an elegiac couplet: 'If thy strength had only been equal to thy purposes, Demosthenes, never would the Greeks have been ruled by a Macedonian Ares', ἐπὶ τῆς εἰκόνος αὐτοῦ ἐλεγεῖον ἐπιγεγραμμένον ὑπὸ τῶν Ἀθηναίων ὕστερον·

εἴπερ ἴσην ῥώμην γνώμῃ Δημόσθενες ἔσχες
οὔποτ' ἂν Ἑλλήνων ἦρχεν Ἄρης Μακεδών.

Cf. Wycherley, *Testimonia*, pp. 210f., no. 698.

Pausanias (I, 8, 2 and 4) mentions this same statue as standing in the agora with other statues, after those of the eponymoi: ἔστι δὲ καὶ Δημοσθένης.

From Plut., *Demosth.* 30, 5–31, 1, comes the additional information that the statue was of bronze, that its hands were interlaced, and that a soldier once placed some gold inside the hands of the statue, and, on returning some time later, found the gold intact, hidden by the leaves of a neighbouring plane tree, Τούτῳ μὲν ὀλίγον ὕστερον (i.e. after Demosthenes' death) ὁ τῶν Ἀθηναίων δῆμος . . . εἰκόνα τε χαλκῆν ἀνέστησε. . . . ἕστηκε δὲ τοὺς δακτύλους συνέχων δι' ἀλλήλων, καὶ παραπέφυκεν οὐ μεγάλη πλάτανος. This, people said, showed the incorruptibility of Demosthenes (cf. also Suidas, s.v. Demosthenes).

3. Christ., *Ecphr.* in *Gk. Anth.* II, 23ff. cites a bronze statue in the Zeuxippos at Constantinople, without any factual description.

4. Cicero, *Orat.*, 110, refers to a bronze bust in the villa of M. Brutus at Tusculum: Demosthenes quidem, cujus nuper inter imagines tuas, cum ad te in Tusculanum venissem, imaginem ex aere vidi.

5. The sophist Polemon of Smyrna (time of Hadrian) dedicated a bronze statue of Demosthenes in the Asklepieion at Pergamon: Πολέμων ὁ Ἰωνικὸς σοφιστὴς Δημοσθένους τοῦ ῥήτορος εἰκόνα χαλκῆν ἐν Ἀσκληπιοῦ τοῦ ἐν Περγάμῳ τῇ Μυσίᾳ ἀναθεὶς ἐπέγραψεν ἐπίγραμμα τοιόνδε Δημοσθένη Παιανιέα Πολέμων κατ' ὄναρ (cf. Phrynichos, *Epit.*, p. 421, ed. Lobeck).

The portraits cited in nos. 4, 5, were of course Roman copies of a Greek original; perhaps also that cited in no. 3. This leaves only no. 2 as a certain statue recorded as having been erected to Demosthenes in Greek times. We shall see that the many extant portraits all go back to one original; and it is likely that this was the statue by Polyeuktos in Athens, of which we, moreover, know the exact date (cf. *supra*).

PORTRAITS EXTANT AND ONCE EXTANT
WORKS IN THE ROUND

1. Statue in the Braccio Nuovo, Vatican, inv. 2255. Acquired in 1823. Formerly in the Villa Aldobrandini at Frascati (appears there in the inventory of 1709); so perhaps found in the region of Tusculum. According to another report it was taken in 1687 by Morosini to Venice from Athens (A. Nibby, *Mus. Chiar.* II, pp. 54ff., pl. 24).

FIGS. 1397, 1404–1406

Height 2·07 m.; ht. of head 27·9 cm.

Restorations: End of nose, pieces on right eyebrow, on forehead, and on left temple, part of neck, a large piece on right upper arm, both forearms, many pieces on the right foot, most of plinth (preserved only under the feet). The restored hands shown holding a scroll have now been removed.

Michaelis, *Die Bildnisse des Demosthenes* (henceforth cited as Michaelis), p. 402, no. B.
Bernoulli II, p. 69, no. 2.
Helbig, *F.³*, no. 22; Helbig, *F.⁴*-Speier, no. 431.
Arndt-Br., 574.
Amelung, *Vat. Kat.* I, p. 80, no. 62, pl. XI.

Pair of clasped hands, found in the garden of the Palazzo Barberini, and now in the Vatican (inv. 15060. Length 21·3 cm., ht. c. 12 cm.) Thought by Hartwig to have come from a statue of Demosthenes. Cursorily worked and made in a separate piece for attachment to the forearms of a statue (there are dowel holes at the bottom); perhaps an ancient repair? It belonged neither to the statue in the Vatican (no. 1), nor to that in Copenhagen (cf. no. 32), but apparently to a third example, which must have been a little larger than life, to judge by the dimensions. FIG. 1407

A sandalled right foot, similar to and of the same dimensions as that of the Vatican statue, was found in the same excavations in the Barberini gardens, and has been thought to have belonged to the same statue as the hands; cf. Hartwig, *J.d.I.* XVIII, 1903, pp. 26f., figs. 2–4. But it is not identical with the foot of either the Vatican or the Copenhagen statue, the straps being different; and since it is life-size and the hands larger than life, the two can hardly have belonged to the same statue. FIG. 1408

2. Head, mounted on a modern herm, in the Sala delle Muse, Vatican, inv. 289. Acquired under Pius VI, before 1792.   FIG. 1430
Height with neck, 32 cm.; ht. of head 24·5 cm.
The nose is restored.
Michaelis, p. 409, x.
Bernoulli II, p. 69, no. 4.
Helbig, F.³, no. 280.
Lippold, *Vat. Kat.* III, 1, p. 38, no. 506, pl. 16.

3. Bust, on a round base, in the Museo Chiaramonti, Vatican, inv. 1555. From the Barberini Collection. Drapery on left shoulder.   FIGS. 1410–1412
Height 50·5 cm.; ht. of head 28·6 cm.
Restorations: End of nose, pieces on the lower part of the base.
Michaelis, p. 409, w.
Bernoulli II, p. 69, no. 3 (wonders whether this bust was perhaps the pendant of the Aischines mentioned by Visconti, *Ic. gr.* I, p. 364; cf. p. 213).
Amelung, *Vat. Kat.* I, no. 422, pl. 61.
Helbig, F.⁴-Speier, no, 340.

4. Head, mounted on a modern herm, in the Capitoline Museum, Stanza dei Filosofi, no. 43. Probably from the Albani Collection.   FIGS. 1416–1418
Height, with neck, 33 cm.; ht. of head 25·5 cm.
Restorations: Part of the back of the head, most of the nose, the right eyebrow and adjoining parts.
Michaelis, p. 401, u.
Bernoulli II, p. 69, no. 1.
Stuart Jones, *Cat.*, p. 232, no. 31, pl. 58.

5. Head, mounted on an alien bust, in the National Museum of the Terme, Rome, inv. 8581. From the Ludovisi Collection. Probably from the Villa Cesi.   FIG. 1431
Height 31 cm.; ht. of head c. 27 cm.
The whole nose is restored.
Schreiber, *Villa Ludovisi*, p. 45, no. 5.
Michaelis, p. 409, v.
Bernoulli II, p. 69, no. 5.
Felletti Maj, *Ritratti*, no. 18.

6. Head in a small double herm, with Aischines (q.v.), in the Museo Nazionale delle Terme, Rome, inv. 125840. Of the other head only the hair on the left temple and part of the beard on the cheek are preserved. The coupling of the two orators is of great interest (cf. p. 213). FIGS. 1425–1427
Height 25 cm.; ht. of head 16 cm.
No restorations.
Faccenna, *Not. d. Sc.* 1951, pp. 69f., fig. 15.
Felletti Maj, *Ritratti*, p. 19, under no. 18.
Richter, *Gk. Portr.* IV, pp. 37f.

7. Head in the Barracco Museum, Rome, Acquired in Rome.   FIGS. 1419–1421
Height, with neck, 29 cm.; ht. of head 26·5 cm.
The nose is restored, the eyebrows are patched. The bottom of the neck has been cut.
Bernoulli II, p. 70, no. 6.

Helbig and Barracco, *Collection Barracco*, p. 47, pl. 62 *bis*.
Pietrangeli, *Guida*, 1949, p. 84, no. 140; 1960, p. 107, no. 140.

8. Herm in the Roman house under the church of S. Cecilia, Trastevere, Rome. Found in the ruins of this house in 1899.   FIGS. 1413–1415
Height 49 cm.; ht. of head 28 cm.
No restorations: Only the nose, the rim of the left ear, and a few slivers are missing.
Mentioned by Felletti Maj, *Ritratti*, p. 19, under no. 18.
Arndt-Br., mentioned in text to pl. 1120.
Here illustrated for the first time. Unfortunately the surface of the herm is covered with modern graffiti (which withstand washing).

9. Bust in relief, on a medallion in the Villa Doria Pamphili, Rome. On the scroll in the background the name Δημοσ-θένης is inscribed in four lines. Mantle on left shoulder. The first mention of the medallion is in the Pamphili—Aldobrandini inventory of 1709: Due busti di marmo antico, ciascheduno di basso rilievo in un tondo . . . , largo in diametro ogni tondo del marmo dui palmi et un quarto (*Doc. ined.* III, 180). The other medallion is that of 'Aischines' (cf. p. 214), the two apparently having been pendants.
FIGS. 1403, 1409
Diam. c. 50 cm.
Restorations: Nose and part of the background.
Matz–Duhn III, no. 3610.
Visconti, *Ic. gr.* I, pp. 358, pl. XXIXa, no. 2.
Michaelis, p. 410, β.
Bernoulli II, p. 75, no. 37.
E.A., 2355–2356.
C.I.G., 6037.
Kaibel, *I.G.* XIV, 1147.
Huelsen, no. 8.

10. Another marble medallion said (by Faber in the text to Gallaeus) to have been found in Tarragona, is now 'lost'. It is illustrated in Gallaeus' *Imag.*, 55, from a drawing sent to F. Ursinus by the Archbishop Augustin (d. 1586) (cf. also Gronov, *Thes.* II, 93; Bellori, *Imag.* 79). On the background, on one side, is the inscription Δημοσθένης, in three lines. On the other side is a scroll. Demosthenes is represented without a beard; the mantle is on the right instead of the left shoulder.
Michaelis, p. 411, γ.
Bernoulli, p. 75, no. 38.

11. Head in the Museum of Ostia, inv. no. 1519. From the Episcopio di Porto.   FIGS. 1422–1424
Height, with neck, 28 cm.; ht. of head, 24 cm.
No restorations, but much damaged. Once a fine portrait.
R. Calza, *Museo Ostiense*, 2nd ed. (1962), p. 35, Sala IV, 3.
Felletti Maj, *Ritratti*, p. 19, no. 10 of her list of portraits of Demosthenes.

For the head R. Calza, *Museo Ostiense* (1947), p. 20, no. 92, 2nd ed. (1962), p. 36, Sala IV, no. 4, see my p. 221, no. 11*.

12. Small bronze bust in the National Museum, Naples, inv. 5467. Found on November 3, 1753, in the villa of the

Pisoni, Herculaneum, together with the small busts of Zenon, Epikouros, and Hermarchos. Drapery on left shoulder. On the chest is the inscription: Δημοσθένης. FIGS. 1438–1440
Height 13 cm.; ht. of head 9 cm.
No restorations.
Visconti, *Ic. gr.* I, pp. 358f., pl. XXIXa.
Comparetti and De Petra, *Villa ercol.*, pl. XII, 4, p. 262, no. 11.
Michaelis, p. 407, m.
Bernoulli II, p. 70, no. 7.
Ruesch, *Guida*, no. 893.
Kaibel, *I.G.* XIV, no. 707.
C.I.G., 6036.

13. Small bronze bust in the National Museum, Naples, inv. 5469. Found in 1752 in the same villa as the preceding. Of better quality, but uninscribed. Drapery on left shoulder.
FIGS. 1441–1443
Height 22 cm.; ht. of head 14 cm.
No restorations, except a small piece at the bottom of the bust.
Comparetti and De Petra, *Villa ercol.*, p. 262, no. 12, pl. XII, 1.
Michaelis, p. 407, n.
Bernoulli II, p. 70, no. 8.
Ruesch, *Guida*, no. 901.

14. Bust found in 1842 in Pompeii. Now? Not found in the National Museum, Naples.
Life-size.
Minervini, *Bull. arch. Napol.* I, 1843, p. 95 ('di grandezza naturale').
Michaelis, p. 407, o ('nicht näher bekannt').
Bernoulli II, p. 70, no. 9.

15. Small herm in the National Museum, Naples, inv. 111399. Found 1878 in Pompeii. Flattened at back, but not cut, so not part of a double herm.
FIG. 1428
Height 31 cm.; ht. of head 29 cm.
Restorations: The nose, parts of the hair at the back, and back corner of herm.
Comparetti and De Petra, *Villa ercol.*, pl. III, 2, p. 34.
Michaelis, p. 407, p.
Bernoulli, p. 70, no. 10.
Ruesch, *Guida*, no. 1076.

16. A bust, said to be from Canosa was until 1837 in the possession of the Archbishop Rossi. Drapery on left shoulder. On the chest is a metric inscription, with a dedication to Athena: Θεῷ Ἀθανᾷ Δυνάμιος Δαμοσθένην.
Now?
'Natürliche Grösse' (Michaelis).
Restorations: The nose, once restored, is now missing.
Avellino, *Not. di un busto di Demostene*, Naples, 1841, pp. 1ff.
Welcker, *Rhein. Mus.* III 1845, p. 274, no. 54.
Michaelis, p. 406, f.
Bernoulli II, p. 70, no. 11.
Kaibel, *I.G.* XIV, Addenda, 1146a.

17. Head, mounted on a modern herm, in the Uffizi, Florence, inv. 1914, no. 391. Acquired in 1788.
FIG. 1432
Height, with neck, 29 cm.; ht. of head 21 cm.
Restorations: Nose, most of ears, almost the whole upper lip with the moustache. Surface somewhat corroded.
Dütschke III, no. 306.
Michaelis, p. 406, g.
Bernoulli II, p. 70, no. 12.
Mansuelli, *Cat.*, no. 6.

18. Fragment of a head, in the Uffizi, Florence, inv. 1914, no. 411. Only the right side of the face, with part of the left side and of the neck remains. The piece is inserted in a modern medallion.
FIG. 1433
Height 21 cm.
Restorations: Nose, right eyebrow, chin, part of the left ear, edge of the bust.
Dütschke III, no. 394.
Michaelis, p. 406, h.
Bernoulli II, p. 70, no. 13.
Mansuelli, *Cat.*, no. 5.

19. Head, mounted on a modern bust, in the Uffizi, Florence, inv. 1914, no. 34.
FIG. 1434
Height, with neck, 31 cm.; ht. of head 24 cm.
Restorations: Part of nose, chin with part of left jaw, patch on left cheek.
Dütschke III, no. 20.
Michaelis, p. 406, f'.
Bernoulli II, p. 73 'vielleicht ein verfehlter Demosthenes'.
Mansuelli, *Cat.*, no. 7 (has some doubts regarding the antiquity of the piece).
I am inclined to think that it has been worked over (as shown by the contrast of the surface of the face and of the back), but that it is a genuine Demosthenes, somewhat resembling the Ludovisi example in the Terme Museum (cf. p. 217, no. 5).

20. Bust in the Museo di Antichità, Turin.
FIG. 1429
Height 32 cm.
Restorations: Nose, left shoulder, and small pieces. On the edge of the bust is the modern inscription M. BRUTUS.
Dütschke IV, no. 157.
Michaelis, p. 409, z.
Bernoulli II, p. 70, no. 14.

21. Head, in the Louvre, Ma 79b. Formerly in the Villa Montalto. Taken to France by Napoleon. Once mounted on an alien statue (cf. under Pindar).
FIG. 1435
Height c. 28 cm.
Restorations: Nose, left ear.
Cat. sommaire (1922), p. 5, no. 79.
Michaelis, p. 408, q.
Bernoulli II, p. 71, no. 15.
Dontas, *Eikones*, p. 45, pl. 17.

22. Bust, in the Louvre, Ma 237. From the Villa Albani. Came to Paris in the time of Napoleon. FIGS. 1444–1446
Height 47 cm.; ht. of head 28·8 cm.
Restorations: Only the end of the nose.
Visconti, *Ic. gr.* I, p. 356, pl. XXIX, 1, 2.
Cat. sommaire (1922), p. 19. no. 237.
Michaelis, p. 408, r.
Bernoulli, p. 71, no. 16.

23. Head, mounted on a modern bust, in the Louvre, Ma 349. From the Villa Borghese.   FIGS. 1447–1449
Height c. 28 cm.
Restorations: Nose, upper lip, chin, lower part of forehead; the lower lip is recut.
Cat. sommaire (1922), p. 19, no. 349.
Bernoulli II, p. 71, no. 17.

24. Head, mounted on a modern herm, in the Louvre, Ma 244. From the Borghese Collection.   FIGS. 1450–1452
Height 27 cm.
Restorations: Nose, mouth, left ear.
Cat. sommaire (1922), p. 18, no. 244.
Michaelis, p. 408, s.
Bernoulli II, p. 71, no. 18.

25. Head, mounted on a modern bust, in the Museum of Tours. Formerly in the castle of Cardinal Richelieu.
FIGS. 1436–1437
Height, with bust, 82 cm. The draped bust will have been added in Rome when the bust was acquired.
The nose is restored.
S. Reinach, *Rev. arch.* VIII, 1906, p. 322.

26. Head, mounted on a modern bust, in the British Museum, no. 1840.   FIGS. 1453–1455
Height 26·7 cm.
Restorations: Nose, right side of head with edge of ear, part of left cheek, left ear, neck.
Michaelis, p. 406, j.
Bernoulli II, p. 71, no. 21.
Casson, *J.H.S.* XLVI, 1926, p. 76.
A. H. Smith, *Cat.*, no. 1840.

27. Head in the Ashmolean Museum, Oxford. Purchased in 1923 from Mr. L. T. Bower, a British officer, who had bought it in Constantinople. It is said to have come from Eski-Shehr, the ancient Dorylaion, in Asia Minor.
FIGS. 1464–1467
Height 30 cm.; ht. of head 28·3 cm.
No restorations; even the nose is ancient; parts of the beard are missing.
Casson, *J.H.S.* XLVI, 1926, pp. 72ff., fig. 1, pl. V.

28. Bust in Brocklesby Park, in the Collection of Lord Yarborough. From the Worsley Collection, so presumably from Italy.
FIGS. 1458–1460
Height of head, with neck, 34 cm.; ht. of head 28 cm.
Restorations: Nose, part of upper lip, of right ear, and of bust.
Michaelis, pp. 405f., e; and *Anc. Marbl.*, p. 230, no. 18.
E.A., 3008–3010.
Bernoulli II, p. 72, no. 24.

29. Head, mounted on a modern herm, in Northwick Park, once in the collection of the late Captain Spencer Churchill. From Shobden Court.   FIGS. 1461–1463
Height of ancient part 36 cm.
Restorations: End of nose, part of right ear. The surface is

curiously fresh and uniform. Perhaps copied from no. 3?
Casson, *J.H.S.* XLVI, 1926, p. 76.
Vermeule and von Bothmer, *A.J.A.* LXIII, 1959, p. 339, pl. 80, fig. 21.
E. Strong, *Catalogue of the Melchett Collection* (1928), p. 27, fig. 14.
Von Heintze, in Hekler, *Bild. b. Gr.*[3], p. 64, no. 31 ('antik?').

30. Head, mounted on a modern herm, formerly in the Melchett Collection, and in that of Charles Robinson; now in the Liverpool Public Museums, 53.115.30.
FIGS. 1456–1457
Height of ancient part 29 cm.
Restorations: Most of the nose, rim of the left ear.
Casson, *J.H.S.* XLVI, 1926, p. 76.
Burlington Fine Arts Club, Cat. of Greek Art, 1904, p. 258, pl. XXVI, no. 68.
E. Strong, *Catalogue of the Melchett Collection*, 1928, no. 21, pl. XXIX.
Vermeule and von Bothmer, *A.J.A.* LXIII, 1959, p. 163, no. 26.

31. Statuette on which is mounted a modern head of Sophokles. Collection of Major E. R. F. Compton, Newby Hall, Yorkshire.
Height 1·19 m.
Restorations: Forearms, with hands, feet, scrinium.
Michaelis, *Anc. Marbl.*, p. 525, no. 7, and *Bild. des Dem.*, p. 403, under C.
E.A., no. 3116 (identified as Demosthenes).
Arndt-Br., in text of no. 1120 ('doch wohl Replik').
Vermeule, *A.J.A.* LIX, 1955, p. 143.

32. Statue in the Ny Carlsberg Glyptothek, Copenhagen, I.N. 2782. Acquired in 1929. Said to have been found in the eighteenth century in Campania; then went to the Palazzo Columbrano, Naples; then was from 1770 to 1929 in Knole Park, Kent. Wears no chiton, but himation and sandals.   FIGS. 1398–1402
Height 2·02 m.; without plinth, 1·92 m.; ht. of head 28 cm.
Restorations: Nose, toes of left foot, and two toes of the right foot. The clasped hands are of plaster, made with the help of a mould of the hands found in the garden of the Palazzo Barberini (cf. p. 216).
Michaelis, *Anc. Marbl.*, p. 417, no. 1; *Bild. des Dem.*, pp. 401f., A.
Bernoulli II, pp. 71f., no. 22.
F. Poulsen, *Cat.*, no. 436a, and in Arndt-Br., 1111–1114.
V. Poulsen, *Portr. gr.*, no. 27.

33. Head in the Ny Carlsberg Glyptothek, Copenhagen, I.N. 1532. Acquired in Naples in 1896.   FIGS. 1471–1472
Height 26 cm.
The end of the nose is restored. In 1952 the other restorations were removed, namely the top of the skull and the back of the head. This showed that the head came from a double herm but not the same as that of Hypereides (cf. p. 211, no. 4).
Bernoulli II, p. 72, no. 29, pl. XII.
F. Poulsen, *Cat.*, no. 436; and in Arndt-Br., 1118–1119.
V. Poulsen, *Portr. gr.*, no. 28.

34. Head, mounted on a modern herm, in the Staatliche Museen, Berlin, no. 302. Acquired in 1766 from the Natali Collection, Rome. Formerly in the Sanssouci Palace.
Height 44 cm.

Restorations: Back of head, nose, neck.
Michaelis, p. 405, c.
Conze, *Beschreibung*, no. 302.
Bernoulli II, p. 72, no. 25.
Arndt-Br., 138.

35. Head, in the Staatliche Museen, Berlin, no. 303. From the Baireuth Collection, which was formed in Italy.

FIG. 1478

Height 48·5 cm.
Restorations: Nose, left eyebrow, pieces in the lips, the chin, most of neck, the chest.
Michaelis, p. 405, d.
Bernoulli II, p. 72, no. 26.
Conze, *Beschreibung*, no. 303.

36. Herm, in the Glyptothek, Munich. Found in 1825 in the Circus Maxentius, Rome. Acquired 1828 for King Ludwig of Bavaria. FIGS. 1476–1477, 1481
Height 1·89 m.
Restorations: Nose, piece in lower lip, and the lower part of each ear.
A. Nibby, *Del circo volgarmente detto di Caracalla*, 1825, pp. 45f.
Furtwängler, *Beschreibung*, no. 292.
Arndt-Br., nos. 136–137.
Michaelis, pp. 406f., l.
Bernoulli II, p. 72, no. 28.

37. Herm, once in Dr. Lederer's possession in Berlin. Said to be from Greece. Inscribed at the bottom of the herm: Δημοσθένης Δημοσθένους Παιανιεύς.

FIGS. 1496–1497

Height 36 cm.; width 25 cm.
Arndt-Br., in text to pl. 1120 (there apparently accepted as genuine).
V. Poulsen, *Portr. gr.*, under no. 27 ('d'après l'examen de la photographie, un hermès de marbre . . . n'inspire pas grande confiance').
Richter, *Gr. Portr.* IV, p. 36, figs. 42, 43.
I have not been able to find out the present whereabouts of this herm. Dr. Blümel knew nothing of it; nor did Dr. Weickert.
M. Guarducci and B. Meritt, judging from the photograph, thought the inscription genuine.

38. Head, mounted on a modern bust, formerly in the Museum of Arolsen, no. 5. Said to have come from Pompeii. Present location not known to me.
Height, with modern bust, 54 cm.
The nose is restored.
Michaelis, p. 405, a.
Bernoulli II, p. 72, no. 27.
Gädechens, *Antiken des Museums zu Arolsen* (1862), p. 23, 5.

39. Head, mounted on a modern bust, in the Hermitage, Leningrad, inv. 2349. From the Campana Collection.

FIGS. 1473–1475

Height of ancient part 28 cm.; ht. of head 25 cm.
Restorations: Tip of nose, right eyebrow. Formerly set on an alien statue.
D'Escamps, *Musée Campana*, p. 49.
Campana Cat. VII, no. 100.

Michaelis, p. 408, t, p. 404, G.
Bernoulli II, p. 73, no. 30.
Waldhauer, *Die antiken Skulpturen der Ermitage* I (1928), no. 68, pl. XLIV.
Dontas, *Eikones*, p. 95, pl. 37, γ.

40. Head, mounted on a modern herm, in the Prado, Madrid. FIGS. 1482–1484
Height 58 cm.
Restorations: Nose, part of upper lip, ears.
Hübner, no. 153.
Michaelis, p. 406, k.
Bernoulli II, p. 71, no. 19.
Ricard, *Marbres antiques*, no. 98, pl. XLV.
Blanco, *Cat.*, no. 77E, pl. XXXVII.

41. Head in the National Museum, Athens, 327. Found in the royal gardens in Athens in 1849. FIGS. 1489–1490
Height 28 cm.
No restorations, but most of nose and of left cheek are missing.
Michaelis, p. 405, b.
Bernoulli II, p. 73, no. 31.
Casson, *J.H.S.* XLVI, 1926, p. 74, fig. 2.
Arndt-Br., 1117.
Kastriotes, *Glypta*, no. 327.

42. Small head in the National Museum, Athens, 1761. From Attica. FIGS. 1491–1493
Height, with neck, c. 18 cm.
No restorations, but a few pieces missing.
Casson, *J.H.S.* XLVI, 1926, p. 76, fig. 4.
Kastriotes, *Glypta*, no. 1761.
A fairly faithful but still free copy, as seen, for instance, in the design of the locks of the hair on the right side.

43. Small head, mounted on a modern bust, in the National Museum, Athens, 1760. Found in Athens. FIGS. 1479–1480
Height, with neck, c. 12 cm.
Restorations: Most of the back of the head with part of the right ear.
Kastriotes, *Glypta*, no. 1760.
Quite free copy.

44. Fragment of a moulded base of a large statuette inscribed Δημοσθένης, once at the entrance of the Akropolis, in the 'Invalidenhaus'; now in the Epigraphical Museum, Athens, no. 9623. On its upper surface are traces of the two feet. The forms of the letters of the inscription suggest a date in the second century A.D. (Wycherley).
Present length 25 cm.; height 6·5–7·5 cm.; thickness 17 cm.; length of feet 9·5 cm. The statuette must have been about one-third life size. The stance of the feet is not quite the same as in the Vatican and Copenhagen statues; it must have been a free, not an exact copy. FIG. 1498
Sybel, no. 4752.
'Αθήναιον, 6, 1877, p. 278.
Michaelis, p. 403, D.
Bernoulli II, p. 73, no. 32.
Wycherley, *Testimonia*, p. 211, under no. 699.
I.G. II–III², no. 4263.

45. A statue base in the Epigraphical Museum, Athens, no. 1927, is inscribed Δημοσθέν[ει] at end of line, in letters of the 2nd century A.D., cut on an earlier, mostly erased inscription. The base itself was used several times, right side up and upside down (Mitzos, Meritt). Its first use, as indicated by the form of the moulding, must have been in 'the middle or third quarter of the fourth century B.C.' (L. Shoe); then, in Roman times, it was used to support a statue of Demosthenes. FIG. 1495
Height 68 cm.; width 61 cm.; thickness 43. On the top face is a cutting for a standing figure 32·5 cm. wide by 25 cm. Back left unfinished.
Mitzos, *Eph. Arch.* 1960 (1963), pp. 38ff.

46. Bust in the Museum of Cyrene, acc. no. C 17141. Found in the valley east of the agora. FIGS. 1485–1488
Height 69 cm.; ht. of head 25·5 cm.
No restorations. Drapery on left shoulder.
Rosenbaum, *Cyrenaican Portrait Sculpture*, no. 4, pl. VII (where the whole bust is included).

47. Head formerly in the Smithsonian Institution, Washington, inv. 86.612. From the Alden Sampson Collection. Now in the Princeton Art Museum, 62.133, a gift of Edward Sampson. FIGS. 1468–1470
Height 32·8 cm.; ht. of head without neck, 22 cm.
No restorations.
Fraser, *A.J.A.* XLI, 1937, pp. 212ff., fig. 1.
Richter, *Gr. Portr.* (1), p. 36, figs. 27–28.
F. F. Jones, *Record of the Art Museum, Princeton University* XXI, 1962, p. 52, figs. 7–9.

DOUBTFUL EXAMPLES

The following heads somewhat resemble Demosthenes, and were sometimes thought to represent him, but have now been mostly discarded (some are listed by Bernoulli II, pp. 73f., nos. 33ff., under 'zweifelhaft'):

1*. Head in the Galleria Geografica, Vatican. Michaelis, p. 409, γ; Lippold, *Vat. Kat.* III, 2, p. 454, no. 14a, pl. 194.

2*. Head in the British Museum, Smith, *Catalogue* III, no. 1841; Michaelis, op. cit., p. 406, h.

3*. Head in the Stanza dei Filosofi, Capitoline Museum, no. 21. Michaelis, op. cit., p. 408, u'; Stuart Jones, *Cat.*, p. 232, no. 32.

4*. Head in the Villa Albani (Coffee House). Michaelis, op. cit., p. 408, t".

5*. Head in the Museo Torlonia. Visconti, *Museo Torlonia*, no. 29; Michaelis, p. 409, v'; Benndorf, *Röm. Mitt.* I, 1885, p. 113.

6*. Herm, from Herculaneum, in the National Museum, Naples, inv. 6153. Michaelis, p. 407, n; Comparetti and De Petra, *Villa ercol.*, p. 275, no. 70, pl. 22, 2.

7*. Head in the Louvre, Ma 72. From the Campana Collection. *Cat. sommaire* (1922), p. 21, no. 72; Arndt-Br., 139–140.

8*. Head in Stockholm, mounted on a modern herm inscribed Demosthenes. Michaelis, p. 430, γ'; Farnell, *J.H.S.* IX, 1888, p. 37.

9*. Head, mounted on a modern herm inscribed Δημοσθένης. In the Casa del Labrador, Aranjuez. From the Azara Collection. Hübner, no. 152; Azara, *Vida de Ciceron*, 2, pl. 1; Michaelis, op. cit., p. 405, a'; Blanco, *Cat.*, under no. 77E.

10*. Head in the Barracco Museum. Laurenzi, *Ritratti*, no. 62; Pietrangeli, *Guida*, (1949), p. 64, no. 143, pl. XV, 2; (1960), p. 81, no. 143, pl. XV, 2.

11*. Head in the Ostia Museum, inv. 92. Height, with neck, 34 cm., ht. of head 25 cm. No restorations. R. Calza, *Museo Ostiense*, (1947), p. 20, no. 92; 2nd ed. (1962), p. 36, Sala IV, no. 4. The head deviates in many particulars from the certified type—in the setting of the eyes and in the design of the strands of the hair, especially at the back. The expression is also less harsh and unhappy. In spite, therefore, of an undoubted general resemblance, one may hesitate to include the head as a Demosthenes. FIGS. 1501–1502

12*. Head, in the Musée d'Art et d'Histoire, Geneva, inv. 12424. FIGS. 1499–1500
Height 27 cm. No restorations, but some pieces missing.
Deonna, *L'Acropole, Revue du monde hellénique (Paris)* II, 1927, pp. 10ff.; *Genava* V, 1927, p. 51, and IX, 1931, p. 114, no. 8.
Musée d'Art et d'Histoire, Ville de Genève, Guides illustrés 4, sculpture antique, p. 16, no. 12424.
Cited by Felletti Maj, *Ritratti*, p. 19, under no. 18, as no. 31 of her list.
Though life-size, this head deviates considerably in the design of hair and beard from the accepted type, as well as somewhat in the expression; but the general form of the head is the same. It was either—for some reason worked free-hand, or represents another individual who resembled Demosthenes. But to judge from the photograph, it seems to me to be ancient, though von Heintze, in Hekler, *Bild.b.Gr.*[3], p. 65, thinks 'kaum antik'.

The head in the Uffizi, Florence, inv. 1914, no. 34 (Dütschke, no. 20; Michaelis, p. 406, f. Mansuelli, *Cat.*, no. 7) I take to be a real Demosthenes (cf. no. 19).

SMALL RELIEFS AND STATUETTES

a. Bust, in profile to the right, on a silver emblema, in the Staatliche Museen, Berlin. From Miletopolis. It formed the central medallion of a silver bowl, of which only this emblema is preserved. Apparently a Hellenistic original of the second century B.C. FIG. 1509
Diam. 9·27 cm.
Intact; shows form of nose.

Pernice, *Hellenistisches Silbergerät in Berlin.*
Winnefeld, *68. Berliner Winckelmannsprogramm,* 1908, pp. 13ff., pl. II.
Köster, *Antikes Tafelsilber,* pl. 9.
Bieber, *Sc. of the Hell. Age²,* p. 66, fig. 216.
Richter, *Gr. Portr.* II, p. 18, fig. 13; in *Coll. Latomus* LVIII, *Hommages à A. Grenier,* pp. 1323f., pl. CCLVIII, fig. 1.
If rightly assigned to the second century B.C., this is the only Greek copy of the portrait of Demosthenes—apparently a free rendering of the work of Polyeuktos.

b. Bust, apparently of Demosthenes, in profile to the right, on a terracotta emblema, in the Agora Museum, Athens, P14992. Found in the agora excavations 'in a well in which the filling was of the first century B.C. to the first century A.D.'   FIG. 1494
Diam. 5·3 cm.
The surface is much worn, but what is discernible corresponds with the known portraits of Demosthenes.
Richter, *Gr. Portr.* III, p. 46, fig. 202.

A terracotta statuette, formerly in the Campana Collection, seen in Rome by Michaelis in 1860, thought by Bernoulli (II, p. 71) to be in Paris, but not found in the Louvre or the Cabinet des Médailles. Present whereabouts not known.
Bernoulli II, p. 71: 'Vom Motiv der Braccio Nuovo Statue, aber mit gefalteten Händen. Höchst wahrscheinlich modern'.
Michaelis, op. cit., p. 403, E: 'Die notorische Unzuverlässigkeit Campanischer Terrakotten gebietet grosse Vorsicht hinsichtlich dieser Figur'.

The following two pieces seem to me to be of doubtful antiquity:

Bronze statuette formerly in the collection of Mrs. Herbert Straus, New York. (Now?) It first turned up (in c. 1920) at a merchant in Istanbul, who said that it had been found by shepherds near Ankara, together with a marble statuette of the Farnese Herakles; it subsequently passed to a dealer in Saloniki.   FIGS. 1511–1512
Height 23 cm.
No restorations.
S. Reinach, *B.C.H.* XLVIII, 1924, pp. 504f., fig. 19 ('si cette statuette est authentique...').
Lippold, in Arndt-Br., 1115–1116.
E. Strong, *Catalogue of the Melchett Collection,* note 36 to no. 21, p. 52: 'The statuette recently at a dealer's in Constantinople, which seems, however, of doubtful antiquity....'
Buschor, *Bildnisstufen,* pp. 177ff., fig. 79, and *Porträt,* p. 117, fig. 81.
Bieber, *Sc. of the Hell. Age²,* p. 67, figs. 226–229.
Lippold, Buschor, and Bieber (locc. cit.) accept the statuette as ancient; I have not seen it, so that I cannot form a definite opinion regarding its antiquity; judging from the illustrations, however, I cannot help having a suspicious feeling. There is, moreover, a misunderstanding in the rendering of the pendant fold at the back, a meaningless extra member having been added. For the clasped hands see the Campana statuette *supra.*

Small relief in Trinity College, Dublin. Said to have been found in Hadrian's villa in 1737. Formerly in the possession of the antiquarian Franc. Palazzi in Rome, then purchased by Dr. Meade in London, and, after the sale by auction of Dr. Meade's collection in 1755, was for a long time thought 'lost', until it was rediscovered in Dublin.   FIG. 1513
28 by 20 cm.
No restorations.
Demosthenes is represented sitting in a dejected attitude on an altar, on which is the inscription: Δημωσθένης ἐπιβώμιος (*C.I.Gr.* 6038).
Ficoroni, in Venuti, *Roma antica,* 1741, I, p. 281: 'Nel 1737 fu trovato (in Hadrian's villa) un bassorilievo rappresentante Demostene, con una greca iscrizione, in marmo'.
Michaelis, p. 410, α, with illustration.; *J.d.I.* III, 1888, p. 237.
Visconti, *Ic. gr.* I, pp. 554f.
Bernoulli II, p. 74f., no. 36, pp. 82ff.
T. K. Abbot, *Hermathena* XXXVI, 1910, pp. 1ff., pls. I, II.
Lippold, in text of Arndt-Br., 1120 ('falsch').
Richter, *Gk. Portr.* IV, p. 37, fig. 44.
Michaelis, after accepting the relief as genuine in his *Bildnisse* in 1887, rejected it in his article in the *J.d.I.,* 1888, pointing out the inconsistencies in the style and the mistake in spelling in the inscription. Bernoulli, however, thought that, if the relief was not ancient, it was curious that the forger made Demosthenes resemble the real portraits at a time when they had not yet been identified by the inscribed bust from Herculaneum; also that mistakes in spelling are not uncommon in ancient works. On examination of the photograph kindly sent me by Mr. H. W. Parke, Vice-Provost and Librarian of Trinity College, Dublin, I also think that the style seems suspect; and M. Guarducci, B. Meritt, and G. Daux, to whom I showed the photograph, considered the forms of the letters not ancient; cf. my *Gk. Portr.* IV, p. 37.

ENGRAVED GEMS AND COINS

The following engravings on gems seem to me certainly ancient and the identity as Demosthenes certain:

c. Amethyst ringstone, deeply engraved with a bust of Demosthenes, in slight three-quarter view to his right; with drapery on left shoulder (as seen in impression). Formerly in the collections of the Duke of Piombino and of Sir Arthur Evans, now in a private collection in Italy. In the field is lightly engraved the signature of the artist: Διοσκουρίδου, 'of Dioskourides'.   FIGS. 1504, 1506
20 by 14 mm.
Visconti, *Ic. gr.* I, p. 357, pl. XXIXa, 1.
Michaelis, p. 411, δ.
Bernoulli II, p. 76, b.
Furtwängler, *J.d.I.* III, 1888, p. 222, pl. 26, no. 24; *A.G.,* pl. XLIX, 7.
Casson, *J.H.S.* XLVI, 1926, p. 74, fig. 3.
Lippold, *Gemmen und Kameen,* pl. LXVII, 3.
Richter, *Gr. Portr.* II, p. 17, fig. 11.

d. Glass ringstone engraved with a head of Demosthenes, in profile to the right. Present location not known to me.

Not in Berlin (as Bernoulli thought), so Dr. Greifenhagen informed me.   FIG. 1503
12 by 6 mm.
Bernoulli II, p. 76, d.
Furtwängler *A.G.*, pl. XLIII, 2.

e. Furthermore there is the cameo with a head of Demosthenes in the Cabinet des Médailles, Babelon, *Cat.* no. 314.

f. Bust, in profile to the right, on the obverse of a contorniate, inscribed Δημοσθένης. Drapery on left shoulder. In the Cabinet des Médailles.   FIG. 1510
Diam. 3·7 cm. Surface much corroded.
Bernoulli II, p. 76, a.
Sabatier, *Description générale des médallions contorniates*, p. 45, pl. VI, 6.
Cohen, *Médailles impériales* VIII, p. 281, no. 61.
Casson, *J.H.S.* XLVI, 1926, p. 78.
As far as one can judge in its present corroded state, there is little resemblance to the known portraits of Demosthenes.

A carnelian cameo once in the collection of Peter Leven in Cologne (Michaelis, op. cit., p. 412, θ; F. Fiedler, *Rheinl. Jahrb.* XIV, 1849, p. 23, no. 48) was considered by Urlichs as not ancient, and this estimate is repeated by Bernoulli II, p. 76. Dimensions c. 3·8 by 2·5 cm.
I have not been able to locate the piece. There is no Leven collection in Cologne now, and no one seems to know what has happened to it, so Professor T. Dohrn and W. Binsfeld told me.

In the following example the identity of Demosthenes is problematical:
Glass ringstone (in imitation of nicolo). In the Staatliche Museen, Berlin. Furtwängler, *Geschnittene Steine*, no. 5042; *A.G.*, pl. XLIII, I ('Brustbild ... wie es scheint des Demosthenes, diesem jedenfalls ähnlich').   FIG. 1505

To judge by the photograph and impression kindly sent me by Miss Peredolskaia, I feel uncertain of the antiquity of the following piece:
Carnelian ringstone, engraved with the bust of Demosthenes. In the Hermitage, Leningrad. From the Crozat collection.   FIG. 1508
Michaelis, p. 411, ('von vortrefflicher Arbeit').
Bernoulli II, p. 76, c ('von vortrefflicher Arbeit').
The expression is fiercer than in the known portraits of Demosthenes, the nose is more curved, the lips are slightly parted instead of being compressed with the lower lip recessed. Furthermore, the curious wavy edge of the drapery on the right shoulder makes one pause. Miss Peredolskaia wrote me that Miss Maximova also felt that 'the psychological character in this portrait does not seem to conform with that of Demosthenes'. I, therefore, suggest that the engraving is an excellent work of the eighteenth century.

The antiquity of the following piece also seems to me uncertain:
Sard ringstone, engraved with the head of Demosthenes, in profile to the right. In the British Museum. From the Castellani Collection. 14 by 11 mm.   FIG. 1507
H. B. Walters, *Cat.*, no. 1959 (accepted as ancient).
Bernoulli II, p. 76, f. There called sardonyx and of 'verdächtigem Altertum'.
Here too the professorial expression seems to me unlike the troubled one that one meets in all the portraits of Demosthenes, in more or less accentuated form; and the curious renderings of the right shoulder, bust, and drapery are, I think, unparalleled in an ancient work. It seems more likely that the engraving dates from the eighteenth to nineteenth century.

CONCLUSIONS

The physical physiognomy in all the authentic portraits of Demosthenes is always the same. They show a man between 50 and 60 years old, with an oval face, becoming pointed below; lean and lined cheeks; hair carved in short, thick curls; a clipped beard; a high forehead marked by three horizontal, undulating furrows; a long, slightly curved nose; bushy, contracted eyebrows; several deep wrinkles above the bridge of the nose; deep-set eyes, placed rather close together; three crow's feet at the outer corners of the eyes; a straight, thin-lipped, closed mouth, the lower lip drawn in, the upper covered by a thick moustache; ears protruding in their upper part. The expression is harsh, unhappy, determined—that of a noble fanatic, corresponding exactly to what is known of Demosthenes' appearance and life. And the nervous and dignified character is brought out also in the two extant statues, with their simple, diffident pose, and the harmonious composition of the folds, suggestive of his nobility. In both these respects the statue of Aischines (cf. fig. 1369) forms an instructive contrast.

We are particularly fortunate in possessing so many portraits of Demosthenes, in a variety of sizes, in the round and in relief. The life-size examples in the round were evidently all reproduced from the same Greek original, mechanically by the pointing process. The variations observable in some of the copies are simply due to a different surface finish (cf. p. 27). On the other hand, the sometimes fundamental differences in the reduced renderings (cf. no. 43) and in the reliefs (cf. no. 9) are of course due to the fact that they were worked free-hand, but copied from the same original as were the life-size ones; by way of contrast the contorniate (fig. 1510) is a merely invented portrait. In this wealth of material one can in fact evaluate the similarities and differences introduced in the copies from an identical original. It is interesting to observe that of the almost 50 extant marble portraits nearly all were found in Italy, only a few in the East—three heads (and two bases) in Attica, one in Macedonia, one in Cyrene—an eloquent testimony to Demosthenes' popularity in the West in Roman times. Also instructive is the fact that, though several statues to Demosthenes are recorded in ancient literature, all extant copies go back to the same Greek original (cf. p. 216).

LEODAMAS

Of Acharnai, Attica. Orator of the time of Aischines and Demosthenes. Pupil of Isokrates (Ps.-Plutarch, *Vit. X orat.*, Isokr., 837d).

Took part in the intrigues against Chabrias, and opposed Demosthenes in the suit against Leptines (355/4 B.C.). Cf. Demosthenes, *Orat. in Leptin.*, 146f. Was much esteemed as an orator.

A double herm, in the sixteenth century in the Villa Cesi, property of the Duke of Aqua Sparta, was inscribed . . . δαμας. Now lost, but drawings of it exist: Ursinus, *Imag.*, 76; Statius, xv; Gallaeus-Faber. 84; all rather different from one another. Cf. Visconti, *Ic. gr.* I, pl. xxx, 2, p. 366. As, in Visconti's opinion, there was room only for three, not four, letters, before damas, the name should be Leodamas rather than, for instance, Alkidamas, the orator of the fourth century B.C. This, however, cannot now be verified. Of neither individual is there a record of a statue having been set up.

On a modern herm in the Stanza dei Filosofi, Capitoline Museum, is the inscribed name Leodamas (in the Latin form). Cf. Stuart Jones, *Cat.*, p. 242, no. 56, pl. 55, where it is suggested that the name was added on account of a supposed likeness to the head of the Cesi collection. But the resemblance is at best slight; cf. Bernoulli II, p. 85; Arndt-Br., nos. 367-368. A replica of the Capitoline head was, in 1892, in the Roman antiquity market, and is illustrated in Arndt-Br., 369–370.

THEODEKTES

c. 375–334 B.C. Born in Phaselis, Lycia. Orator and tragedian (Cf. Ps.-Plut., *Vit. X orat.*, Isocrat., 837 c–d). Lived chiefly in Athens, where he studied with Plato, Isokrates, and Aristotle. Was buried on the road to Eleusis. On his grave was a monument (μνῆμα), with representations (statues?) of poets, of which that of Homer was the only one that had still survived (cf. p. 45, no. 2). Presumably a statue of Theodektes was included.

Drexel, *Ath. Mitt.* XXXVII, 1912, pp. 119ff.

DEMOCHARES

c. 355–275 B.C., Athenian orator and democratic statesman. Nephew of Demosthenes.

In 322 B.C. made a public protest against the surrender of the anti-Macedonian orators.

280/279. Had a decree passed honouring his uncle Demosthenes, and directing that a statue of him should be erected in the agora.

According to Ps.-Plutarch, *Vit. X orat.*, Demosth., 847, d, e, a bronze statue of Demochares was set up in the Athenian agora in 271 B.C., and was later removed to the Prytaneion. It represented him 'wearing a sword with his himation, for in this manner he is said to have made his speech when Antipatros was demanding the orators', ἔστι δ' αὐτοῦ εἰκὼν ἐν τῷ πρυτανείῳ . . . περιεζωσμένος ἅμα τῷ ἱματίῳ καὶ ξίφος. Wycherley, *Testimonia*, p. 170, no. 559.

4. POETS

MENANDER

c. 342/1–293/2 B.C. Foremost representative of the New Comedy. Athenian. Son of Diopeithes of Kephisia, and of Hegesistrate.

LIFE

His parents being well-to-do, he lived in comfortable circumstances in his youth: λαμπρὸς καὶ βίῳ καὶ γένει (Anon., Περὶ κωμ.). Studied with Theophrastos (Diog. Laert. v, 36): διδάσκαλος Μενάνδρου τοῦ κωμικοῦ. Was a friend of Demetrios of Phaleron, and so was in danger after the latter's fall in 307 B.C. (Diog. Laert. v, 79). Ptolemy Soter invited him to his court, but the invitation was refused. Associated with Epikouros, who was his συνέφηβος.

Was initiated into the art of comedy writing by the poet Alexis (372–270 B.C.), cf. Anonymus, Περὶ κωμ., 17.

321 Produced his first play, entitled *Orge*.

315 Won his first victory (*Marm. Par.* B, ep. 14; Jacoby, p. 198). During his short life he wrote over 100 comedies. Of these, one, discovered in 1958 in a private library in Switzerland, is preserved practically entire (ὁ Δύσκολος, 'the Misanthrope'), several others have survived in considerable fragments, and of the majority the titles are known; cf. the list given by Körte, in Pauly-Wissowa, *R.E.*, col. 718, and *Menandri quae supersunt*[3] (1958–59); Edmonds, *Frgt. Att. Com.*, III B.

293/2 Died, perhaps while bathing in the sea off the Piraeus (cf. Scholion, Ovid, *Ibis*, 593).

Though not greatly appreciated during his lifetime (at least he won few victories, cf. Martial v, 10: Rara coronato plausere theatra Menandro), he became famous after his death (cf. Quintil., *Inst. or*, III, 7, 18: quidam, sicut Menander, iustiora posteriorum quam suae aetatis iudicia sunt consecuti). His plays were revived on the Athenian stage. Aristophanes of Byzantion (257–180 B.C.) considered him the greatest poet after Homer (cf. p. 226), and his fame continued throughout early Roman imperial times. Plutarch (A.D. 46

to after 120), in his σύγκρισις Ἀριστοφάνους καὶ Μενάνδρου, 1, greatly prefers Menander to his predecessor Aristophanes: ὡς μὲν κοινῶς καὶ καθόλου εἰπεῖν, πολλῷ προκρίνει τὸν Μένανδρον.

Latin authors, for instance Plautus, Terence, and Caecilius Statius, imitated him. He was read by young and old, and considered the greatest of comic poets (Quintil., *Inst.* x, 1, 69–72: ille quidem omnibus eiusdem operis auctoribus abstulit nomen et fulgore quodam suae claritatis tenebras obduxit). Ovid thought he was worthy of immortality (*Amor.* I, 15, 17f.; cf. also his *Tristia* II, 369; Plutarch, *Quaest, conv.* VII, 712b). Scenes from his plays and his portrait appear in Roman mosaics, cf. Bieber, *Theater²*, p. 88, fig. 315; Orlandos, *Ergon, kata to* 1961, pp. 214ff., fig. 229, *kata to* 1962, p. 155, fig. 186; Vanderpool, *A.J.A.* LXVI, 1962, pp. 390, pl. III, figs. 9–10, LXVII, 1963, p. 282, pl. 64, fig. 14; Daux, *B.C.H.* LXXXVII, 1963, p. 823; Dimitrov, *La Bulgarie, pays de civilisations anciennes*, p. 26, fig. 36.

Later his fame gradually diminished. Phrynichos (*Epit.*, p. 418, ed. Lobeck) attacked his language for its lack of Attic purity; cf. also Pollux III, 29. Though still extensively read during the third and fourth centuries A.D., he presently suffered an eclipse.

Inevitably, anecdotes, many untrustworthy, were told of him. The best known are his love affairs with Glykera (cf. Martial, Athenaios (XIII, 594d), and Alkiphron) and with Thais (cf. Martial XIV, 187).

Instead of the subjects from mythology preferred by the poets of the Old Comedy, Menander chose his from the everyday life of his time, and developed both plot and characters with skill and insight. The love plot is the central theme. The protagonists are ordinary human beings, the story is told simply, with dramatic instinct, and with delicate humour; cf. Gallius: illud Menandri de vita hominum media sumptum, simplex et verum et delectabile. There are no great poetic flights in Menander's writings, but their human appeal ensured them the long popularity that they enjoyed. 'Menander is the fountain head of the whole modern comedy of manners' (Warrington in *Everyman's Classical Dictionary*).

APPEARANCE AND CHARACTER

Athenaios (VI, 248d and VIII, 264d) calls Menander ὁ καλός. Phaedrus (*Fabulae Aesopiae* V, 1, 12ff.=Perry, *Aesopica*, no. 523) describes Menander's appearance when he first met Demetrios of Phaleron: 'anointed with perfume, effeminate in dress, walking with delicate and languid steps', unguento delibutus, vestitu affluens, veniebat gressu delicato et languido.

Suidas says that he was cross-eyed, but of nimble mind, στραβὸς τὰς ὄψεις, ὀξὺς δὲ τὸν νοῦν.

Menander, in a letter to Glykera (Alkiphron, *Epist.* IV, 18, 4), speaks of his feeble health, which is thought by his friends to be self-indulgence and swagger: οἶσθα γάρ μου τὰς συνήθεις ἀσθενείας, ἃς οἱ μὴ φιλοῦντές με τρυφὰς καὶ σαλακωνίας καλεῖν εἰώθασιν.

STATUES RECORDED BY ANCIENT AUTHORS AND IN INSCRIPTIONS

1. Pausanias (I, 21, 1): 'In the theatre the Athenians have portrait statues of poets, both tragic and comic, but they are mostly of undistinguished persons. With the exception of Menander no poet of comedy represented here won a reputation, but tragedy has two illustrious representatives, Euripides and Sophokles', Εἰσὶ δὲ Ἀθηναίοις εἰκόνες ἐν τῷ θεάτρῳ καὶ τραγῳδίας καὶ κωμῳδίας ποιητῶν, αἱ πολλαὶ τῶν ἀφανεστέρων· ὅτι μὴ γὰρ Μένανδρος, οὐδεὶς ἦν ποιητὴς κωμῳδίας τῶν ἐς δόξαν ἡκόντων, τραγῳδίας δὲ κεῖνται τῶν φανερῶν Εὐριπίδης καὶ Σοφοκλῆς. (Cf. also Dio Chrys. XXXI, 116-117.)

The base of this statue of Menander was found in 1862, embedded in a wall behind the stage of the theatre in Athens. On the top face is a recess (35 cm. deep, 96 cm. long, 41 cm. wide) and on the bottom a similar recess (35 cm. deep) 'for lightening the weight' (H. A. Thompson). On the front face is the inscription: Μένανδρος; and lower down Κηφισόδοτος Τίμαρχος ἐποίησαν in much smaller letters. The dimensions of the base (height 1·10 m.; width 59 cm.; length 1·10 cm.) show that the statue must have been seated. It is generally thought to have been of bronze, though this is nowhere specifically recorded. Kephisodotos and Timarchos were the sons of Praxiteles, and their floruit is given by Pliny (XXXIV, 51) as the 121st Olympiad (292 B.C.): CXXI Olympiade floruere Cephisodotus, Timarchus; Pausanias (I, 8, 4; IX, 12, 4): οἱ παῖδες οἱ Πραξιτέλους. Cf. also Ps.-Plut., *Vit. X orat.*, Lykourg., p. 843f. FIGS. 1518–1520

Rhousopoulos, *Arch. Eph.* I, 1862, cols. 158f., 178f., no. 183 (ill.).
Bernoulli II, p. 107, g.
Löwy, *Inschriften, no. 108.*

Studniczka, *Das Bildnis Menanders* (henceforth cited as Studniczka), p. 4, fig. 1, gives a reconstruction of the base with the addition of the projecting members. Of these, according to Miss Shoe, the bottom one is necessary, the top one possible (but probably was not as high as drawn by Studniczka). The date, to judge by the extant mouldings, she thinks, should be late fourth century or possibly early third.

2. Marble base found near the theatre of Eretria, with other marbles. Inscribed Μένανδρος, in letters probably of the early third century B.C. FIG. 1521

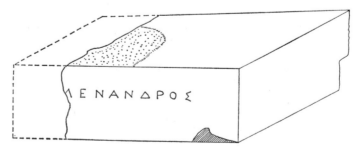

Marble base for a statue of Menander. From Eretria

Height 46 cm.; width c. 72 cm.; length 1·08 m.; ht. of letters 4–4·5 cm.

'The back is roughly worked and is cut back below as if to be set against something. The upper half is dressed with a fine point, the lower half with a coarse point. On top, towards the left, is an area that has been dressed down later with a point, evidently during a re-use of the block. The base must have had another block placed on top of it, for there are no cuttings' (B. Petrakos, as communicated to me by E. Vanderpool).

Kourouniotes *Eph. Arch.* 1897, p. 151, no. 4: 'It does not appear to belong to a tomb monument'.

Studniczka, p. 4.

I.G. XII, 9, no. 280.

The statue mounted on it may have been another early third-century portrait of Menander.

Now in the Eretria Museum, no. I g, XII, 9, 280.

3. Christodoros (*Ecphr.*, in *Gk. Anth.* II, 361f.) mentions a statue of Menander in the Zeuxippos at Constantinople: 'There stood also Menander, who in well towered Athens was the bright star of the New Comedy',

Εἱστήκει δὲ Μένανδρος, ὃς εὐπύργοισιν Ἀθήναις
ὁπλοτέρου κώμοιο σελασφόρος ἔπρεπεν ἀστήρ.

4. Headless herm inscribed Μένανδρος and with three epigrams, of which the last reads: 'Not without reason

Lost herm of Menander. Ursinus, *Imag.*, 33

have I placed you, dear Menander, alongside and opposite the gaze of the head of Homer, inasmuch as the wise grammarian Aristophanes, excellent judge of your writings, gave you second place immediately after the great genius' (tr. A. M. Friend),

οὐκ ἄλλως] ἔστησα κατ' ὀφθαλμούς σε, Μένανδ[ρε
    γείτον' Ὁ]μηρείης, φίλτατέ μοι κεφαλῆς
εἴ σέ γε δεύτ]ερα ἔταξε σοφὸς κρείνειν, μετ' ἐκεῖνον
    [γραμματι]κὸς κλεινὸς πρόσθεν Ἀριστοφάνης.

On the different readings—of the now missing left part of the inscription—by Ursinus and others, see Kaibel and Huelsen, locc. cit.

Found, together with a headless herm of Homer (p. 46), outside the Porta Trigemina in Rome; first shown in the Mausoleum Augusti, now in the University of Turin. Cf. Ursinus, *Imag.* 33; Studniczka, *M.*, p. 5, fig. 3, Bernoulli II, p. 107f.; Körte, *Hermes* 71, 1936, pp. 221f.; Kaibel, *I.G.* XIV, 1183; Huelsen, no. 27.

5. Headless herm, inscribed Μένανδρος, found in 1887 on the site of an ancient villa near Nemi, but now lost.

Cf. Borsari, *Not. d. Sc.* 1888, p. 195; Kaibel, *I.G.* XIV, add. 1184 a; Studniczka, p. 5.

As the upper face of the herm was worked for insertion of a separately made head, Studniczka (loc. cit.) thought that a head of this Menander type, found about the same time at Nemi and worked for insertion in a herm (cf. p. 234, no. 50) might have belonged to it; in which case one would have an inscribed portrait of Menander, and the question of identification would be settled. In spite of repeated efforts, the herm has not been rediscovered.

6. An inscription on a four-sided plaque of Roman date, once in the collection of F. Ursinus (*Imag.*, 33), is now 'lost': 'Menander, the son of Diopeithes, of Kephisia, was born under the archonship of Sosigenes [=342/1 B.C.] and died 52 years old, under the archonship of Philippos [=293/2 B.C.], in the 32nd year of king Ptolemy Soter'.

Plaque perhaps from a portrait statue of Menander. Ursinus, *Imag.*, 33

As Körte has pointed out, the dates of Menander's birth and death are slightly different from those given in some of the literary sources. Studniczka (p. 5, fig. 2) suggested that the plaque might have been attached to the base of a portrait statue of Menander, in which case it would be trustworthy evidence also for the dates.

Kirchner, *Prosop. Att.* II, no. 9875.
Kaibel, *I.G.* XIV, 1184.
Körte, in Pauly-Wissowa, *R.E.* XV, 1, s.v. Menandros, cols. 707f.
Huelsen, no. 28.

We have here, therefore, the record of one certain, and a second possible statue erected to Menander presumably shortly after his death. Whether the statue mentioned by Christodoros (no. 3) was of a third type, or a copy of either (1) or (2) there is no telling. Nos. 4, 5, 6, being of Roman date, must have belonged to portraits copied from earlier ones. In addition, of course, there may have been a number of unrecorded portrait statues.

EVIDENCE FOR IDENTIFICATION

As is well known, the identification of Menander has long been debated. I shall first cite the miscellaneous evidence that exists for a possible identification, then list the many heads of the type that was identified as Menander by Studniczka; and finally discuss this intricate problem.

First and foremost come three medallions*, two of which are inscribed with Menander's name. Cf. now my 'The Menander Medallions', *Ath. Mitt.*, 77, 1962, pp. 250ff.(Festschrift Kunze).

1. Once in the possession of F. Ursinus, now 'lost'. Kaibel, *I.G.* XIV, 1182. Found outside Porta Aurelia, in Rome, with another medallion representing Sophokles (q.v.), of the same small dimensions (c. 20 cm. diam., i.e., about one-third life size), both used as decorations of a poet's tomb. On the frame of the medallion, at the bottom, is the inscription Μένανδρος. Though lost, it is preserved in several drawings (cf. p. 228):

(a) One made in 1570 (cf. Ursinus, *Imag.*, pag. 33; Bellori 55; Gronov II, 98; Studniczka, pl. 4, no. 1), which shows a youngish, clean-shaven man, wearing chiton and mantle, with plentiful hair arranged in curly tufts, a wide mouth with finely curving lips, lean cheeks, an oval face, and a slender neck.

(b) Another by Pirro Ligorio (in two versions), both made soon after 1570; cf. his *Delle Antichità*, XXIII; Studniczka, pl. VII, nos. 4, 6). Now in the state archives in Turin (*Manoscritti Ligoriani nell' Archivio di Stato di Torino* XXIII, 32f.). Here the head, in spite of its strong Renaissance flavour, is easily recognizable as the same man as that in the Ursinus medallion —with curly hair, arranged in separate tufts, full lips, lean cheeks, a slender neck, and a forehead protruding in its lower part; the medallion, however, has been changed into a herm, in one case with the three epigrams of the Turin herm (cf. p. 226, no. 4) added, in the other merely inscribed Μένανδρος, and with a myrtle wreath placed on the head.

(c) A third, made in 1598 (cf. Gallaeus-Faber, 90; Studniczka, pl. IV, no. 2), and reproduced as an engraving in

*I use the word medallion instead of 'imago clipeata' for such round reliefs, when no shield-frame is indicated. For the distinction cf. also Becatti, *Enc. dell' Arte antica* II, s.v. Clipeatae, Immagini, p. 719, bottom.

the Codex Capponianus 228, in the Vatican Library; cf. Studniczka, pl. VIII, no. 2. The drawing was evidently made for the engraving, and the direction is, therefore, reversed. The individual is here shown with a quite different physiognomy from that in a and b; he has a squarish, instead of an oval face; compact, slightly wavy hair, instead of divided into separate, curly tufts; full instead of lean cheeks; a short instead of a slender neck. The expression is also different— not gay and friendly as in the Ursinus drawing, but serious, almost grumpy, and he seems to be an older man, of a less imaginative outlook. (From Gallaeus' drawing was evidently derived that reproduced by Visconti, *Ic, gr.* I, pl. VI.) For a possible explanation of the difference in features and personality in the drawings a and b, on the one hand, and c, on the other, all supposedly copied from the same original, see p. 235.

2. Medallion once in Marbury Hall, Cheshire, inscribed Μένανδρος on the lower part of the frame. In the field a scroll. Height 55 cm.; length 48 cm.; diam. 23 cm. The tip of the nose is restored. FIGS. 1528–1530
Most of the antiquities of Marbury Hall were sold at two auctions on March 15–16, 1933, and on July 29, 1946, cf. Vermeule, *A.J.A.* LIX, 1955, p. 142, and LX, 1956, p. 337. The Menander medallion was evidently sold later, for it is no longer at Marbury Hall (so Mr. Donald Strong, who went to investigate, has informed me). Where it is now is not known.
Cf. Scharf, *Transactions of the Royal Society of Literature*, new ser. IV, 1853), pp. 381ff., fig. 3, on pl. opposite p. 384.
Michaelis, *Anc. Marbl.*, p. 514, no. 40.
Bernoulli II, p. 105, fig. 8.
Studniczka, pp. 11ff., pl. 6, no. 2, pl. 7, no. 2.
Kaibel, *I.G.* XIV, 1181.
The portrait is that of a clean shaven, youngish man, in full front view, wearing chiton and mantle, with hair arranged in curling tufts, three strands in the middle of the forehead being directed from (spectator's) right to left, a high forehead marked by two horizontal grooves, lean cheeks, half-open lips, an oval face, a small but prominent chin, and a slender neck, on which the Adam's apple is prominent.

3. Medallion, uninscribed, once in the Greek Εὐαγγελικὴ Σχολή in Smyrna, destroyed during the last war. Said to be from Aphrodisias. Width 49 cm.; thickness c. 3·5 cm. No restorations. FIGS. 1522–1523
E.A., 3204–3205.
Lippold, *Röm. Mitt.* XXXIII, 1918, p. 8.
Studniczka, p. 23, pl. 6, no. 5.
Sieveking, *Phil. Wochenschr.* LVI, 1936, col. 340.
Schefold, *B.*, p. 209.
Though there is no name inscribed, the medallion, as Sieveking, loc. cit., pointed out, may be used as evidence in the identification, since the portrait markedly resembles that in the Marbury Hall medallion on the one hand, and some of the sculptured heads listed below on the other (cf. *infra*, p. 236).

1 (c) Engraving after the drawing by Gallaeus   1 (c) Drawing by Gallaeus   1 (a) Ursinus, *Imag.*, 33

MEDALLIONS OF MENANDER

In addition to these medallions there are miscellaneous portraits either inscribed Menandros or related to the poet on other grounds.

4. Bone theatre ticket, of the Roman period, found at Pergamon. On one side is a beardless bust in profile to the right, wearing an ivy wreath and holding a mask; at the back are Roman and Greek numerals and the inscription [M]ένανδρο[ς. Diam. 3 cm.
Cf. A. E. Kondoleon, *Ath. Mitt.* XIV, 1889, p. 130, no. 44.

5. Bone theatre ticket, of the Roman period, found at Alexandria, similar to 4, also inscribed Μένανδρος.
FIGS. 1531–1532
Cf. Noir, *Bulletin de la Société royale d'archéologie, Alexandrie*, XXXII, 1938, p. 157, fig. 1.
Herbig, *Röm. Mitt.* LIX, 1944, pp. 82f., note 3, fig. 4 (on p. 85).
Bieber, *Sc. of the Hell. Age*[2], p. 53, fig. 153, and *Theater*[2], p. 90, fig. 320.

6. On the mosaic by Monnus of the third century A.D. in the Landesmuseum, Trier (cf. p. 55), is included a bust inscribed Μεν . . (δρος). Though the head is mostly lost, enough remains to show that the individual was beardless and that he wore chiton and mantle.
FIG. 1516
Hettner, *Ant. Denk.* I, pl. 48, no. 4.
Bernoulli II, p. 105, c.
Herbig, *Röm. Mitt.* LIX, 1944, p. 82, note 3, p. 78, fig. 2.
Parlasca, *Mosaiken*, p. 42, pl. 46, no. 3.

7. Wall painting, representing a young man, seated in a cathedra, holding a scroll in his left hand. On the base the inscription: Menander; and on the open page held by Menander: Menander, Hic primus (novam) com(o)ediam scripsit. . . . Found in the Casa del Menandro, Pompeii. First century A.D.
FIG. 1515
Maiuri, *Casa del Menandro* (1933), pp. 106ff., figs. 50, 52, 53, pl. XII.
Schefold, *B.*, pp. 164f., no. 1.
Dontas, *Eikones*, pp. 35f., pl. 9, α.
Bieber, *Theater*[2], pp. 90f., figs. 322, a–c.

1 (b) Menander. Drawing by Pirro Ligorio of the medallion shown in Ursinus, *Imag.*, 33

Menander. Head from a lost medallion, once in Smyrna.
Studniczka, *Menander*, pl. 6, no. 5

8, 9. Two mosaics found at Antioch, now in the Art Museum of Princeton University. One shows Menander, Glykera, and Komoedia, all three with names inscribed;

the two former are reclining on a couch, the latter is standing by. The other mosaic is much destroyed, but there remain the two inscriptions. FIG. 1514

Stillwell, *Antioch on the Orontes III Excavations*, 1937–39, no. 131, pl. 63.
Friend, *ibid.*, pp. 248ff., 'Menander and Glykera', pp. 185f., p. 176, no. 10, pl. 50.
Bieber, *Theater*², p. 90, fig. 321.

10. Mosaic found by S. J. Charitonides at Mytilene in 1962 in the same building in which were previously found the mosaics with scenes from Menander's plays (cf. p. 225). It represents a draped bust inscribed Menandros. Tentatively dated in the early fourth century A.D. FIG. 1517

Vanderpool, *A.J.A.* LXVII, 1963, p. 282, pl. 64, fig. 14.
Daux, *B.C.H.* LXXXVII, 1963, p. 823, fig. 5 (on p. 819).

11. Relief formerly in the Lateran Museum, now transferred to the Vatican Museum, inv. 9985, representing a seated comic poet holding a mask and a standing female figure (Glykera?, Personification of Skene?, Muse?). The presence of three comic masks and other attributes show that the seated figure must be a comic poet, and therefore perhaps the most celebrated of them, Menander. FIGS. 1525, 1527
Height 40 cm.; width 56 cm.
Restorations: The nose of the seated figure.
Complete on both sides.
Benndorf and Schöne, *Lateran*, no. 245.
Helbig, *F.*³, no. 1183; Helbig, *F.*⁴-Speier, no. 1069.
Studniczka, pp. 25ff.
Sieveking, in Brunn-Bruckmann, *Denk.*, pl. 626, b.
Bieber, *Theater*², pp. 89f., figs. 317 a–c, and in *Festschrift A. Rumpf*, pp. 14f.

12. Relief formerly in the Stroganoff Collection, now in the Art Museum of Princeton University. It is a replica of the relief in the Lateran, but with the female figure omitted. FIG. 1526
Height 49·5 cm.; width 68·3 cm. (Bieber). Complete on both sides.
Restorations: the part of the head above the mouth, the legs of the seat, and the stretchers of the table.
Cf. Pollak and Muñoz, *Pièces de choix de la collection du Comte Grégoire Stroganoff à Rome* I, (1912), p. 8, pl. X.
Sieveking in Brunn-Bruckmann, *Denk.*, pl. 626a.
Bieber, in *Festschrift A. Rumpf*, (1952), pp. 14ff., and *Theater*², pp. 89f., fig. 316.
F. F. Jones, *Ancient Art in the Art Museum, Princeton University* (1960), pp. 44f.
An adaptation of this relief, with only the figure of the seated poet holding a comic mask, is in the Staatliche Museen, Berlin. Acquired in 1858 in Aquileia. FIG. 1524
Height 28 cm.; width 24 cm.
The edges on both sides are ancient.
Conze, *Beschreibung*, no. 951.
Sieveking, in Brunn-Bruckmann, *Denk.*, text to pl. 626, figs. 3, 4.
Krüger, *Ath. Mitt.* XXVI, 1901, pp. 136f.
Here the features of the poet are generalized.

13. Small herm with portrait of the same type as those listed below, pp. 229–234, but cursorily worked (cf. p.230, no. 14). Found in the peristyle of the Casa degli Amorini dorati, Pompeii, together with herms and reliefs of Dionysos, Ariadne, satyrs, Erotes, centaurs, Marsyas, theatrical masks, Melpomene and Pan. The presence of this one portrait in the midst of other small sculptures that relate to the theatre suggests that the individual is a dramatist. FIGS. 1561–1563

14. Skeleton of Menander, inscribed Μένανδρος, on one of the two silver cups from Boscoreale, now in the Louvre. He is shown holding up a female mask; by his side is the skeleton of Archilochos, with a lyre. FIG. 1702

Héron de Villefosse, *Mon. Piot* V, 1899, p. 65, pl. VII, 1.
Winter, *Arch. Anz.*, 1896, col. 82.
Bernoulli II, p. 107, e.
Schefold, B., p. 167, no. 3.
Bieber, *Theater*², p. 91.

For the statue in the Vatican, found with the statue of Poseidippos (Arndt-Br., 1225–1227), once thought to represent Menander, now thought to be that of an unidentified Roman, see pp. 235, 238. As Bernoulli II, pp. 108ff. pointed out, the two statues need by no means have originally been intended to be pendants, for the poses in the two are different; it is more likely that the two were combined in Roman times. Cf. Amelung, *Vat. Kat.* II, p. 54, no. 390.

THE EXTANT PORTRAITS OF THE TYPE IDENTIFIED BY STUDNICZKA AS MENANDER

Let us now examine the more than forty examples of the type identified by Studniczka as Menander, and then see what they can teach us. They consist of heads full-size and reduced.

1. Bust in the Museo Chiaramonti, Vatican, inv. 1453. Formerly in the Mattei Collection. FIGS. 1533–1535
Height, without the modern support, 41 cm.; ht. of head 27 cm.
Restorations: Nose, lips, chin, right eyebrow, most of left eyebrow, rim of left ear.
Amelung, *Vat. Kat.* I, p. 645, no. 508, pl. 69.
Bernoulli II, p. 111, no. 1.
Helbig, *F.*³, no. 94; Helbig, *F.*⁴-Speier, no. 353.
Crome, *Das Bildnis Vergils* (henceforth cited as Crome, *Bildnis*), p. 69, no. 27.

2. Head in the Museo Chiaramonti, Vatican, inv. 1681. FIGS. 1536–1538
Height, with neck, 37 cm.; ht. of head 25 cm.
Restorations: Nose, support of bust.
Amelung, *Vat. Kat.* I, p. 594, no. 431, pl. 62.
Bernoulli II, p. 113, no. 20 ('zweifelhaft').
Crome, *Bildnis*, p. 70, no. 28.

3. Head, mounted on a modern herm, in the Galleria Geografica, Vatican, inv. 2859. FIGS. 1539–1540

Height, with neck, 31·4 cm.; ht. of head 25·5 cm.
Restorations: Nose, chin, the hair above the right ear, the top of the head at the back.
Lippold, *Vat. Kat.* III, 2, pp. 479f., no. 48, pl. 214.
Bernoulli II, p. 111, no. 3.
Crome, *Bildnis*, p. 70, no. 29.

4. Head in the Museo Nazionale delle Terme, Rome, inv. 58703. Found in a Roman villa at Genazzano.
                                         FIGS. 1542–1544
Height 28 cm.
Restorations: Nose, a large part of the lips, the chin.
Crome, *Bildnis*, p. 69, no. 24.
Felletti Maj, *Ritratti*, no. 26.
It is noteworthy that the restored lips are very different from the preserved ones in the other examples.

5. Head, mounted on a modern bust, in the Museo Nazionale delle Terme, Rome, inv. 8613. From the Ludovisi Collection.   FIGS. 1545–1547
Height of head 28 cm.
Restorations: Nose, ears, end of chin, bottom of neck, most of eyebrows.
Schreiber, *Villa Ludovisi*, p. 119, no. 98.
Bernoulli II, p. 112, no. 6.
Crome, *Bildnis*, p. 69, no. 25.
Felletti Maj, *Ritratti*, no. 27.

6. Head, mounted on a modern bust, in the Museo Nazionale delle Terme, Rome, inv. 8630. From the Ludovisi Collection.   FIG. 1550
Height, with neck, 39 cm.; ht. of head 27 cm.
Restorations: Nose, a piece in the right eyebrow, large parts of both ears.
Schreiber, *Villa Ludovisi*, p. 131, no. 109.
Bernoulli II, p. 112, no. 7.
Studniczka, pl. 6, no. 6.
Crome, *Bildnis*, p. 69, no. 26.
Felletti Maj, *Ritratti*, no. 28.

7. Head in a double herm, with one of Homer of the Apollonios of Tyana type (cf. p. 48, no. 3). In the Museo Nazionale delle Terme, Rome, inv. 124490. Found near the Via Appia Nuova, on the estate of Conte Alessandro Martini Marescotti.   FIGS. 1548–1549
Height 41·5 cm. A little over life size.
Restorations: The right (spectator's) side of the herm. A piece on the right side of the head, including the ear, was worked separately and is missing.
R. Paribeni, *Not. d. Sc.*, 1929, pp. 351ff., pls. XVI, b, XVII.
Crome, *Bildnis*, p. 14, no. 1, p. 69, no. 23, figs. 2–4.
Lippold, *D.L.Z.* LVIII, 1937, p. 672.
Felletti Maj, *Ritratti*, no. 21.

8. Head in a double herm, with one of the Pseudo-Seneca type (p. 59, no. 6), in the Villa Albani, Rome, no. 67. Provenance not known.   FIGS. 1551–1552
Height of head 26·2 cm.
Restorations: Nose, part of the right eyebrow, rim of the right ear, a few patches here and there, herm with the lower part of the neck.
Comparetti and De Petra, *Villa ercol.*, p. 38, pl. 4, nos. 3, 4.
Bernoulli II, p. 111, no. 4, p. 162, no. 9.
Helbig, *F.*[3], no. 1826.
Arndt-Br., 1217–1219.
Crome, *Bildnis*, pp. 59ff., p. 70, no. 30.

9. Head mounted on a partly modern herm, in the Stanza dei Filosofi, Capitoline Museum, no. 45. FIGS. 1553–1555
Height, with neck, 32 cm.; ht. of head 23 cm.
Restorations: End of nose, piece on upper lip, portions of the herm. The surface has been worked over.
Bernoulli II, p. 90.
Arndt-Br., 1220–1221.
Stuart Jones, *Cat.*, p. 240, no. 53.
Crome, *Il Volto di Vergilio*, p. 8, no. 43.

10. Head, mounted on an alien statue, in the Borghese Gallery, Salone, no. 12.   FIG. 1541
Life-size.
Restorations: Nose, ears, chin. Surface weathered.
Bernoulli II, p. 112, no. 5.
Crome, *Bildnis*, p. 70, no. 32.

The head cited by Crome, *Bildnis Vergils*, p. 70, no. 31 (without illustration), as being in the Villa Doria Pamfili, Rome, must be due to a misunderstanding of Studniczka's remark in *Menander*, p. 14, n. 2, and of Matz-Duhn I, no. 1832.

11. Fragment of a head in the Antiquario Comunale, Rome. Only the right side of the head is preserved. From the Ara Sacra del Largo Argentino.   FIG. 1560
Height 28 cm.
No restorations.
Hekler, *B.b.G.*, p. 34; 3rd ed., revised by von Heintze, p. 65, no. 18.
Crome, *Il Volto di Vergilio*, p. 7, no. 40, pl. VIII.
Marchetti-Longhi, *L'Area Sacra del Largo Argentino, Itinerario* 102, pl. XXXIII, 2.

12. Head in a private collection in Rome. Listed by von Heintze, in Hekler, *B.b.G.*[3], p. 66, no. 49, as 'unveröffentlicht'.

13. Head found in 1961 at Velia. In the Museum of Paestum.   FIG. 1558
Height 32·5 cm.; ht. of head (from chin to top of brow) 22·8 cm.
No restorations.
Van Buren, *A.J.A.* LXV, 1961, p. 380.
von Heintze, in Hekler, *B.b.G.*[3], p. 65, no. 17.
To be published by Mr. Sestieri, to whose kindness I owe the photograph here reproduced.

14. Small bust, set in a herm. In the Casa degli Amorini dorati, Pompeii. Found with other small heads (cf. p. 229).
                                         FIGS. 1561–1563
Height, with herm, 1·09 m.; ht. without herm, 25 cm.; ht. of face 11·5 cm.
No restorations.
Sogliano, *Not. d. Sc.* 1907, p. 589, fig. 31 (on p. 582).

Studniczka, *J.d.I.*, 38–39, 1923, p. 68, note 1.
L. Curtius, *Röm. Mitt.* LIV, 1939, pp. 120f., pls. 25, 26 (there identified as Agrippa).
Carettoni, *Mem. Acc. Pont.*, serie 3, vol. VI, note 1, 1943, p. 65.
Herbig, *Röm. Mitt.* LIX, 1944, p. 86, note 1.
Crome, *Volto di Vergilio*, p. 8, no. 41, figs. 9, 10.
A. de Franciscis, *Il ritratto romano a Pompei*, 1951, fig. 9, p. 24.
Della Corte, *Case e abitanti di Pompei*, 1926, pp. 61ff., pl. X; 2nd ed., 1954, pp. 62f.
Laurenzi, *Rivista dell'Ist. Naz. d'Arch. e St. d'Arte*, N.S. IV, 1955, pp. 195ff.
T. Dohrn, *Gymnasium*, 68, 1961, p. 351.

15. Bust in the Seminario Patriarcale of S. Maria della Salute, Venice. Found in Athens before 1760. Formerly in the Museo Nani, then in the possession of Canon Moschini. Underside rough, with remains of an iron dowel. Made for insertion in another member. Wears chiton and mantle. Height 40 cm.   FIGS. 1573–1576
No restorations.
Paciaudi, *Monumenta Peloponnesia* (1761), II, p. 176 (there reproduced in a drawing labelled: Ex Athenis 1760).
Studniczka, p. 17, fig. 4.
Crome, *Bildnis*, p. 70, no. 36.
Campanile, *Bull. Comunale* LVI, 1928, pp. 187ff., pls. I, II.
Schefold, B., pp. 114f., 209.

16. Head, mounted on a modern bust, in the Uffizi, Florence, inv. 1914, no. 26.   FIG. 1566

EX Athenis 1760 Alt.pal.R. 2.

Menander. Drawing made in 1761 of the bust in Venice (cf. fig. 1574). Paciaudi, *Mon. Pel.* II, p. 176

Height, with neck, 36 cm.; ht. of head 26 cm.
Restorations: Nose, chin, part of the left cheek.
Dütschke III, no. 15.
Bernoulli II, p. 112, no. 8.
Crome, *Bildnis*, p. 68, no. 9.
Mansuelli, *Cat.*, no. 8.

17. Head, mounted on an alien bust, in the Museo Archeologico al Teatro Romano, Verona. From the Veronese Collection Alessandri.   FIGS. 1564–1565
Height 27·5 cm.
No restorations.
Bernoulli II, p. 112, no. 10.
Studniczka, p. 19, note 1.
Crome, *Bildnis*, p. 70, no. 35.

18. Head, in a small double herm, with an unidentified portrait (Aristophanes?, cf. p. 235). In the Akademische Kunstmuseum, Bonn. Gift of F. G. Welcker. Found on the site of Tusculum.   FIGS. 1580–1582
Height 26 cm.
Restorations: Nose, part of the herm, piece of the neck.
Welcker, *Ann. dell'Inst.*, 1853, pp. 250ff.
Bernoulli II, p. 113, no. 23.
Arndt-Br., 124.
Studniczka, p. 13, note 2 ('unsicher').
Bieber, *Röm. Mitt.* XXXII, 1917, pp. 129f.
Lippold, *Röm. Mitt.* XXXIII, 1918, p. 17.
Crome, *Bildnis*, p. 14, no. 2, p. 67, no. 3.
Kekule, *Kunstmuseum*, no. 688, pl. II, 1.
Richter, *Gk. Portr.* II, pp. 23f., fig. 31.

19. Head in the Staatliche Kunstsammlungen, Dresden.
                    FIGS. 1583–1584
Height 27·5 cm.
The back of the head is missing.
Hermann, *Verzeichnis*, no. 198.
Studniczka, pp. 13, 19.
Crome, *Bildnis*, p. 67, no. 7, figs. 26, 27.

20. Head, mounted on a modern bust. In Castle Erbach.
                    FIGS. 1586–1587
Life-size.
Restorations: Nose, mouth, and chin.
Bernoulli II, p. 113, no. 16.
E.A., no. 1446.
Crome, *Bildnis*, p. 67, no. 8.

21. Small head, mounted on a modern bust, in the Archaeological Institute, Leipzig.
Height 9 cm.
Restorations: Nose, chin, neck. Surface cleaned (Studniczka).
Studniczka, p. 24, note 1, pl. 8, no. 3.
Crome, *Bildnis*, p. 68, no. 16.

22. Head in the Archaeological Institute, Leipzig. From Italy.
Height 31 cm.
The tip of the nose is restored.
Studniczka, p. 13.
Crome, *Bildnis*, p. 68, no. 17, figs. 33, 34.

23. Head, mounted on a modern bust. In the Musée d'Art et d'Histoire, Geneva, inv. 8118.   FIGS. 1577–1579
Height 25 cm.
Restorations: Eyebrows, nose, chin.
Crome, *Bildnis*, p. 68, no. 10.
Deonna, *Catalogue des sculptures antiques* (1923), p. 86, no. 121 (ill. on p. 85).
Guides illustrés, no. 4, *Sculpture antique*, 1957, p. 20.

24. Head, mounted on an alien statue, in the cemetery of Gerzensee, Kanton Bern. Purchased in Switzerland, but presumably from Italy.   FIGS. 1567–1568
Life-size.
No restorations.
Unpublished. I owe my knowledge of the piece to E. Langlotz, and the photographs here reproduced to Dr. Jucker.

25. Herm in a private collection in Biel, Switzerland. Said to be from Greece.
Height 25 cm.
No restorations, but in poor condition.
Shown in the exhibition held March 10—April 15, 1962, in the Städtische Galerie Biel; cf. catalogue by Margot-Schmidt, no. 71 (not illustrated).
I owe my knowledge of this head to Prof. H. Jucker.

26. Head, mounted on an alien bust, in the Ashmolean Museum, Oxford. Ivy wreath on head, tied at back in a knot.   FIGS. 1592–1595
Height, with neck, 33 cm.; ht. of head 27 cm.
Restorations: Nose, left part of forehead, mouth, eyebrows, lower eyelids, parts of eyeballs.
Michaelis, *Anc. Marbl.*, p. 557, no. 66.
Studniczka, p. 16, note 5.
Crome, *Bildnis*, p. 69, no. 21, figs. 41–43 (43 before restoration).

27. Head, mounted on a modern bust, in Ince Blundell Hall. From the Villa Borioni.   FIG. 1588
Height 29 cm.
Restorations: Nose, neck, patches on the right cheek and on the top of the head.
Bernoulli II, p. 112, no. 13.
Crome, *Bildnis*, p. 68, no. 12.
F. Poulsen, *English Country Houses*, no. 15.
Ashmole, *Cat.*, no. 110, pl. 30.

28. Head, mounted on a modern bust. In Ince Blundell Hall. Unknown provenance.   FIG. 1585
Height of ancient part 26 cm.; ht. with restored chin 32 cm.
Restorations: Nose, patch on chin and one on left eyebrow, both ears, lower half of neck.
Bernoulli II, p. 113, no. 22.
Studniczka, p. 13, note 2.
Crome, *Bildnis*, p. 68, no. 13.
F. Poulsen, *English Country Houses*, no. 14.

29. Head, mounted on the statue of a togatus. In the garden of Chiswick House. Perhaps from 'the old Arundel House collection' (Vermeule).
Vermeule, *A.J.A.* LIX, 1955, p. 132.

30. Head, in a small double herm, combined with a bearded head (Aristophanes?, cf. p. 235). In Wilton House.
          FIG. 1591
Height 27 cm.
Restorations: Tip of nose. Surface cleaned (F. Poulsen).
Michaelis, *Anc. Marbl.*, p. 679, no. 35.
Lippold, *Röm. Mitt.* XXXIII, 1918, p. 17, note 2.
Boehringer, *Homer*, p. 71, no. XVI, pl. 42.
F. Poulsen, *English Country Houses*, p. 36, no. 8.
Crome, *Volto di Vergilio*, p. 8, no. 42.
Bernoulli II, p. 114.
Richter, *Gk. Portr.* II, pp. 23f., fig. 32.

31. Head, mounted on a modern herm, in the Prado, Madrid. From the Azara Collection.   FIGS. 1605–1607
Height, with bust, 42 cm.
Restorations: Nose, chin, patch on beard.
Bernoulli II, p. 112, no. 12.
Hübner, no. 149.
Ricard, no. 97.
Blanco, *Cat.*, no. 81E.
Crome, *Bildnis*, p. 69, no. 20.

32. Head in the Casa di Pilatos, Seville.   FIGS. 1602–1603
Life-size.
The tip of the nose is restored.
Hübner, no. 860.
E. A., nos. 1842–1843.
Crome, Bildnis, p. 70, no. 33, figs. 35–36.

33. Herm in the collection of T. J. B. Hoff, Oslo, Norway.
          FIG. 1620
Height 60 cm., ht. of head 28·5 cm.
No restorations, but the face is much injured.
L'Orange, 'Romerske skulpturer IV, *Farmand*, no. 30, July 28, 1956, p. 20 (with 2 ills.).

34. Head in the collection of Mr. H. Throne-Holst, Djursholm, Sweden.   FIG. 1604
Height 17·5 cm.
No restorations. Most of the left side is missing.
O. Vessberg, *Bulletin Medelhavsmuseet*, Stockholm II, 1962, pp. 46ff., figs. 6–8.

35. Head in the Ny Carlsberg Glyptothek, Copenhagen, I.N. 577. Acquired in 1889 from Martinetti, Rome. Part of drapery at back.   FIGS. 1589–1590
Height 34 cm.
The former restorations have been removed.
Bernoulli II, p, 113, no. 17.
Studniczka, p. 17.
Crome, *Bildnis*, p. 66, no. 14.
F. Poulsen, *Ik. Misc.*, p. 31; *From the Collections* III, 1942, p. 96; *Cat.*, no. 429.
V. Poulsen, *Portr. gr.*, no. 41.

36. Head, with neck, in the Hermitage, Leningrad, inv. 851. Formerly in the Gatschina Palace.   FIGS. 1596–1598
Height 35 cm.
Restorations: Nose, chin, pieces on the left eyebrow, parts of left ear. Surface weathered.

Waldhauer, *Studies in the History of Antique Portraiture* (in Russian), pp. 132f., figs. 47, 48; *Antique Scultpure*, no. 491.
Crome, *Bildnis*, p. 69, no. 19, figs. 30, 31.

37. Head, with part of neck, mounted on a modern bust. In the Hermitage, Leningrad, inv. 850. Formerly in the Gatschina Palace.   FIGS. 1599–1601
Height 32 cm.
Restorations: Nose, chin, part of the lower lip, parts of both ears, pieces at back.
Waldhauer, *Antique Sculpture* (1923), no. 492; *Studies in the History of Antique Portraiture* (in Russian), 1938, p. 129, pls. 44–46.
Crome, *Bildnis*, p. 68, no. 18, figs. 28, 29.

38. Herm in the Museum of Fine Arts, Boston, inv. 97.288. From the neighbourhood of Torre Annunziata. Acquired from the Catherine Page Perkins Collection in 1897.
                                                              FIGS. 1621–1623
Height 51·5 cm.; ht. of face 19·6 cm.
No restorations.
Studniczka, p. 17, pl. 6, no. 1, pl. 7, no. 3.
Bernoulli II, p. 113, no. 18, pl. XIV.
Crome, *Bildnis*, p. 67, no. 5, figs. 19–21.
L. D. Caskey, *Cat.*, no. 86.

39. Head in the Dumbarton Oaks Collection, Washington, D.C., inv. 46.2. From Tarquinia (Corneto). Formerly in the collection of Mrs. E. D. Brandegee. Exhibited in the Museo Civico at Tarquinia, and in the Museum of Fine Arts, Boston.   FIGS. 1611–1613
Height 34 cm. Made for insertion in another member.
No restorations. Even the nose is ancient.
Bernoulli II, p. 112, no. 9.
Studniczka, p. 23, pl. 6, no. 3, pl. 7, no. 1, pl. 9, no. 3.
Crome, *Bildnis*, p. 67, no. 4.
Richter, *Cat.*, *Dumbarton Oaks Coll.*, no. 4, pl. II.

The head in the Royal Ontario Museum, Toronto, 925, 13.44, is now considered to be a modern copy of the head in Dumbarton Oaks (my no. 39).   FIG. 1614
Height 31·4 cm.
Bulletin of the Royal Ontario Museum, 1926, p. 2.
S. Reinach, *Gazette des Beaux-Arts* V, 1931, pp. 90ff., figs. 21, 22.
Crome, *Bildnis*, p. 71, no. 38, j (there listed as modern).

40. Head in the University Museum, Philadelphia. Gift of Mrs. L. W. Drexel, 1901. Found in 1897 at Montecelio, Latium. Formerly in the collection of Mr. Edward Warren, Lewes House, Sussex.   FIGS. 1608–1610
Height, with neck, 40 cm. Made for insertion in another member.
The Museum Journal, Pennsylvania University V, 1914, p. 122, fig. 68.
Bernoulli II, p. 112, no. 15.
Mariani, *Not. d. Sc.* 1897, p. 148, b.
Studniczka, pp. 14, 18, pl. 8, no. 1.
Crome, *Bildnis*, p. 69, no. 22, figs. 14, 15.

41. Head, with part of bust, formerly in the collection of D. M. Robinson. Bequeathed by him to the University of Mississippi. Said to have been found at Tarentum in 1938.
                                                                FIG. 1617
Height 37·5 cm. Made for insertion in a statue.

'The only restoration is a small patch of plaster on the upper lip' (Turnbull). There is a large oblong hole (5 cm. by 7 cm., and 5 cm. deep) at the top of the head and a smaller one at the bottom—the former modern, the other ancient, according to D. M. Robinson (op. cit., p. 466).
D. M. Robinson, *Proceedings of the American Philosophical Society*, vol. 83, no. 3, 1940, pp. 465ff., pl. I, 1–4.
Crome, *Volto di Vergilio*, p. 9 (there considered modern).

42. Head in the Museum of Corinth. Formerly mounted on an alien reclining funerary figure. Exact provenance not known, but 'it was among the antiquities which were brought from the Demarchion in New Corinth' (E. Harrison, to whom I owe the knowledge of this piece).
                                                              FIGS. 1624–1626
Height 26 cm.; ht. of head 24 cm.
No restorations, but battered. Top of head missing.
Deltion IV, 1918, Parartema, pp. 4–5, no. 7, fig. 7.
Here reproduced with the kind permission of Edward Capps Jr., who will include the head in a forthcoming volume of *Corinth*.

43. Head in the Museum of Corfu. Found in Corfu.
                                                              FIGS. 1633–1635
Height 29·5 cm.; ht. of head 28 cm.
No restorations.
Bernoulli II, p. 112, no. 11.
Studniczka, p. 17.
E.A., nos. 610, 611.
Crome, *Bildnis*, p. 68, no. 15, figs. 16–18.

44. Head in the National Museum, Athens, inv. no. 3292. Found in Athens.   FIGS. 1630–1632
Height 18 cm. Less than life-size.
No restorations. Much of the face is missing.
Studniczka, p. 17.
Crome, *Bildnis*, p. 66, no. 2.

45. Head in the Museum of Rhodes. Found in 1937, in a heap of débris left by the Turks in Rhodes.
                                                              FIGS. 1627–1629
Height 33 cm.
No restorations, but face injured in part.
Laurenzi, *Critica d'Arte* IV, 1, 1939–40, pp. 28ff., pls. XVI–XVII.
Crome, *Volto di Vergilio*, p. 7, no. 39, figs. 6, 7.

46. Draped bust in the Museum of Konya (Ikonium), Asia Minor. First said to have been found at Ikonium, then at Yalovatch=Antiocheia Pisidiae (cf. Crome, *Volto*).
                                                                FIG. 1637
Height 50 cm.
No restorations.
Buckler, Calder, and Cox, *J.R.S.* XIV, 1924, p. 46, no. 33, pl. VII.
Crome, *Bildnis*, p. 68, no. 11, fig. 44, and *Volto di Vergilio*, p. 6.

47. Head in the Museum of Ephesos. From Smyrna?
                                                                FIG. 1636
Life-size.
No restorations.
Here published with the kind permission of F. Eichler.

48. Small herm in the Museum of Alexandria. From Alexandria.   FIGS. 1618–1619
About half life-size.
No restorations, but most of the face is missing.
Studniczka, p. 16.
Crome, *Bildnis*, p. 67, no. 1.

49. For the head in high relief on a marble medallion (c. 49 cm. wide), said to have been found at Aphrodisias, formerly in the Εὐαγγελικὴ Σχολή, Smyrna, but destroyed during the last war cf. p. 227).   FIGS. 1522–1523
In addition, several portraits of this type have been recorded but are now 'lost':

50. Head formerly in the villa of General Biancardi at Castelgandolfo, said to be from Nemi (cf. p. 226, no. 5).

51. Head, mounted on a modern bust, formerly in the possession of the antiquaire Jandolo, in the Via Babuino, and there seen by Arndt and Hartwig. According to Arndt's notes the nose is restored. Cf. Crome, *Bildnis*, p. 70, no. 37: 'Altes Palast-Stück mit Renaissancepolitur. Gute Arbeit, sass auf nackter Büste, die bis unter den Nabel ging, mit Schnitt ansass, hinten ausgehöhlt war. Sie war nicht zugehörig'. Not identical with the head now in the University of Mississippi (no. 41), as has been thought (cf. D. M. Robinson, *Proc. Am. Philosoph. Soc.*, vol. 83, 1940, p. 265, note 1).

52. Head, of which a photograph, once in Professor Amelung's possession, is in the German Institute in Rome, 38.555. To judge by this photograph, the nose, the chin, the eyebrows, and the bust appear to be restored. Cf. Crome, *Bildnis*, p. 71, no. 38, fig. 32.   FIG. 1559

53. Bust in 1935 in the antiquity market, Rome, and at that time photographed for O. Deubner, but not acquired by him (so he informed me). Present whereabouts unknown to me. Perhaps originally formed part of a medallion, which would explain the forward inclination.   FIGS. 1569–1572
Height 30 cm.
No restorations.
Crome, *Il Volto di Vergilio*, p. 8, no. 44, figs. 11, 12.
H. von Heintze, in Hekler, *Bildn. b. Gr.*[3], p. 65, no. 31.

54. Head in 1938 in the antiquity market in Rome. Now? German Institute photographs 38.1317, 1318.
                                FIGS. 1556–1557
H. von Heintze, *Hekler, Bild. b. Gr.*[3], p. 65, no. 12.
A portrait which appears on a number of glass gems has been interpreted as representing the same individual as the heads above listed; cf. K. Kraft, *Jahrbuch für Numismatik* XIII, 1963, p. 10, pl. I, 29–40, pl. II, 1, 4.

DOUBTFUL EXAMPLES
A head in high relief, found at Saloniki, and now in the Museum there, resembles this type of head in many particulars—in the general contour, the form of the skull, the lean cheeks, the prominent Adam's apple, etc.—and has, therefore, been thought by some to represent Menander, cf. e.g.

Ch. Picard, *Rev. arch.* XLIX–L, 1957, p. 236. But there are also divergencies, especially in the composition of the locks and in the expression. These may—or may not—exceed the differences that would result from the piece having been carved free-hand, not mechanically. Andronikos, *Mon. Piot* LI, 1960, pp. 37ff., in his publication of the head considered it to be a creation of the Roman Republican period, independent of the Menander type. It would then presumably have been a tomb monument. To judge by the photograph, I, personally, am impressed by the strong resemblance to the Menander type.   FIGS. 1638–1640

An unfinished marble herm in the Museo Archeologico, Aquileia, inv. 479, has been thought to have been intended for a portrait of this type; cf. Squarciapino, *Aquileia Nostra* XXI, 1950, pp. 10ff. Height 42 cm.; ht. of head 25 cm. Provenance Udine.   FIGS. 1641–1643
The identification is made difficult by the unfinished state of the head. Nevertheless, though in general and in the particulars listed by Squarciapino, it resembles the type in question, in certain important details it does not. For instance, the hair does not continue far down on the nape of the neck, as it invariably does on the many examples of the type, but stops at the level of the lobe of the ear; furthermore, though it is true that the strands of hair over the forehead are directed from (the spectator's) right to left, the characteristic long lock ending in the middle of the forehead is absent. It seems to me, therefore, that the identification is doubtful. F. Poulsen, in his *Porträtstudien in Norditalienischen Provinzmuseen* (1928), p. 19, no. 17, figs. 31, 32, merely called the herm 'Kopf eines Griechen, abbozziert, offenbar ein hellenistisches Porträt, sehr wahrscheinlich ein hellenistischer Herrscher'.

The type seems to have found favour with modern copyists; cf. the lists given by Crome, *Bildnis*, p. 71, and *Volto di Vergilio*, p. 9; also *supra*. To these examples could now be added also that in the Prado, cited as modern by Blanco as no. 330E (without giving an illustration, however).

CONCLUSIONS
The type presented by the heads listed on pp. 229 ff. is that of a sensitive person, between 40 and 50 years of age, clean-shaven, with plentiful hair, an oval face, a high forehead that bulges out in its lower part, lean cheeks, finely curving lips, a thin, straight nose slightly curving below the bridge (cf. nos. 15, 38, 39), a small, round, rather prominent chin with a pronounced groove between it and the lower lip, and a slender neck with a prominent Adam's apple. The distinguishing details that indicate a mechanical reproduction from the same Greek original are as usual especially evident in the carving of the hair. It is arranged in a series of wavy tufts going in different directions and forming a lively design; in the middle of the forehead there regularly are several such tufts, directed from right to left, two of which are almost horizontal, the others directed downwards; and over the temples are similar but longer tufts which descend

as far as the ears, but leave the latter uncovered. At the back, at the base of the skull, is a marked indentation, below which the hair grows again in little tufts. To visualize the Greek original of these many Roman reproductions, one must confine one's study to the life-size copies in the round, which were evidently made by the pointing process; for, in spite of many variations, the basic form is the same in all. In fact, from these many extant portraits of one type one can learn much concerning the ancient pointing process—how relatively few subsidiary points were taken and how between these points each copyist could deviate from the original. Nevertheless, the points, though few, ensured that the copy had the same proportions as the original and the same all-over design in details (cf. p. 27).

Who can this individual be who was so extraordinarily popular in Roman times that almost more copies of his portrait have survived than of any other person? As is well known, the two chief candidates have been Menander, first proposed by Studniczka and endorsed by many since, and Vergil, first proposed by Lippold, and then sponsored by Crome (*Bildnis*), Carpenter (*Memoirs of the American Academy* XVIII, 1941, pp. 96ff.), and others.

The chief arguments used for the identification as Menander are the following:

1. The person was presumably a poet, since he wears a wreath (cf. p. 232, no. 26).

2. The general appearance of the portrait conforms with what is known of Menander from literary sources (cf. p. 225) —the face of a poet, imaginative, sensitive, somewhat effeminate, not vigorous.

3. Since Menander was exceedingly popular in Roman times, it is natural that many portraits of him should have survived.

4. A head of this type is coupled with Homer in the double herm in the Terme Museum (cf. no. 7), and this bears out the estimate of him that he ranked second only to Homer (cf. p. 226). One might add that in two double herms the portrait is coupled with a bearded head that may represent Aristophanes (cf. nos. 18, 30, above), in which case the chief representative of the Old Comedy would have been shown with the chief representative of the New Comedy. Unfortunately, the identification of the bearded head, first proposed by Welcker (cf. my p. 141), still awaits confirmation.

5. A small head of this type appears, as the only portrait of a human individual in the peristyle of a private house in Pompeii, with other small heads and reliefs, practically all of Dionysiac character (cf. p. 230, no. 14). This should indicate that the person represented was a dramatic poet.

6. Stylistically the portrait may be placed around 300 B.C., approximately the time when Menander died, and when a statue of him may have been erected. (For this date, which has been disputed, cf. p. 41.)

7. The resemblance of the portrait to the heads in the two medallions inscribed Menandros (cf. p. 227).

8. Finally, the resemblance of the portrait to the head on the mosaic recently found in Mytilene (cf. p. 229). Though in the mosaic the expression has been changed to conform to its late period (probably fourth century A.D.)—as is the case also in the late Roman portrait of Plato (cf. p. 167, no. 20)—the all-over form is not unlike the Studniczka Menander. Furthermore, the arrangement of the drapery is strikingly similar to that in the marble herm in Venice (cf. p. 231, no. 15)—and, incidentally, not like that in the statue which Crome (*Bildnis*, p. 50, figs. 56, 57) thought might belong to this type of head; for there the folds of the mantle descend from the left shoulder diagonally across the chest, instead of vertically.

In evaluating these various arguments we must first try to remove a serious difficulty, namely that Gallaeus' drawing of Ursinus' medallion, made in 1598, substantially differs from the two other drawings of the same medallion made in 1570 and soon afterwards. Gallaeus' Menander seems to represent an entirely different personality from that shown in the earlier drawings (cf. pp. 227 f.) and in the Marbury medallion (figs. 1528–30). Studniczka, influenced by Gallaeus' usual trustworthiness, accepted his rendering of Ursinus' medallion as the most reliable, and, in my opinion, thereby weakened his case for his identification of Menander's portrait. I have tried to solve this problem in a recent article (cf. *Ath. Mitt.*, 77, 1962, pp. 250ff.), in which I suggested that Gallaeus in this case was influenced by the then newly discovered statues of Poseidippos and 'Menander', now in the Vatican, and altered the physiognomy of the Ursinus medallion accordingly; and that, therefore, his version may be discarded in favour of the earlier, unprejudiced drawing in Ursinus' *Imagines*, 33, and in Pirro Ligorio's adaptations. Ursinus' version, moreover (as Bernoulli II, p. 104, pointed out), would be a better pendant to the Sophokles medallion found with it, for in both the iris and pupil are incised, whereas in Gallaeus' version that is not the case.

With this difficulty removed, the road seems clear. The earlier drawings (figs. 227–228) are close enough to the Marbury relief to indicate that they portray the same person, allowing, of course, for the inevitable sixteenth-century flavour that has entered into the drawings. In both we find the same shape of head, the same clean-shaven, youngish face with a high forehead, full, curving lips, a prominent, indented chin, eyes set far apart, slender neck with a prominent Adam's apple, and a similar disposition of the curly hair over the forehead and temples; and in both appear both chiton and mantle. There can be no doubt that the inscribed name Menander can in each case be taken as trustworthy evidence for the identity.

The other evidence, moreover, seems to be consistent with these medallions. The inscribed theatre tickets (cf. p. 228), small and negligible though they are, substantially agree; the heads on the Lateran and Stroganoff reliefs (figs. 1525–1527)—if intended for Menander—are not unlike; the painting from Pompeii (fig. 1515) and the mosaics from Trier and Antioch (figs. 1516, 1514), though of little iconographical value, do not contradict. The skeleton on the

Boscoreale cup and the headless herms (cf. pp. 229, 226) do not enter into the discussion, except in contributing evidence of the widespread popularity of Menander in Roman times.

Lastly, the inscribed portrait on the mosaic from Mytilene (fig. 1517) adds a weighty argument in favour of the identification. The important question now remains: is the resemblance of the sculptured heads in the round, my nos. pp. 229 ff., close enough to the portrait on the Marbury medallion to indicate identity of person? There are, it is true, many divergencies between the two, and these have been thought by some to preclude such an identity. Herbig, in particular, in a detailed analysis of these differences, has pointed out how different is the design of the strands of hair in the two, and that this 'Lockenphilologie' is often a decisive criterion in determining identity. This is true, but there is, I think, a simple explanation for the differences. The life-size heads in the round were all made mechanically by the pointing process, and so are basically alike. The head in the Marbury medallion, on the other hand, is in relief, and was evidently made free-hand, with the usual inevitable divergencies. Such differences may also be observed in the medallions with the heads of Demosthenes and of Sokrates (cf. figs. 1403, 1409, 1512), and in reduced portraits, also mostly made free-hand (cf. p. 9). So different are they sometimes from the full-size heads in the round that the identity of the persons portrayed, and even the authenticity of the piece, has occasionally been questioned. Such deviations apart, the Marbury Hall medallion surely sufficiently resembles the heads in question to suggest the identity.

In this connexion Sieveking has added an important argument. In his review of Crome's 'Bildnis Vergils' in the *Philologische Wochenschrift* LVI, 1926, col. 339, he pointed out the strong resemblance on the one hand between the portraits on the Marbury and Smyrna medallions (cf. p. 227, nos. 2–3), and on the other hand between the Smyrna medallion and the head from Konya (cf. p. 233, no. 46), which showed that the three must represent the same person: 'Ganz unverständlich bleibt mir aber, wie man den Kopf auf dem Clipeus in Marbury Hall mit dem Namen Menanders für eine andere Person erklären will als die Schildbüste in Smyrna, und auch die Zusammenstellung der Büste von Konia mit ersterem bestätigt nur die Identität der Dargestellten und damit für alle drei den Menander'.

The identification with Vergil has been based on the following arguments:

1. As shown by the rendering of the hair at the back of the head in the portraits in question, the individual is not a Greek but a Roman; for only in heads of the Augustan period does this treatment occur—hair shown growing low on the back of the neck, with a marked indentation at the base of the skull, etc. Moreover the person is represented wearing a Roman tunica.

2. Vergil, as the foremost poet of this period, would be a likely candidate.

3. The lack of correspondence between the heads in question with the Ursinus medallion as drawn by Gallaeus is decisive for not accepting the identification as Menander.

4. The comparative lack of correspondence between the heads in question and that on the Marbury Hall medallion makes the identification with Menander questionable.

5. The combination of the head in question with Homer would make the identification as Vergil appropriate.

Of these arguments, nos. 3 and 4, which are the most serious, I have already tried to answer (cf. *supra*). The argument concerning the rendering of the hair has been countered at length by F. Poulsen and others (cf. especially F. Poulsen, *Ik. Misc.*, 1921, p. 42, and *Gnomon* XII, 1936, pp. 92f.; Sieveking, op. cit., cols. 340f.). As has been pointed out, the liveliness in the design of the strands of hair as rendered in the heads in question is in marked contrast with the more linear treatment on Augustan heads, and sufficiently shows that the person is a Greek, not a Roman, quite apart from the general appearance and the expression.

Furthermore, if V. Poulsen's brilliant, though admittedly tentative, identification of Vergil in several heads in Copenhagen and the Lateran Museum (to which H. von Heintze has added another in Leipzig; cf. *Röm. Mitt.* LXVII, 1960, pp. 103ff., pls. 30, 32) should prove correct, Vergil can be eliminated from the discussion (cf. *Opus nobile*, no. 12).

With regard to the other individuals that have been proposed for the type in question, e.g., Theokritos by Möbius (*Bull. van Vereniging . . . Antike Beschaving* XXIX–XXXI, 1951, pp. 57ff.), and Kallimachos by V. Poulsen (*Portr. gr.*, no. 41), they would be more persuasive if they did not have so strong a rival in Menander.

Taken all in all, therefore, the identification of the type in question with Menander, though it lacks the clinching evidence of an inscribed name on a life-size portrait in the round, seems practically assured. The original Greek statue can well have been shown seated, to judge by the inclination of the head in some of the examples; and so be the statue that was erected in the Athenian theatre, of which the very base has survived, with the signature of the artists, Kephisodotos and Timarchos, the sons of Praxiteles (cf. p. 225). The prominent place of this original would also help to explain why all the many copies were derived from it.

PHILEMON

361–263 B.C. Writer of comedies. Of Syracuse (Suidas, s.v., and Anon., *De comoedia*), but according to Strabo (XIV, p. 671) from Soloi-Pompeiopolis. Son of Damon (Suidas). The second most famous of the Alexandrian comedy writers after Menander; cf. Quintilian, *Inst. Orat.*, X, 1, 72; Philemon . . . consensu omnium meruit credi secundus.

He perhaps lived for some time at the court of Ptolemy I of Egypt (Alkiphron, *Epist.* IV, 18, 5 and 17).

Lived also in Athens and was granted Athenian citizenship. He died at an advanced age, and left 97 comedies, two of which are known from reworkings by Plautus and other Latin writers, viz. the Ἔμπορος and the Θησαυρός (=Mercator and Trinummus). For the extant fragments cf. Edmondson, *Frgts. Att. Com.* III A, pp. 6ff.

No statue erected to Philemon is recorded in ancient literature, but that his portraits must have been current in antiquity is shown by two herms inscribed with his name:

1. According to Ligorius, a herm inscribed Φιλήμων was once in the library of Cardinal Rodolphi (Ursinus, *Imag.*, 34; Bernoulli II, p. 103; Huelsen, no. 42).

2. Faber (no. 104) mentions a herm inscribed Φιλήμων Δάμωνος Συρακόσιος as having been found at Tivoli (Kaibel, *I.G.* XIV, no. 1221; Huelsen, no. 43; Bernoulli II, p. 103).

There are also two herms with modern inscriptions; cf. Kaibel, *I.G.* XIV, 269*, 263*, 2; Huelsen, nos, 155*, 156*.

A head on a late Roman bronze coin of Soloi-Pompeiopolis, c. 240 A.D., was thought by Imhoof-Blumer (*J.H.S.* XVIII, 1898, p. 168, no. 22, pl. XII, 9) perhaps to represent Philemon, since he was the only famous person, besides Aratos and Chrysippos, to have come from that city. But apart from the fact that Philemon's connexion with Soloi is problematical (see above), the physiognomy of the person portrayed seems hardly appropriate for a poet. As Bernoulli (II, p. 103) said, the individual might more likely have been some magistrate of the city or a benefactor who had won the esteem of his fellow citizens and was honoured by having his portrait put on a coin. Either theory is a mere guess, as an informative inscription is lacking.   FIG. 1651

Bernoulli II, pp. 102f., 1, Münztafel II, 13.

Schefold, B., pp. 173f., no. 29, p. 221.

F. Poulsen once suggested Philemon as the person represented in the Pseudo-Seneca type (cf. p. 64, no. 7).

Still another supposition is that by Schefold (*Gnomon* XXXV, 1963, cols 811f.) namely that V. Poulsen's Vergil (cf. p. 236) represents Philemon. And, as he thinks Pseudo-Seneca= Aristophanes, the coupling of these two poets of comedy in the Copenhagen herm would be appropriate. But see p. 65.

DIPHILOS

c. 355/350 until after 289 or 263 B.C. Contemporary of Menander (Anon., *De com.* III). Born at Sinope (Strabo XII, 546). Poet of the Attic Comedy. He worked chiefly in Athens (Athen. XIII, 583f.). Produced c. 100 comedies (Anon., *De com.*), the titles of some of which are listed by Athenaios, with short citations. Many were later used by Plautus in his plays, from which one can still realize the lively wit of the dialogues.

After 289 (or 263) B.C. Died in Smyrna (Anon. *De com.*, 2, 18). On Diphilos see now J. M. Edmonds, *The Fragments of Attic Comedy*, vol. III A, Leiden, 1961, pp. 96–97.

SUGGESTED IDENTIFICATION

S. Karouzou (*Deltion arch.* XII, 1929, pp. 225ff.) suggested that a head in the Kunsthistorische Museum, Vienna, inv. I 1282 (cf. Hekler, *Oest. Jahr.* XII, 1909, pp. 198f., pl. VIII; nose restored) represents Diphilos. The evidence cited is that the individual looks like a man from Asia Minor (the hair resembles that of Maussolos, q.v.); that he appears to be a poet rather than a philosopher; and that the serious expression is in conformity with the somewhat pessimistic outlook shown in what is left of his writings. FIGS. 1644–1645 Also that there are three replicas, indicating that the man was famous:

1. Head in the Terme Museum, inv. 299. Felletti Maj, *Ritratti*, no. 16. Nose restored.   FIG. 1646

2. Herm in the Museum of Thermos. Karouzou, op. cit., p. 227.

3. The drawing of a herm once in the collection of Cardinal Carpi. Statius, *Ill. vir. vult.* (1569), XXXVIII; Karouzou, op. cit., pp. 225f., fig. 1.   Cf. *infra*.

The style of these heads certainly would fit the first quarter of the third century B.C., when one may suppose that a statue might have been erected to Diphilos soon after his death.

Mrs. Karouzou aptly quotes the following passage to bring

Herm of Diphilos once in the collection of Cardinal Carpi.
Drawing by Statius

out Diphilos' sad disposition (ed. Edmonds III A, p. 140, no. 88):

οὐκ ἔστι βίος ὃς οὐ⟨χὶ⟩ κέκτηται κακά,
λύπας, μερίμνας, ἁρπαγάς, στρέβλας, νόσους,
τούτων ὁ θάνατος καθάπερ ἰατρὸς φανεὶς
ἀπέλυσε (MS. ἀνέπαυσεν) τοὺς ἔχοντας ἀναπαύσας ὕπνῳ.

'There is no life free from suffering—from sorrows, anxieties, losses, tortures, disease; and then death appears, like a physician, and rescues the sufferers by putting them to sleep'.

The inscribed slab used on the tomb of Diphilos, of his father Dion, and of his brother Diodoros was found in Athens; cf. Wilhelm, *Urkunden*, 60.

POSEIDIPPOS

c. 316–c. 250 B.C. Poet of the New comedy. Son of Kyniskos. Born at Kassandreia (Potideia), in Macedonia. Suidas, s.v. Posidippos.

291–290 Came forward as a writer of comedies soon after Menander's death (Suidas) and was for a time the most popular dramatist of the Attic stage. Won four prizes at the Great Dionysia (*I.G.* II–III², 2325).

Of the thirty comedies that he is known to have written, eighteen titles are known, and some fragments survive. The cook is said to have played a prominent role in his plays, and this incidentally throws light on their character (cf. E. M. Rankin, *The role of the μάγειροι in the life of the ancient Greeks* (1907), pp. 20f.; Edmonds, *Frgts. Att. Com.* III A, pp. 229ff.

Poseidippos was much honoured during his lifetime. A building called Poseidippeion in Athens is referred to in inscriptions; cf. Wilhelm, *Urkunden*, pp. 223ff. In Roman times his writings were popular and imitated; cf. Gell. II, 23, 1: comoedias lectitamus nostrorum poetarum sumptas ac versas de Graecis Menandro aut Posidippo aut Apollodoro aut Alexide.

STATUES RECORDED

No statue of Poseidippos is mentioned in extant ancient literature, but an inscribed base, which perhaps had belonged to such a statue, was found in front of the temple of Apollo at Delos.

Height 24 cm.; width, as preserved, 42 cm.; thickness 99 cm.
The inscription reads: Ποσείδιππον Κασσανδρει.
Homolle, *B.C.H.* III, 1879, p. 369: 'Le rapprochement du nom de Poseidippos et de la ville de Cassandra, semblerait indiquer qu'il est question de Poseidippos, le poète comique, qui était né en cette ville . . .; mais la paléographie du monument ne paraît pas autoriser cette hypothèse'. But, as Wilhelm, *Urkunden*, p. 118, points out, the statue may have been erected sometime after Poseidippos' death; and, since the base is broken on the right side, he suggests that the inscription may have read:

Ποσείδιππον [Κυνίσκου
Κασσανδρε[ῖς ἀνέθηκαν

PORTRAITS EXTANT

Statue in the Galleria delle Statue, Vatican, inv. 735. Inscribed Ποσείδιππος on the plinth. Found on the Viminal, together with another statue, once thought to represent Menander (cf. p. 229, and Amelung, *Vat. Kat.* II, no. 390, pl. 54), near S. Lorenzo in Panisperna under Sixtus V (1585–1590). It was first placed in the Villa Montalto, later acquired by Thomas Jenkins, and finally secured for the Vatican under Pius VI. Under Napoleon it was in Paris.   FIGS. 1647–1650

Height 1·47 m.; ht. of head 26·7 cm.
Restorations: Left thumb, piece at the bottom of the throat, piece of the mantle adjoining the left forearm. Surface reworked: 'Es scheint die ganze Marmoroberfläche übergegangen zu sein' (Amelung).
The hole at the top of the skull shows that the statue was placed out of doors and had a meniskos. The oxydation and consequent swelling of this (iron) peg evidently caused the various cracks visible on the top and sides of the head. Thus the face was broken from the back of the head, and the surface perhaps injured, necessitating some reworking.

Bellori, 61; Gron. *Thes.* II, 100.
Visconti, *Ic. gr.* I, pp. 118f., pl. VIA.
Amelung, *Vat. Kat.* II, p. 469, no. 271.
Helbig, *F.*³, no. 195; Helbig, *F.*⁴-Speier, no. 129.
Pfuhl, *J.d.I.* XLV, 1930, p. 57.
Lippold, in Arndt-Br., 1222–1224.
Bernoulli II, pp. 141ff., fig. 12, pl. XXI.
Horn, Gewandstatuen, *Röm. Mitt.*, 2. Ergänzungsheft, 1931, pp. 31f.
Dontas, *Eikones*, pp. 48f., pl. 18, α.
H. von Heintze, *Röm. Mitt.* LXVIII, 1961, pp. 80ff. (She thinks the original surface has been removed to the extent of ·5–1 cm.)

There seems little doubt that the man represented in the Vatican statue is the comic poet Poseidippos, the only bearer of that name sufficiently important to have had a statue erected to him, and one, as we saw, popular in Roman times. He is shown as a man of about fifty, with short hair, clean-shaven, sitting at ease on a cushioned chair (klismos); he wears a chiton, a himation, and shoes, and holds a scroll in his right hand. The expression is serious and concentrated, clearly that of a writer, a thinker, not a man of action.

The relatively simple folds of the drapery, the still restrained rendering of the face (as far as one can judge in its present condition), and the quiet pose suggest a date for the Greek original around the middle of the third century B.C., that is, in the early, not the late, Hellenistic period. The massive form of the chair is also of the Hellenistic type which was frequently copied in the Roman period (cf. Richter, *Ancient Furniture*, p. 52, figs. 148, 149, p. 127, figs. 303, 306). The inscribed name shows that the statue was intended to portray a Greek, not a Roman, individual; and the type of face also suggests this. Though most third-century philosophers are bearded, the poet Menander—on the inscribed medallion of Marbury Hall (cf. p. 227)—is clean-shaven; and he also wears a chiton in addition to the himation, like Poseidippos. The latter's shoes, instead of the customary Greek sandals, may, as has been suggested, be a change introduced by the Roman copyist, in order to make the statue conform to its pendant (the ex-Menander), which presumably represents a Roman poet (=Plautus?, cf. Schefold, B., p. 164, no. 2); though this figure also was doubtless copied from a Greek original and given the head of a Roman, in the well-known custom of the time.

No replicas of the Vatican Poseidippos have so far been recognized.

As has often been observed, and as H. von Heintze (loc. cit.) has recently again pointed out, there is a distinct resemblance between the face of Poseidippos and the Menander of the Ursinus medallion as drawn by Gallaeus (p. 228). Cf. my article in *Ath. Mitt.* LXXVII, 1962, pp. 250ff., Beilage 70 (Festschrift for E. Kunze).

H. von Heintze furthermore has drawn attention to the resemblance between Poseidippos and one of the heads in a double herm in the National Museum, Naples, inv. 6236; Ruesch, *Guida*, no. 1135. But they clearly represent two different persons.

ARATOS

c. 310–c. 245 B.C., of Soloi, Cilicia. Poet and astronomer. Son of Athenodoros (Suidas) and Letophila, who, though citizens of Soloi, perhaps originally came from Tarsos.

LIFE

Went early to Athens and there met many famous people, among them Zeno, whose Stoic teachings made a lasting impression on him.

Was introduced to Antigonos Gonatas of Macedon and, at the latter's request, wrote the astronomical poem *Phainomena*, based on a prose treatise by Eudoxos of Knidos (c. 390–337 B.C.).

c. 276 Was invited by Antigonos to the Macedonian court, where he wrote a *Hymn to Pan* in celebration of the king's marriage to Phila, daughter of Seleukos. Remained in Macedon as a member of the literary circle that had gathered round Antigonos.

274 After the sudden invasion by Pyrrhos he went to Syria and joined the court of Antiochos Soter, brother-in-law of Antigonos. There, at the request of the king, he completed a new edition of the *Odyssey* and projected one of the *Iliad*. After the death of Pyrrhos he returned to Macedon.

c. 240/230 Died there, sometime before Antigonos (Suidas). Aratos' poem *Phainomena*, which is still extant, achieved immediate fame (*Gk. Anth.* IX, 25). The simple, direct style of the poem—in which the influence of Hesiod is apparent (*Gk. Anth.* IX, 507)—and Aratos' imaginative interpretations appealed to his contemporaries. Its scientific correctness was, however, severely attacked by astronomers of the second century B.C. (e.g. by Hipparchos, 190–120 B.C.). In Roman times it was much admired (cf. Cicero, *De Or.* I, 69), and Latin translations with commentaries (called *Aratia*) were made by Cicero, Germanicus, and Avienus.

As a source of the astronomical knowledge of the time it is an interesting record; it describes the northern and southern fixed stars (26–453), the circles of the celestial spheres (462–558), and the risings and settings of the stars (559–732), as well as weather signs (773–1154). Aratos wrote many other poems, one of them on the stars, Ἀστρικά, of which, however, only fragments remain.

STATUES RECORDED

Pompon. Mela, *Chorogr.* I, §71, says that a memorial was erected to Aratos by his native city: Nunc Pompejopolis tunc Soloe. Juxta in parvo tumulo Arati poetae monumentum. Perhaps the portrait on the Roman coins of Soloi (see below) was copied from that statue.

APPEARANCE

There is no specific description of Aratos' appearance in extant ancient writings. But, judging from the fact that his parents were respected people and that he himself spent much time at the courts of the Hellenistic rulers, one expects him to have been a polished man of the world, in addition to being a studious poet.

PORTRAITS EXTANT

a. On the obverse and reverse of bronze coins of Soloi (Pompeiopolis) of A.D. 163 are represented two portraits of bearded men in advanced years. Since Aratos and Chrysippos are the most famous men that Soloi produced, it is probable that they are here represented (cf. Galen, *Protrept.* 7, 14: Τίς δ᾽ αὖ Σόλων, εἰ μὴ δι Ἄρατόν τε καὶ Χρύσιππον). After a long period of uncertainty as to which head represented whom, a headless herm in Athens (cf. p. 192, no. 16), of which the bare neck and chest remain and which is inscribed τὸν Χρ(ύ)σιππον, showed that the long-bearded man, not the short-bearded one must represent Aratos. He is shown as a man of about sixty, apparently not bald, his long beard hiding his chest, with an enveloping mantle pulled up to cover his neck, his left hand raised to the beard.   FIG. 1653

Visconti, *Ic. gr.* I, p. 122, pl. VII, 5.
Bürchner, *Ztschr. für Numism.* IX, 1882, pl. IV, no. 12, p. 118.
Bernoulli II, p. 146, I, Münztaf, II, 12.
Schefold, B., pp. 173f., no. 28.

Aratos. Roman bronze coin of Soloi (Ursinus, *Imag.* 35)

b. A similar portrait occurs on bronze coins struck under the emperor Philippus (A.D. 244–249).   FIG. 1654
Imhoof Blumer, *J.H.S.* XVIII, 1898, p. 169, pl. XII, 20.
Bernoulli II, p. 148, I Münzt. II, no. 14.

c. On the mosaic by Monnus, found in 1884 in Trier, and now in the Museum there, a distinguished-looking, bearded man, not bald, wrapped in a mantle, and inscribed ARATOS, is shown seated opposite a standing Muse, inscribed URANIA; between the two figures is a capillary globe on a stand. Third century A.D.   FIG. 1656
Bernoulli II, p. 146, fig. 13.
Antike Denkmäler I, pl. 48, no. 3.
Schefold, *B.*, pp. 168f., no. 5, p. 217.
Richter, *Hommages à Léon Herrmann, Collection Latomus* XLIV, (1960), p. 675, pl. XLVI, I.
Parlasca, *Mosaiken*, p. 42, pl. 441.

d. A similar representation occurs on a twelfth-century manuscript, the codex Arateia, in Madrid (cf. my fig. 1657, reproduced from a direct photograph kindly given me by Mr. Davis Wright of Harvard). Aratos is shown seated, holding a scroll in his left hand, in his right a pair of compasses with which he is pointing to a globe. Opposite him is again a standing Muse; in the background a peristyle.
Bethe, *Rhein. Mus.*, N.F. 48, 1893, p. 91.
Bernoulli II, p. 146, b.
Picard, *Mon. Piot* XLV, 1950, pp. 55ff., fig. I, pl. V, I.
Richter, *Hommages à Léon Herrmann, Coll. Latomus*, XLIV, (1960), p. 676, pl. XLVI, 2.

e. On a Coptic textile in the Benaki Museum, Athens, a man with a shortish beard and an eager face, looking upward, is inscribed Ἄρατος; to the right and left are the Muses Ourania and Kalliope.   FIGS. 1658–1659
It has been argued (by Apostolakis and Picard, locc. cit.) that since this Aratos, with his head tilted upward, somewhat resembles the head on the coin with the short instead of the long beard, it is the former that must have been intended for Aratos, and the other for Chrysippos. But it is a well-known fact that late textiles and mosaics are not reliable criteria for the identification of the portraits represented on them (cf. p. 12), whereas the evidence for the identification of the short-bearded type as Chrysippos is too strong to be discarded (cf. p. 191). So the fact that the Aratos on this textile does not resemble the long-bearded type on the coin cannot be taken as a valid argument.
Apostolakis, Εἴκων τοῦ ᾿Αράτου ἐπὶ ὑφάσματος (1938), pp. 2ff., figs. I, 2.
Picard, *Mon. Piot*, XLIV, 1950, pp. 56f., fig. 2.
Richter, *MMA Sc. Cat.*, under no. 188.

SUGGESTED IDENTIFICATIONS

On account of its similarity to the coin portraits, a herm in the Villa Albani (no. 610) has been persuasively identified as Aratos; for it shows the same type of distinguished, studious man, not bald, with a long beard falling on his chest, and wrapped in a mantle that covers his neck (the last an unusual feature).   FIG. 1655

Height 37.5 cm.
Restorations: The whole nose, patches on forehead and left eyebrow, on right cheek and on beard, both shoulders of the herm.
Visconti, *Ic. gr.* I, p. 281, pl. 23a, nos. 4, 5.
Bernoulli II, pp. 155f., figs. 16, 17.
Helbig, *F.³*, no. 1914.
Arndt-Br., 995, 996.
Schefold, *B.*, pp. 109f., no. 3.

On a silver cup from Berthouville, in the Bibliothèque Nationale in Paris, is a relief with a man standing and pointing to a globe with a stick; in front of him is a Muse, and between them a lyre. So the man should be a poet, and, therefore, it was thought, perhaps Aratos.   FIG. 1660
Schefold, *B.*, p. 47, fig. 12, pp. 216f.
Picard, *Mon. Piot* XLIX, 1950, pp. 55ff.

Aratos(?). On a silver cup in the Cabinet des Médailles, Paris. Cf. fig. 1660.
Picard, *Mon. Piot*, XLIV, 1950, p. 55, fig. I

Likewise the figure with a stick, pointing toward an armillary globe, on the well-known mosaic from Torre Annunziata in the National Museum, Naples (cf. p. 82), has been interpreted as Aratos.
Brendel, *Röm. Mitt.* LI, 1936, p. 10.
Picard, op. cit., pp. 75f., fig. 13 (=Thales).
Schefold, *B.*, pp. 154f., no. I, p. 214.
Richter, *Gr. Portr.* II, p. 27.

Still another representation of Aratos may be the astronomer engraved on a lapis lazuli in the Fitzwilliam Museum, Cambridge. He is shown sitting in front of an armillary globe, holding a pair of compasses and looking up at the sun, moon, and stars. But, of course, another astronomer may have been intended, for instance, Hipparchos.   FIG. 1652
Urlichs, *Bonner Winckelmannsprogramm*, 1846, pp. 10f., no. VIII.
Martin, in Daremberg-Saglio, *Dictionnaire* I (1877), p. 491, fig. 587.
Bernoulli II, p. 187 (there as a possible Hipparchos).
Catalogue of Ancient Greek Art, Burlington Fine Arts Club, 1904, M65 (on p. 193, pl. CVIII).
(J. D. Beazley), *Sotheby Sale Catalogue of the Story-Maskeleyne Collection*, July 4–5, 1921, no. 176, pl. III.
Schlachter, *Der Globus*, 1927, p. 61.
Richter, *Hommages à Léon Herrmann, Coll. Latomus* XLIV, 1960, pp. 674ff., pl. XLIV, fig. 2.

For a theory that Pseudo-Seneca=Aratos cf. p. 64, no. 4.

CONCLUSIONS

Of all these more or less authenticated as well as frankly hypothetical representations of Aratos, the only ones that have any iconographical value are the bust on the coin of Soloi (figs. 1653–54) and the marble herm in the Villa Albani (fig. 1655). They show a man of mature years, not yet quite bald, with a skull rounded at the back, a long beard falling on his chest, a long moustache, and a mantle pulled up to cover his neck. The expression is serious, but affable. The general appearance is that of a studious man of the world, such as one would expect Aratos to have been, not an original genius, but a gifted man of many parts.

That only one marble portrait of him has so far been identified (no replicas of the Albani head have as yet been recognized) would seem strange considering Aratos' popularity in Roman times, except for the fact that he was popular only in literary circles, not with the general public. This too is an argument in favour of the identification of this type of head as Aratos rather than Chrysippos; for a great many sculptured portraits resembling the other coin type have been found (cf. pp. 191 ff.), corresponding to the widespread popularity of Chrysippos.

KALLIMACHOS

c. 310–c. 235 B.C. Elegiac poet (princeps elegiae, Quint., *Inst. orat.*, x, 1, 58) and scholar. From Cyrene (Suidas, s.v.); said to be a descendant of Battos, founder of Cyrene (Strabo XVII, 837).

Studied in Athens together with Aratos.

Began his teachings in Alexandria. Among his pupils were Eratosthenes, Aristophanes of Byzantion, and Apollonios Rhodios, the last afterwards his opponent.

c. 260 B.C. Was made head of the library of Alexandria by Ptolemy Philadelphos, and wrote a famous poem on a lock of hair of Berenike, Philadelphos' wife.

He combined scholarship with poetic gifts. He left 800 books, both in prose and verse. Was popular in Roman times, and was imitated and translated by Latin writers, e.g., by Catullus and Ovid.

There is no record of a statue having been erected to Kallimachos. Tentative suggestions for his portrait have been: by Dilthey the Pseudo-Seneca type (cf. p. 63); by V. Poulsen (*Portr. gr.*, p. 74) the Menander type; by Schefold (*B.*, pp. 128f., no. 2, p. 211) an interesting head in Copenhagen (I.N. 2740, V. Poulsen, op. cit., no. 56), for which the fillet in the hair would tally with Quintilian's appellation (see above), and the serious physiognomy and the style would fit; by Lippold (*Gr. Portr.*, p. 67) the portrait which was by Amelung and others tentatively identified as Apollonios Rhodios (q.v.). With so little to go on, it is difficult, in fact, to advance any convincing theory.

THEOKRITOS

c. 310–245 B.C. Bucolic poet; founder of pastoral poetry in Greece. Probably of Syracuse (*Gk. Anth.* IX, 434; Athen. VII, 284a). Son of Praxagoras and Philine. Friend of the poet Aratos of Soloi and of the physician Nikias of Miletos. Also had connexions with Kos. Studied with Philetas and Asklepiades of Samos. Went to Alexandria while Ptolemy Soter was still ruler. Obtained also the patronage of Ptolemy Philadelphos, for whom he wrote several idylls. Later returned to Syracuse and lived there under Hieron II.

About thirty of his idylls have survived. They are mostly in literary Doric and picture idealized rural life. They were popular in Roman times, and were imitated by Latin poets, especially by Vergil.

There is no mention in ancient literature of a statue having been erected for him; and little is known of his personality, except what one learns from his poems. A few suggestions for his portrait have, however, been made:

Studniczka (*J.d.I.* 38/39, 1923/1924, pp. 57ff., and *Phil. Woch.* LIV, 1924, cols. 1276f.) pointed out a certain resemblance between the figure inscribed Theokritos dedicating his syrinx to Pan, on a fourteenth-century MS. in the Bibliothèque Nationale (cf. *Mon. Piot* XII, 1905, pl. 12), and that of a shepherd, sitting on a rock surrounded by animals, on a silver dish in the Hermitage, Leningrad (Matzuliewitsch, *Byzantinische Antike* IV, p. 112, no. 4, pls. 31f.; diameter 24 cm.), and thought that the latter could, therefore, represent Theokritos, and perhaps serve for the identification of other portraits of him. It is a possibility. The concentrated expression of the youth on the silver dish may indicate that he is not an ordinary shepherd, and one cannot deny a resemblance to the man on the MS. On the other hand, such MSS. portraits are generally merely invented (cf. p. 12); so that little reliance can be placed on this one. Cf. Rumpf, *Bursian* 245B, 1934, p. 108; M. Mayer, *J.d.I.* XLIV, 1929, p. 295. FIGS. 1662–1663

The suggestion that the Pseudo-Seneca type represents Theokritos (cf. p. 64) would seem to be in contradiction with the gay and light spirit evinced in Theokritos' poems. Cf. Bernoulli II, p. 144.

Picard (*Mon. Piot* XLIV, 1950, pp. 72ff., fig. 11, pl. VIII) suggested that the seated figure on a silver cup from Berthouville in the Cabinet des Médailles perhaps was intended for Theokritos, as a pendant to Menedemos (see my p. 244) on the other side of the cup. Cf. Dontas, *Eikones*, pp. 92f., pl. 37, α. FIG. 1661

It was thought that a profile head wearing a pine wreath on a marble diskos, once in F. Ursinus' collection, may have been intended for Theokritos (cf. Gallaeus-Faber, *Imag.* 142; Bellori, 66; Gronov, *Thes.* III, pl. e). But it is now lost and the drawings, as Bernoulli (II, p. 144) points out, are hardly sufficient to determine even whether a portrait was intended.

APOLLONIOS RHODIOS

c. 295 or 280–c. 215 or 200 B.C. The most important of the Alexandrian epic poets. Of Alexandria (Suidas; Strabo, XIV, p. 655), or Naukratis (Athen. VII, p. 283d; Aelian, N.A. XV, 23); but generally called Rhodios. Son of Silleus. Taught the young prince who afterwards became Ptolemy III Euergetes. Like Kallimachos, he combined scholarly and poetic gifts. Through jealousy of Kallimachos he left Egypt for Rhodes, where he became so popular that he was given the Rhodian franchise.

Later, probably after Kallimachos' death, he returned to Alexandria, and became head of the library.

His most famous work 'Αργοναυτικά is preserved in four books (with the scholia). Varro Atacinus and Valerius Flaccus imitated it, and grammarians annotated it.

No statue erected to him has been recorded.

SUGGESTED IDENTIFICATION

A bronze bust, found in the sea near Livorno with others of Homer, Sophokles, and Aischylos? (q.v.), and now in the Archaeological Museum, Florence, inv. 1647, has been thought to be a portrait of Apollonios Rhodios (cf. Amelung, *Führer*, nos. 271–274, and *Mem. Pont. Acc. Arch.* I, 2, 1924, pp. 122f.; Schefold, *B.*, pp. 128f., no. 1, p. 211; Crome, *Bemerkungen* . . . , pp. 3ff.). The evidence cited for the identification is: (1) that the bust was apparently made as a pendant of that of Homer (both are similarly draped), and should therefore represent an epic poet, but in this case evidently not an invented portrait, like that of Homer, but a real likeness; (2) the style would fit the time of Apollonios Rhodios. All one can say is that the scholarly appearance of the individual in the Florence portrait would tally with what is known of Apollonios, whose *Argonautica* somewhat suffers from being too learned for a poem. Lippold, *Gr. Portr.*, pp. 66f., suggested Kallimachos for this head (cf. p. 241).

FIGS. 1670–1672

Some have thought that this bust represents not Apollonios Rhodios but Hermarchos. But in spite of obvious similarities, there are, I think, too many divergencies to make it likely that the two types are derived from the same Greek original. The drapery in the bronze bust, furthermore, is quite unlike that in the marble figures of Hermarchos (cf. figs. 1319–1320).

PHILISKOS

(Φιλίσκος, Φίλικος), of Korkyra. Son of Philotas. Writer of tragedies and some lyric poetry. Lived at the time of Ptolemy Philadelphos (285–247 B.C.).

Was priest of Dionysos at Alexandria (Suidas).

According to Suidas, he wrote 42 tragedies, but practically nothing has survived. The title of one of them perhaps was *Themistokles*.

According to Pliny (XXXV, 106), Philiskos was represented in a painting by Protogenes in a meditative attitude; (Protogenes) fecit et Philiscum tragoediarum scriptorem meditantem. Based on this statement, Th. Schreiber, *Die hellenistischen Reliefbilder*, text to pl. 84, once suggested that Philiskos was represented in the well known relief in the Lateran Museum with a seated poet holding up a mask (cf. under Menander, p. 229). But the figure there is not really in a meditative attitude, and the mask he is holding is comic, not tragic; cf. Bernoulli II, p. 143.

MOSCHION

Tragic poet, has been dated both in the fourth century and in the early third (cf. bibliography). Several fragments of his plays survive, one entitled *Themistokles*, another *Telephos*, a third *Pheraoi*, i.e. men of Pherai. In the last is mentioned the death of Alexander of Pherai, tyrant 369–358, which supplies a post quem date. If the Moschion whose skeleton appears on a cup from Boscoreale (cf. *infra*) is identical with this tragic poet, he was an Athenian, for he is there inscribed 'Αθηναῖος.

EXTANT PORTRAITS

1. It is this Moschion—rather than some others known by name, e.g., a general of Antigonos, a little known comic writer, a philosopher who died c. 185 B.C., and a physician of the first century B.C.; cf. *R.E.*, s.v. Moschion—who probably was represented in the well-known statuette with modern head and neck, in the National Museum, Naples, inv. 6238. On the plinth the inscription Μοσχίων. From the Farnese Collection. Once in the possession of Hier. Garimbertus. FIGS. 1666–1667

Height with head, 62 cm.; ht. of ancient part 51 cm.

Restorations, besides the head: Left forearm with the scroll, right hand, half of the left foot, folds of the mantle on the left shoulder.

Ursinus, *Imag.*, 30.

Visconti, *Ic. gr.* I, p. 120, pl. VII, 1–3,

Bernoulli II, pp. 55f.

Lippold, *Gr. Portr.*, pp. 62f., fig. 10.

Ruesch, *Guida*, no. 1132.

Dontas, *Eikones*, pp. 45f., pl. 16, β.

Kaibel, *I.G.* XIV, 1187.

Huelsen, no. 32.

The figure is shown seated on a cushioned chair, clothed in a himation, resting his sandalled feet on a footstool. Different heads and hands have from time to time been added to the figure; the present combination, for instance, is different from those shown in Ursinus' *Imagines* or by Visconti.

The date of the Greek original of this statuette may well go back to the fourth century B.C.

There are three replicas of this figure, differing, however, in the addition of a chiton or tunica. Two are life-size, the third is a statuette:

2. The so-called Marcellus, in the Stanza dei Filosofi, Capitoline Museum, no. 75. With alien head. From the Giustiniani Collection.   FIG. 1669
Height 1·70 m.
Restorations: The right shoulder with part of the right upper arm, right hand with scroll, left leg, patches on drapery, corners of cushion, greater part of legs of chair.
Galleria Giustiniani I, 113.
Bernoulli II, p. 56.
Stuart Jones, *Cat.*, p. 258, no. 98.

3. The statue signed by Zenon of Aphrodisias, from the Ludovisi Collection, now in the National Museum of the Terme, inv. 8641. Head alien.   FIG. 1668
Height 1·56 m.; with plinth 1·67 m.
Restorations in body: Right arm, left forearm, front part of right foot, left foot with adjoining drapery, small piece of drapery on right knee, and a large part of the base (except the back portion).
Schreiber, *Ludovisi*, p. 54, no. 16.
Loewy, *Inschriften*, no. 365.
Bernoulli II, p. 56.
Helbig, *F.³*, no. 1315.
Felletti Maj, *Ritratti*, no. 92.
Dontas, *Eikones*, p. 94, pl. 38, α.

4. Headless statuette in the Uffizi, Florence.
Height 35 cm.
Restorations: Head, right hand with scroll, both feet, and front part of base.
Bernoulli II, p. 56.
Dütschke III, p. 172, no. 344.
Mansuelli, *Cat.*, no. 52.

The statuette in Naples inscribed Moschion must directly reproduce the Greek original statue, whereas its near-replicas, where an undergarment is added in addition to the himation, are presumably modifications to serve as Roman portrait statues, according to the well known Roman practice; cf. Lippold, *Kopien und Umbildungen*, 1923, p. 105; Schefold, *B.*, p. 209; Richter, *Proceedings of the American Philosophical Society*, vol. 95, no. 2, 1951, pp. 186ff., and *Three Critical Periods*, pp. 59f.

On one of the silver cups from Boscoreale in the Louvre on which the skeletons of famous Greeks are shown in lively action appears also one inscribed Μοσχίων Ἀθηναῖος, coupled with Sophokles (q.v.). Héron de Villefosse, *Mon. Piot* V, 1899, pp. 60f., pl. VIII.   FIG. 1697

LYKOPHRON

Born at Chalkis in Euboea c. 320 B.C. Son of Lykos. Poet and grammarian.
Frequented the lectures of the philosopher Menedemos at Eretria.
c. 284–283 B.C. went to Alexandria, where he was entrusted by Ptolemy II Philadelphos with the putting in order of the collection of comedies in the Library. The result of this work probably was the lexical compilation Περὶ κωμῳδίας in c. nine books (Athen. XI, 485d).
He wrote 64 (or 46) tragedies (Tzetzes, p. 4, 20. 7, 3 Sch.), of which Suidas gives the titles of twenty. There survives only the *Alexandria*, called by Suidas 'the obscure poem', which has as its subject the fall of Troy and Kassandra's prophecies, couched in intricate language.
Picard, *Mon. Piot* XLIV, 1950, pp. 60ff., fig. 5, pl. VI, suggested that Lykophron was represented on one of the silver cups from Berthouville in the Cabinet des Médailles—shown seated, holding a knotted stick, in conversation with Kassandra; a tragic mask and the prophetic urn are placed between them.   FIGS. 1664–1665
As an alternative to Lykophron, Schefold, *B.*, pp. 216f., suggested Thespis (q.v.), who as founder of tragedy would be an appropriate pendant to Aratos (q.v.) founder of astronomical poetry, represented on the other side of the cup, each accompanied by a Muse.

5. VARIOUS OTHERS

ANAXARCHOS

Of Abdera, Thrace. Time of Alexander the Great. Philosopher; follower of Demokritos, with the same sceptical tendencies. Was nicknamed Εὐδαιμονικός for his belief that happiness was the chief end in life.
Lived at the court of Alexander the Great, whom he accompanied on his Asian campaigns.

After Alexander's death, on his return home, he was seized by Nikokreon, tyrant of Cyprus, whom he had offended in his speeches, and cruelly put to death (Diogenes Laert., IX, 58ff.).
On a contorniate in the Cabinet des Médailles, heads of Anaxarchos and Nikokreon are placed opposite to each other, with names inscribed (cf. Sabatier, *Méd. contorn.*, pl. X, 2; Bernoulli II, p. 99, 1, Münzt. II, no. 10; Cohen,

*Méd. Imp.*², VIII, p. 283, no. 75). On the reverse is the inscription οὐδὲν ἐμοῦ σοῦ ἔσται ἀκκιζυμένου, which Cohen translates 'rien de ce qui est à moi sera à toi, si tu fais le méchant'. Cohen quotes Hase as having doubted the authenticity of the medallion, on account of the forms of the letters; and M. Guarducci, whom I consulted, is of the same opinion. She points out that the forms of the letters in the inscribed names on the obverse and in the inscription on the reverse (note e.g. the δ, ε, ω, μ) are earlier than the fourth century, the period of the contorniates.   FIGS. 1081–1082

Alföldi, in *Late Classical and Medieval Studies in honor of A. M. Friend* (1955), pp. 15f., thought that the same two personages, Anaxarchos and Nikokreon, were represented on a gem in Baltimore.

DION

Of Ephesos. Philosopher, c. 350–280 B.C.? Only known from the base cited below.

On a base, now lost, once in the Villa Mattei, an inscription was noted as follows: Δίων φιλόσοφος Ἐφέσιος, Σθέννι[ς] ἐποίει. Cf. Spon, *Voyage d'Italie* (1678), III, 1, p. 138; Loewy, *Inschriften*, no. 481; Kaibel, *I.G.* XIV, 1149.

Sthennis, of Olynthos and Athens, was a contemporary of Lysippos, and active from the time of Alexander the Great to c. 280 B.C. (Pliny XXXIV, 51; Lippold, *R.E.* 2. Reihe, III, A2, col. 2479). Since the Mattei base belongs to a group (all decorated with an egg moulding) of a later period than that of Sthennis (cf. Loewy, *Inschriften*, nos. 481–484), some have thought that it must have supported a copy of Sthennis' statue, not the original. But as the Roman copyists practically never cited the name of the Greek creator of the statue that they were reproducing, it seems more likely that this and the other statues were Greek originals, brought to Italy in Roman times, the bases having, as usual, been left behind, and new ones supplied. For the other bases cf. my pp. 160, 210.

MENEDEMOS

Of Eretria, born c. 319 B.C. Son of Kleisthenes. Of a good but poor family. Philosopher and statesman.

He is said first to have been a soldier, but to have abandoned the military life on meeting Plato (Diog. Laert. II, 125). Pupil of Stilpo at Megara and of Pheidon in Elis (Diog. Laert. II, 126).

Returned to Eretria and founded his own school of philosophy there.

Was sent as an envoy to Ptolemy and to Lysimachos.

Was accused of intrigues with Antigonos Gonatas.

Died when 74 years old.

PORTRAITS RECORDED AND SUGGESTED

Diogenes Laertios (II, 132) refers to a 'small statue', εἰκόνιον, of Menedemos, which represented him almost naked, in the stadium at Eretria.

Ch. Picard (*Mon. Piot* XLIV, 1950, pp. 67ff., fig. 9, pl. VII) made the suggestion that a figure on one of the silver cups from Berthouville, in the Cabinet des Médailles, was intended for Menedemos. He would be a pendant to Theokritos (q.v.) shown on the other side of the cup.   FIG. 1073

Studniczka, in his article on Imagines Illustrium (*J.d.I.* XXXVIII–IX, 1923–24, pp. 64ff.), in which he tried to identify the figures on the Boscoreale frescoes as members of the Macedonian family, suggested that the elderly man with a philosopher-like mien, leaning on his stick, was Menedemos, teacher of Antigonos Gonatas (cf. his p. 81 and pl. II).

EUDOXOS

c. 408–c. 355 B.C. Mathematician, physician, and astronomer. Of Knidos. Pupil of Archytas in geometry and of Philistion and Theomedon in medicine. Son of Aischines. Cf. Diog. Laert. VIII, 86–89.

When he was 23 years old he went to Athens and attended Plato's lectures. Then returned to Knidos.

381–380 Studied astronomy in Egypt.

c. 368 Went to Athens; later returned again to Knidos.

Some of his theories are included in Euclid's books.

He is said to have been the first to have explained the motions of the planets in Greece.

Aratos' *Phainomena* is said to have been a versification of Eudoxos' prose work of the same title; and Euclid's *Elements of Geometry* to have been largely based on Eudoxos' writings. Strabo IX, 390–391, calls him μαθηματικὸς ἀνήρ.

PORTRAIT EXTANT

On a relief in the National Museum of Budapest, inv. 4778, inscribed Εὔδοξος, is a seated man, enveloped in a himation, bending forward (head missing).   FIG. 1679 Height c. 26·5 cm.

Cf. Hekler, *Oest Jahr.* XI, 1908, Beibl., cols. 196f, and *Sammlung antiker Skulpturen* (1929), pp. 60f., fig. 49; Schefold, *B.*, pp. 156f., no. 4; Lippold, *Gr. Portr.*, p. 59, fig. 9. The attitude suggests that Eudoxos was shown in the act of teaching, with perhaps a companion in front of him (cf. Lippold, loc. cit.).

EUCLID (Εὐκλείδης)

Of Alexandria. Born c. 330 B.C. Active under Ptolemy I (306–283 B.C.). Famous mathematician. Founded a school in Alexandria.

Little is known of his life, but a number of his writings have survived. His fame rests on his text-book *The Elements* (τὰ στοιχεῖα), in 13 parts—on plane geometry, proportion, properties of numbers, incommensurable magnitudes, and solid geometry. Full use is made of the work of his predecessors, but much new is added. It remained the text-book on geometry in all schools for centuries, and has only recently been superseded. For this and his other works cf. Hultsch, *R.E.* VI, 1 (1907), cols. 1003ff.

It is said of him that when his royal pupil asked him a shorter way to geometry, he replied 'There is no royal short cut to geometry', μὴ εἶναι βασιλικὴν ἀτραπὸν πρὸς γεωμετρίαν (Geminos, μαθημάτων θεωρία; Hultsch, op. cit., col. 1004).

Sidonius Apollinaris (*Epist.* IX, 14) describes a portrait of Euclid as digitis propter mensurarum spatia laxatis.

It has been thought that a reflection of this portrait is preserved in a miniature drawing of the sixth century A.D., the so-called Codex Arcerianus in the library of Wolfenbüttel (no. 2403), which represents a seated, bearded man, wearing a taenia and mantle, holding an open scroll in his left hand, and the fingers of his right hand extended; cf. F. Marx, 'Digitis computans', in Fleckeisens *Jahrbücher*, 27, Suppl. 1902, pp. 195ff.; also Bernoulli II, pp. 121f; Schefold, *B.*, pp. 170; H. Swarzenski, *Art Bull.* XXII, 1940, p. 10, fig. 6. The gesture of a raised hand with fingers extended is, however, a common one and not restricted to this drawing (cf. p. 191).

ARCHIMEDES

c. 287–212 B.C., of Syracuse. The greatest mathematician of antiquity. Son of the astronomer Pheidias.

He studied for some time at Alexandria where he came in contact with the famous mathematicians Konon, Dositheos, and Eratosthenes, to all of whom he dedicated some of his writings. Later he returned to Syracuse where he was on intimate terms with king Hieron II and his son Gelon.

Famous for his inventions, for instance, of the water-screw (κοχλίας) and of the machines which were used against the Roman besiegers of Syracuse.

212 B.C. He was killed by a Roman soldier at the sack of Syracuse, while busy on some mathematical problem. M. Claudius Marcellus (who had given special instructions that Archimedes should be spared) gave him an honorary burial and cared for his surviving family. His tomb, marked with a cylinder circumscribing a sphere—of which the mutual proportions had been discovered by him—was found by Cicero beneath a tangle of thorns in 75 B.C. (Cic., *Tusc.* V, 64ff.).

Some of Archimedes' writings have been preserved (cf. Hultsch, *R.E.* II, 1, cols. 509ff.).

ATTEMPTED IDENTIFICATIONS

No certain portrait of this famous man survives; but there have been several suggestions:

The mosaic in Frankfurt with a representation of Archimedes threatened by a Roman soldier was once thought to be ancient; cf. Winter, *82. Berl. Winckelmannsprogr.*, who dated it in the Roman period and believed it to be a copy of a Greek painting made soon after Archimedes' death. Since then, however, arguments have been advanced to indicate a date in the Renaissance; cf. Brinckmann in Goethert, *Zur Kunst der römischen Republik*, pp. 56ff., who pointed out that the rendering of the drapery excluded a Roman origin. (On more recent representations of Archimedes cf. A. Zinger, *Weltall*, 34, 1935, pp. 126f.)

Several other representations once believed to refer to Archimedes have also had to be discarded:

The inscription Archimed on the medallion with a head of Sophokles in the Capitoline Museum (cf. p. 126, no. 7) has been shown to be an addition by Nicol. Coroma (cf. Bottari I, p. 47; Bernoulli II, p. 178).

The painted inscription on a herm in Naples, once thought to be 'Αρχιμ . . . ., has been shown to be 'Αρχιδα . . 5 (cf. p. 160).

Various heads on coins and gems thought to represent Archimedes have proved to be modern; cf. Bernoulli II, p. 178.

The head in the Capitoline Museum, once thought to represent Aischylos (cf. p. 123), has on phrenological grounds been identified as a mathematician, and so a possible Archimedes (cf. P. J. Möbius, *Neue Jahrb. für das klassische Alterthum* III, 1900, pp. 161ff.). But see Bernoulli II, p. 179.

Winter, loc. cit., saw a resemblance between the Archimedes on the Frankfurt mosaic and the bronze head from Herculaneum (Schefold, *B.*, p. 125, no. 2), for which, however, other candidates have been suggested (cf. p. 120).

If the figure in the miniature drawing of the sixth century A.D. is not Euclid (cf. *supra*), it has been suggested that it may represent Archimedes. But, in any case, the portrait would have no iconographical value.

SATYROS

Of Elis. Son of Lysianax.

According to Pausanias (VI, 4, 5), Satyros was victorious in boxing five times at Nemea, twice at Delphi, and twice at Olympia, and for this a statue was set up to him at Olympia, the work of Silanion, the Athenian sculptor: Σάτυρος δὲ 'Ηλεῖος Λυσιάνακτος πατρός, γένους δὲ τοῦ 'Ιαμιδῶν, ἐν Νεμέᾳ πεντάκις ἐνίκησε πυκτεύων καὶ Πυθοῖ τε δὶς καὶ δὶς ἐν 'Ολυμπίᾳ. τέχνη δὲ 'Αθηναίου Σιλανίωνος ὁ ἀνδριάς ἐστι.

When a bronze head, presumably broken from a statue, designated as that of a boxer by the swollen cartilages of the ears, and apparently assignable by its style to the fourth century B.C. (cf. *infra*), was found at Olympia, it was tempting to think that it represented Satyros, the work of Silanion, mentioned by Pausanias. That the features are individualized, even though those of an athlete, recalls the statement by Pliny (xxxiv, 16) that in the statues erected for victors in games only those were made to look like the individuals honoured who had been victorious three times. With the long list of victories to his credit, Satyros would have been entitled to have his statue be a real portrait (cf. p. 37). Moreover, this would also account for his relatively advanced age. But of course there are many other possibilities. FIG. 1675

The head is in the National Museum, Athens, 6439.

Height 28 cm.

No restorations.

Furtwängler, *Olympia* IV, pp. 10f., pl. II (suggested the son of Philandrides, victor in the pankration, whose statue was made by Lysippos).

Schmidt, *J.d.I.* XLIX, 1934, pp. 190f.

Laurenzi, *Ritratti*, no. 34.

The date assigned to the head has ranged from the fifth century (Kekule), to the fourth (Schrader, Furtwängler, Laurenzi), and the third (Wolters). Schmidt, loc. cit., saw a stylistic resemblance between it and the head of Plato at Holkham Hall (cf. p. 167, no. 15).

Whatever its date and identity, it is a precious original work by an outstanding Greek sculptor.

PHRYNE

Of Thespiai. Lived during the second and third quarters of the fourth century B.C. A famous hetaira. Loved by Praxiteles and Hypereides.

Her beauty is said to have inspired Apelles in his creation of the Aphrodite Anadyomene, and Praxiteles in that of the Aphrodite of Knidos.

According to Kallistratos in Athenaios XIII, 591d, Phryne offered to rebuild the walls of Thebes if an inscription were added that Alexander destroyed the walls and the hetaira Phryne rebuilt them—a saying that evidently alluded to her enormous wealth: ᾿Αλέξανδρος μὲν κατέσκαψεν, ἀνέστησεν δὲ Φρύνη ἡ ἑταίρα.

STATUES RECORDED

According to Pausanias (IX, 27, 5), there was a marble statue of Phryne by Praxiteles at Thespiai, set up next to one of Aphrodite, also by Praxiteles: ἐνταῦθα καὶ αὐτοῦ Πραξιτέλους, ᾿Αφροδίτη καὶ Φρύνης ἐστὶν εἰκών, λίθου καὶ ἡ Φρύνη καὶ ἡ θεός. Cf. also Alkiphron, *Epist.* IV, 1, fragm. 3.

Pausanias (x, 15, 1) also mentions another statue of Phryne by Praxiteles, of gilded bronze, dedicated by herself at Delphi. This statue of Phryne is mentioned by many other writers (cf. Overbeck, *Schriftquellen*, nos. 1269ff.), and enjoyed great fame. From Dio Chrysost., *Orat.*, 37, 28, we learn that it was placed on a column, like the statue of Gorgias close by (cf. p. 120).

Tatian (*Orat. ad Gr.*, ch. 32, ed. Schwartz, p. 35, 3ff.) records statues of Phryne and Glykera by a sculptor from Olynthos named Herodotos.

ATTEMPTED IDENTIFICATIONS

No reliable identification of a portrait of Phryne has so far been made. Furtwängler, *Masterpieces*, pp. 320f., made the attractive suggestion that the Phryne at Delphi must have looked like the Towneley Aphrodite in the British Museum. In the double herm at Compiègne, where Hypereides is perhaps represented (cf. p. 210), the second head (face missing) has been thought to have been that of Phryne, whom Hypereides defended in a famous lawsuit (cf. p. 210).

B: THE THIRD AND SECOND CENTURIES B.C.

BALAKROS

Son of Meleagros. Third to second century B.C.
The name is inscribed on a statue base found at Pergamon: Βάλακρος Μελεάγρου, in two pieces (inv. II, 134). Found in a Turkish tower.
Cf. Fraenkel, *Die Inschriften von Pergamon*, no. 201, who suggests that this Balakros was the author of Μακεδονικά, a work known through citations by Stephanos of Byzantion. Balakros was a Macedonian name. Cf. under Apollonios.

APOLLONIOS

Son of Philotas. Third to second century B.C.
The name is inscribed on a statue base found in Pergamon, south of the sanctuary of Athena: Ἀ]πο[λ]λώ[νι]ος Φιλώ-[του].
In two pieces, found respectively in 1881 and 1883 (inv. nos. III, 149, II, 119).
Fraenkel, *Die Inschriften von Pergamon* (1890), no. 202, suggests that this Apollonios was the one from Aphrodisias, who wrote the Καρικά. Not so appropriate, according to Fraenkel, would seem to be the Apollonios of Acharnai, author of Περὶ ἑορτῶν, or the historian Apollonios of Askelon, neither of them sufficiently famous.
A similar base, inscribed Balakros, presumably referred to the author of Μακεδονικά (cf. *supra*).

ARISTOMACHOS

Of Soloi, Cilicia. Period uncertain, but has been computed to have lived between the time of Aristotle's *Hist. anim.* IX, and Hyginus' *Liber de apibus*. Cf. Wellmann, *R.E.* II, I (1895), col. 946.
Observed bees for 58 years and wrote a book on the subject entitled μελισσουργικά (Pliny I, II; XIII, 131).
L. Agostini (*Gemme* II, pl. 27) suggested that this Aristomachos was represented on a carnelian in the Dolce collection (Dolce, *Catalogo* II, T, 15; Federigo Dolce, *Dugento Gemme* (Rome, 1792), no. 129; Cades 35, no. 110), where a seated man is shown in a meditative attitude, apparently watching what Agostini thought looked like beehives, attached to an altar-like seat, with two bees hovering round them and a tree right and left. FIG. 1676
Bellori, 6; Gronov, *Thes.* II, 75.
Visconti, *Ic. gr.* I, p. 263, pl. 21a.
Bernoulli II, p. 190 (there said to be in Florence; but I was informed that it was not in the Archaeological Museum).
To judge by a photograph of the Cades impression, which I was able to obtain from the German Institute in Rome, I do not think that either beehives or bees are actually represented, but rather vine leaves and clusters of grapes. Nor do I feel sure of the antiquity of the gem.

On account of a supposed resemblance to the man on the gem, Bottari (I, 59) thought that a bust in the Capitoline Museum (Stuart Jones, *Cat.*, p. 239, no. 50, pl. 54) might represent Aristomachos.

HIPPARCHOS

c. 180–125 B.C. Of Nikaia, Bithynia. Astronomer and founder of trigonometry.
He was the most esteemed astronomer of antiquity, author of a catalogue which comprised 1080 stars. Taught chiefly in Rhodes and Alexandria.
Later, c. A.D. 150, Claudius Ptolemaios gave definite form to Hipparchos' astronomy in his *Syntaxis*, and this remained authoritative until the time of Copernicus (1473–1543).

On bronze coins of Nikaia, Hipparchos is represented as a partly draped, bearded figure, seated in front of a globe set on a pillar: inscribed Ἵππαρχος Νικαιέων or simply Νικαιέων. There are several variations of the same composition, ranging from the time of Commodus to that of Gallienus. FIG. 1677
Cf. Bürchner, pp. 127f., pl. VI, 26; Bernoulli II, p. 186, I, Münzt. II, 15; Schefold, *B.*, pp. 172f., no. 30.

A badly preserved coin of Nikaia, with the head of Antoninus Pius on the obverse, has on the reverse a head in profile to the right, inscribed Ἵππαρχος Νικαιέων. Cf. Bernoulli II, p. 186, I, Münzt. II, 16; Schefold, *B.*, p. 221. FIG. 1678
For some heads on gems tentatively identified as Hipparchos cf. Bernoulli II, p. 187, and my p. 240 (a gem in the Fitzwilliam Museum).

POLYBIOS

Of Megalopolis, c. 203–c. 120 B.C. Historian of Rome. Son of the Achaean general Lykortas.
167/6 Was one of the 1000 hostages taken to Rome, and stayed there for sixteen years.
While in Rome became the friend of prominent Romans (e.g. of Scipio) and of the philosopher Panaitios, studied the Roman constitution, and began his famous history.
150 When his exile terminated he travelled extensively, in the company of Scipio, to Gaul, Spain, and Carthage; and finished his history. In it he posed the questions of the cause of Rome's greatness, and set forth the quality of Greece's contributions.

He was able to act as mediator for his countrymen on several occasions.

c. 120 Died, 82 years old, in consequence of a fall from a horse.

He was much honoured during his lifetime and later. His *Universal History* ('Ιστορίαι), in 40 books, comprised the period 220/19–145/44 B.C. Extensive portions of it are preserved.

PORTRAITS RECORDED

Pausanias mentions a number of figures carved in relief on slabs which were set up in Polybios' honour: in Achaia, in a temple at Mantineia (VIII, 9, 1: ἀνὴρ ἐπείργασται στήλη Πολύβιος ὁ Λυκόρτα); on the market place of Megalopolis (VIII, 30, 8); in the peribolos of the Despoina in Akakesion (VIII, 37, 2); in Tegea (VIII, 48, 8); also a statue (ἀνδριάς) near the temple of Kore in Pallantion (VIII, 44, 5). In Olympia was found a base with the inscription: Ἡ πόλις ἡ τῶν Ἡλείων Πολύβιον Λυκόρτα Μεγαλοπολείτην, 'The city of the Eleans (set it up) for Polybios of Megalopolis, son of Lykortas'. Cf. Dittenberger, *Inschriften aus Olympia*, no. 243.

Also in Olympia were found two inscriptions citing statues erected in honour of two men called Polybios, of the third century A.D.: T. Ph. Polybios. Cf. Dittenberger *Arch. Ztg.* XXXV, 1877, p. 193, nos. 101, 102; Ziegler, *R.E.*, XXI, 2 (1952), col. 1462. That these two men may have been descendants of the historian has been thought likely since in one of the epigrams is mentioned the father named Lykortas—evidently a name recurring in the family:

Τοῦτο Λυκόρτα παιδὶ πόλις περικαλλὲς ἄγαλμα
        ἀντὶ καλῶν ἔργων εἵσατο Πουλυβίῳ.

ATTEMPTED IDENTIFICATION

Milchhöfer (*Arch. Ztg.* XXXIX, 1881, pp. 153ff.) suggested that the stele of a warrior, represented wearing exomis and himation, the right arm extended, a spear in his left hand, a shield and a helmet by his side, was intended for Polybios— the evidence being that the slab was found at Kleitor, that is, in Arcadia, and that it bears the inscription Ἀντὶ καλῶν ἔργων εἵσατο, to which Milchhöfer added Πολυβίῳ for the missing name (since he thought he saw traces of a few letters); furthermore, the same name recurs in a similar dedicatory inscription of the Roman imperial period (cf. *supra*). It is a possibility, and the identification has been accepted by some. The appearance of the man on the stele as a young warrior is, however, not exactly how one imagines the historian Polybios to have been represented; and, incidentally, Kleitor is not one of the places cited by Pausanias as having erected monuments in honour of Polybios. The stele is in the schoolhouse at Mazeïka (Ziegler, loc. cit.), but has by now lost its head and the inscription. A cast of it, with head, was in Berlin, but seems to have been destroyed during the last war, for it cannot now be found—so Frl. Rohde informs me.   FIGS. 1673, 1674
Gurlitt, *Ath. Mitt.* VI, 1881, pp. 154ff., pl. V.

Dittenberger, *Inschriften von Olympia* (1896), no. 449.
Hiller von Gaertringen, *I.G.* V, 2, 370.
Bernoulli II, pp. 185f. (doubtful of the identification).
Wolters, in Friedrichs-Wolters, *Gipsabgüsse in Berlin*, no. 1854 (does not accept identification).
Studniczka, *Sitzungsberichte, Leipzig*, 36, 1911, pp. 3ff. (accepts identification).
Möbius, *J.d.I.* XLIX, 1934, p. 57, figs. 5, 6 (on pp. 52, 53)—accepts identification.
Schefold, B., pp. 146f., no. 5, p. 213 (accepts identification).
Ziegler, *R.E.* XXI, 2 (1952), cols. 1462f. (leaves the question open).

KARNEADES

214/213–129/128 B.C., of Cyrene. Philosopher, founder of the Third, so-called New, Academy in Athens. Son of Epikomos.

Studied philosophy with the Stoic Diogenes of Babylon (Cic., *Acad.* II, 98).

Went to Athens and studied under Hegesinous of Pergamon, who was then the head of the Academy, and whom he presently succeeded (Diog. Laert. IV, 60).

Studied the writings of the Stoics, particularly of Chrysippos, and then attacked them.

156–155 Was a member of the delegation sent to Rome by the Athenians to try to reduce the fine of 500 talents imposed on them for the destruction of Oropos.

While in Rome he delivered lectures which were epoch-making for the study of philosophy in Italy (cf. Cicero, *De orat.* II, 157ff., and *ad Att.* XII, 23, 2). Especially noteworthy were his two lectures on the nature of justice, the first on ideal justice, the second on practical justice. Plutarch (*Cato Major* XXII) has left a vivid account of Karneades' visit: 'Upon the arrival of these philosophers, the most studious of the city's youth hastened to wait upon them, and became their devoted and admiring listeners. The charm (χάρις) of Karneades especially, which had boundless power, and a fame not inferior to its power (ἧς δύναμίς τε πλείστη καὶ δόξα τῆς δυνάμεως οὐκ ἀποδέουσα), won large and sympathetic audiences, and filled the city, like a rushing, mighty wind, with the noise of his praises. Reports spread far and wide that a Greek of amazing talent, who disarmed all opposition by the magic of his eloquence, (ὡς ἀνὴρ Ἕλλην εἰς ἔκπληξιν ὑπερφυὴς πάντα κηλῶν καὶ χειρούμενος) had infused a tremendous passion into the youth of the city, in consequence of which they forsook their other pleasures and pursuits and were enthusiastic about philosophy' (ἐνθουσιῶσι περὶ φιλοσοφίαν). Consequently Cato is said to have ordered Karneades out of the country.

Karneades denied the possibility of knowledge, believing only in probability; he denied validity of the argument with which one can prove the existence of the gods; and attacked the Stoic belief in fatalism. But he combined this scepticism with a practical belief in virtue, for he thought that without it there could be no happiness.

According to Strabo (XVII, 838), Karneades was the greatest

of the Academicians. His fame was due not only to his common-sense philosophy, but to his gift of oratory and dialectics, so that even students of rhetoric would go to his lectures (Diog. Laert. IV, 62–63). Diogenes Laertios (IV, 63) speaks of 'his mighty voice', ἦν δὲ καὶ μεγαλοφωνότατος. Cicero (De orat. III, 18) speaks of his 'quickness of mind and almost divine eloquence', divina quadam celeritate ingenii et dicendi copia Carneades. The school flourished under his presidency, and he was revered by his students (Suidas, s.v.). 137/136 He retired as head of the school, and was succeeded first by the younger Karneades, and after the latter's death by Krates of Tarsos.

129/128 Died 85 years old.

Karneades left no writings, but his teachings are preserved through the notes taken by his pupils, e.g. by Kleitomachos (Diog. Laert. IV, 67; Cicero, Acad. II, 98); and they have come down to us in the writings of Cicero, Plutarch, Sextus, and others. Karneades was the logical product of a sceptical age, and his teachings had a profound effect on the thinking of the Graeco-Roman world.

APPEARANCE

Nothing specific is known regarding his appearance; for one need not take seriously Diogenes Laertios' statement (IV, 62) that he studied so incessantly that he forgot to cut his hair and nails. According to Diogenes Laertios (IV, 66), he suddenly became blind during one night, λέγεται καὶ τὰς ὄψεις νυκτὸς ὑποχυθῆναι.

IDENTIFICATION

The identification of the portraits of Karneades was made possible by a bust inscribed with his name, once in the Farnese collection, now lost, but of which two casts survive (see below). Before the discovery of these casts, the portraits of Karneades, Hippokrates, and Chrysippos were often confused with one another.

STATUE RECORDED

Cicero (De fin., v, 4), after his visit to Athens, speaks of the 'imago' of Karneades: 'All over Athens, I know, there are many reminders of eminent men in the actual places where they lived; but at the present moment it is that hall over there which appeals to me; for not long ago it belonged to Karneades. I fancy I see him now (for his portrait is well known) and I can imagine that the very place where he used to sit misses the sound of his voice and mourns the loss of that mighty intellect', Hoc autem tempore, etsi multa in omne parte Athenarum sunt in ipsis locis indicia summorum virorum, tamen ego illa moveor exhedra: modo enim fuit Carneadis; quem videre videor (est enim nota imago) a sedeque ipsa, tanta ingeni magnitudine orbata desiderari illam vocem puto.

For the base of this statue, found in the Athenian agora, see below.

PORTRAITS ONCE AND NOW EXTANT

1. A bust, inscribed Καρνεα..., horizontally across the folds of the drapery, once in the Piccolo Palazzo Farnese, Rome. After the Farnese collections were moved to Naples, the bust appears in the inventories of 1796 and 1805 (cf. Studniczka, in Arndt-Br., nos. 505–506). Since then it has disappeared. Visconti, in his Ic. gr. (1808–11), had to publish the bust from a cast, though he says he had often seen the original in Rome, where he could assure himself that the head belonged to the bust. Albacuni's cast was subsequently also lost, but a second one was found by Arndt in the Art Historical Museum in Copenhagen (now in the cast collection of the Art Museum). Still another cast is in the Accademia delle Belle Arti in Ravenna, acquired apparently in 1829 (Arias). It was located and photographed for me by Miss Alison Frantz.   FIGS. 1682–1684, 1688

Gallaeus-Faber, 42.
Bellori, Imag. philos., 10; Gronov, Thes., v.
Visconti, Ic. gr., pp. 239f., pl. XIX, 1, 2.
Bernoulli II, pp. 181f., pl. XXIV.
Arndt-Br., 505–506.
Arias, J.d.I. LXVIII, 1953, pp. 119-120, and note 39.
Kaibel, I.G. XIV, 1171,
Huelsen, no. 21.

2. Relief of a head, once evidently part of a medallion, in Holkham Hall. Bought in 1752 by the architect Brettingham from Cavaceppi.   FIG. 1687

Height of head, from crown to end of beard, 28 cm.
Restorations: Back of head, medallion with inscription Karneades, end of nose, rim of ear, parts of forehead and of neck. The upward inclination of the head is certainly exaggerated, but some movement in that direction is implied by the wrinkles on the preserved part of the neck and the shape of the eye (cf. F. Poulsen, loc. cit.).
Michaelis, Anc. Marbl., p. 318, no. 511.
F. Poulsen, English Country Houses, no. 20.
Schefold, B., pp. 140f., 213.
The identification as Karneades in the inscription must be due to Cavaceppi having seen the Farnese bust in Rome as F. Poulsen, loc. cit., said.

3. Herm in the National Museum, Ravenna. Found with other herms north of Porto Corsini in the sea at the mouth of the river Po. Cf. pp. 95, 96.   FIGS. 1693–1696

Height 51 cm.; ht. of face 27 cm.
No restorations. In excellent preservation. The head was broken from the herm, but belongs.
Arias, J.d.I. LXVIII, 1933, pp. 109ff., figs. 19-21.
Jacopi, Le Arti v, 1943, pp. 139f., pl. 57.

4. Head, mounted on a modern herm, in the Palazzo Riccardi, Florence.
Life-size.
Restorations: The nose in marble, a piece of the upper lip in plaster.
Perhaps=Dütschke II, no. 200 ('erinnert im allgemeinen an Homer').
Coco, Cat. (forthcoming). I owe my knowledge of this head to Signora Martinelli Coco.

5. Head in the Antikenmuseum, Basle, inv. 201. It is turned slightly to its right.   FIGS. 1689–1692

Height, with neck, 35 cm.; ht. of head 27·7 cm.

No restorations. Even the nose is ancient.

'The head was evidently made for insertion in a statue, which, since there is no dowel hole at the bottom, was presumably represented seated' (Berger, loc. cit.).

Berger, *Kunstwerke der Antike, Sammlung Käppeli*, A 19.

Lullies, *Griechische Plastik, Vasen, und Kleinkunst aus Privatbesitz.* Staatliche Kunstsammlungen, Kassel, 1964, no. 8.

6. Head, mounted on a modern bust inscribed KARNEADES, in the Casa del Labrador, Aranjuez. From the Azara excavations at Tivoli.   FIGS. 1685–1686

Height, with modern bust, 54 cm.

The nose is restored.

Hübner, no. 166.

Bernoulli II, p. 183.

Arndt-Br., 637–638.

von Heintze, in Hekler, *Bild. b. Gr.*³, p. 70, no. 5.

7. I am inclined to think that the much battered marble head (ht. 28 cm., top and back missing) in the F. J. Dölger-Institut, Bonn, published by H.v. Heintze (*Jahrbuch für Antike und Christentum* VI, 1963, pp. 35ff., and there dated in the last quarter of the 3rd century A.D.), is a late antique version of the portrait of Karneades, comparable to the late version of the portrait of Plato (figs. 938, 941).

8. In the Stoa of Attalos in Athens was found in 1880 the base of a statue inscribed: 'Attalos and Ariarathes dedicated (this statue of) Karneades, the Athenian', Καρνεάδην 'Αζηνιέα "Ατταλος καὶ 'Αριαράθης Συπαλήττι[οι] ἀνέθηκαν. FIG. 1681

Hymettan marble. Broken at back. Height 33 cm.; width 71·5 cm.; depth 82 (originally c. 94) cm.

On the top face are two deep holes evidently for the attachment of the bronze, seated statue. See drawing.

Attalos, 2nd king of Pergamon (159–138 B.C.) and Ariarathes, 5th king of Cappadocia (163–130 B.C.) both were pupils of Karneades. The statue must have been erected round the middle of the second century B.C. Incidentally we learn from this inscription that Karneades obtained Athenian citizenship. The base is now exhibited in the colonnade of the Stoa of Attalos.

Köhler, *Ath. Mitt.* V, 1880, pp. 284ff.

Dittenberger, *Sylloge*³, no. 666.

I.G. II–III², 3781.

H. A. Thompson, *Hesperia* XIX, 1950, pp. 318f.; *Agora Guide*, pp. 133f.

9. A herm with an alien head (of Antisthenes, cf. p. 180, no. 8), inscribed 'Karneades, the son of Philokomos, of Cyrene', Καρνεάδης Φιλοκώμου Κηρηναῖος, was once in the possession of F. Ursinus (cf. Statius, *Illustr. vir. vultus* XIV; Ursinus, *Imag.*, p. 66 (there shown without head). Kaibel, *I.G.* XIV, 1170; Huelsen, no. 20). It has now disappeared.

10. Whether the head on a second herm, also now 'lost', which Faber saw in F. Ursinus' collection and which he

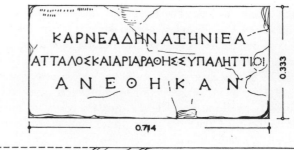

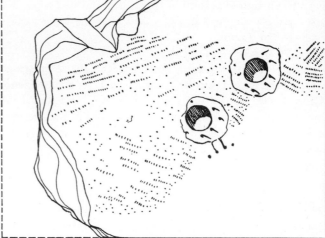

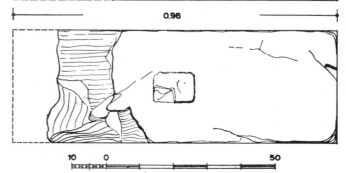

Inscribed base of a statue of Karneades. Agora Museum, Athens

described (*Imag.* to no. 42) as representing Karneades in extreme old age (decrepitus jam et aetatis nimirum senescentis exhibens) really was a portrait of Karneades one cannot tell.

In Bernoulli II, pp. 183f., is given a list of portraits which more or less resemble the certainly identified ones, but are not acceptable as Karneades: In Woburn Abbey (Furtwängler, *Statuenkopien*, pl. 8, p. 47); Aranjuez (Hübner, no. 166; Arndt-Br., 637–638—by me, however, accepted as Karneades, see no. 6); Vatican, Museo Chiaramonti, *Vat. Kat.* I, no. 598 (=Hippokrates, q.v.); Capitoline Museum Stanza dei Filosofi, no. 7 (Stuart Jones, p. 223, *Cat.* no. 8); Museo Torlonia, Visconti, *Cat.* no. 63; Louvre, (Arndt-Br. 139–140); and British Museum 1846 (=Chrysippos, q.v.). To these doubtfuls one should add the head from the Villa dei Pisoni, Herculaneum, in the National Museum, Naples, inv. 6152 (Ruesch, *Guida*, no. 1143; Hekler, *Portraits antiques*, pl. 94a), which was called 'a variant' of the portrait of Karneades by F. Poulsen (*English Country Houses*, p. 47).

Bust of Karneades, now lost. Drawing by Gallaeus

age, and speaks of its resemblance to a painting of a blind man by Giordano (17th century), called by him Karneades. But blindness could only have come to Karneades late in life; and the Pseudo-Seneca type is fundamentally different from the certified portrait of Karneades.

CONCLUSIONS

The portraits listed above under nos. 1–6 show a man of about 50 years of age, wearing chiton and mantle, with a high, wrinkled forehead, a lined face, a deep indentation at the bridge of the nose, a sensitive mouth, with the upper lip much more prominent than the lower. The hair is carved in fairly short, closely adhering locks, the beard is relatively short, the expression alert, testifying to an inquisitive, rather matter of fact mind.

It has been suggested that this portrait may go back to the Greek original erected on the Athenian agora, and this may of course be so.

The Ravenna, Basle, and Farnese heads were evidently mechanically copied from the same Greek original by the pointing process, for the locks of hair and beard closely correspond in the three, with only the usual minor variations. The Holkham relief, on the other hand, must have been worked free-hand, and shows considerable divergencies.

The headless, seated statue, from the Villa Patrizi, now in the Metropolitan Museum, New York, 09.221.4, signed Ζεῦξις ἐποίησεν (cf. Gatti, *Not. d. Sc.*, 1904, p. 226, Richter, *MMA. Sc. Cat.*, no. 190), cannot be the type of figure to which the Karneades portraits belonged, as was thought by Lippold and others; for it was evidently shown playing the kithara, and, therefore, represented a poet, not a philosopher. Moreover, the head in the inscribed bust (no. 1) is turned to the (spectator's) left, whereas the head of the statue must have been turned to the right.   FIG. 1680

D. F. Darcy (*Art Bulletin* XXXIX, 1957, pp. 207ff.) suggested that the Pseudo-Seneca type represented Karneades in old

ZENON

Of Sidon. Epicurean philosopher. Lived at the turn of the second and first century B.C. He was already an old man when Cicero and Atticus heard him in Athens in 79 B.C. Pupil and admirer of Karneades (q.v.).

Only fragments of his writings survive; his doctrines are, however, known through the writings of his pupil Philodemos, which have come to light at Herculaneum.

Some have thought that the portrait inscribed Zenon, which was discovered at Herculaneum, represents the Epicurean Zenon, both on account of its provenance, and because he is known to have been of a quarrelsome disposition, which is suggested by the cast of features in the portrait. But see p. 188.

ILLUSTRATIONS

Figs. 882–884

(Alexa...

Figs. 885–887

(M...

XENOPHON

Fig. 890   (Terme Museum)

888–889   (Naples)

(Copenhagen)   Figs. 892–893   (Vatican)

ARCHIDAMOS III (Figs. 888-889) AND PHOKION (?)

Fig. 894   (Oslo)

Figs. 895–896   (Oslo)

Fig. 897   coin cf
                  Kyzikos

Fig. 898   coin of Kos

Figs. 899–900

(British Museum)

OLYMPIODOROS (Figs. 894–896) · TIMOTHEOS (?) (Fig. 897) · MAUSSOLC

Figs. 901–902   (British Museum)

MAUSSOLOS AND ARTEMISIA

Fig. 903   10 (Berlin)

ΠΛΑΤΩΝ

Fig. 905   10 (Berlin)

ΠΛΑΤΩΝ
ΑΡΙΣΤΩΝΟΣ
ΑΘΗΝΑΙΟΣ

ΑΙΤΙΑ ΕΛΟΜΕ
ΝΩ ΘΕΟΣ·
ΑΝΑΙΤΙΟΣ

ΨΥΧΗ ΔΕ ΠΑΣ
ΑΘΑΝΑΤΟΣ

Fig. 906   8 (Tivoli)

Fig. 904   10 (Berlin)

ΠΛΑΤΩΝ
ΑΡΙΣΤΩΝΟΣ
ΑΘΗΝΑΙΟΣ

ΑΙΤΙΑ ΕΛΟΜΕ
ΝΩ ΘΕΟΣ
ΑΝΑΙΤΙΟΣ

ΨΥΧΗ ΔΕ ΠΑΣΑ
ΑΘΑΝΑΤΟΣ

Fig. 907 (doubtful) (California)

PLATO

Fig. 908   **10** (Berlin)

PLATO

Figs. 909–911

2 (Vatican)

Figs. 912–914

3 (Vatica

PLATO

Figs. 915–917

I (Vatican)

PLATO

Figs. 918–920   **5** (Capitoline Museum)

Figs. 921–923   **9** (Syracuse

Figs. 924–925   **11** (Berlin)   Fig. 926   **4** (Terme Museum

PLATO

Figs. 927–929
15 (Holkham Hall)

Figs. 930–932
12 (Louvre)

Fig. 933
4 (Terme Museum)
Figs. 934–935
6 (Museo Torlonia)

PLATO

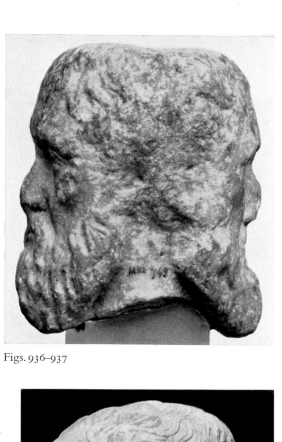

Figs. 936–937   **13** (Louvre)   Fig. 938   **20** (Athens)

Figs. 939–940   **14** (Aix)   Fig. 941   **20** (Athens)

Figs. 942–944   **18** (Boehringer)

PLATO

PLATO

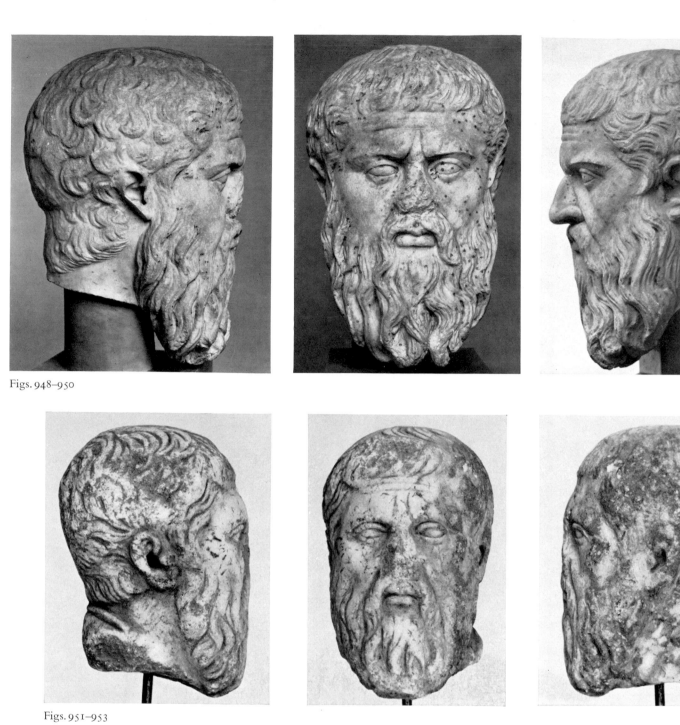

Figs. 948–950

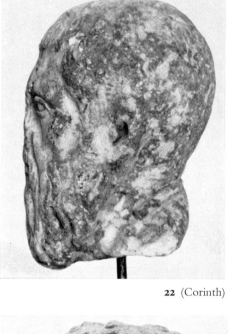

Figs. 951–953

Figs. 954–956

19 (Basel)

PLATO

Figs. 957–959

Fig. 960   Reconstruction   Fig. 961   (Memphis?)

PLATO

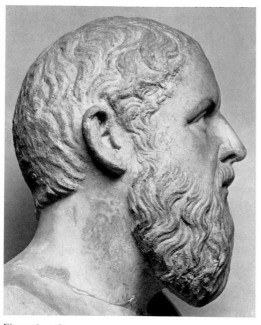

Figs. 962–963　　　　　　　　　　　　　　　　　　　6★ (Vatican)　　Fig. 964　　　　　　　　　　7★ (stolen)

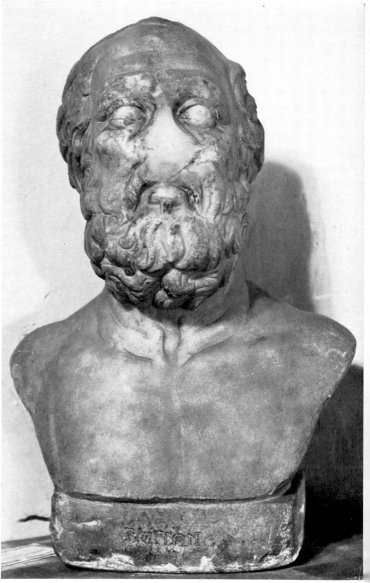

Fig. 965　　　　　　　　　　　　5★ (Athens)　　Fig. 966　　　　　　　　　10★ (Palazzo Riccardi)

PLATO (?)

2★ (Athens)

ig. 970 2★ (Athens) Figs. 971–972 8★ (Thasos)

Figs. 973–975 3★ (Berlin)

PLATO (?)

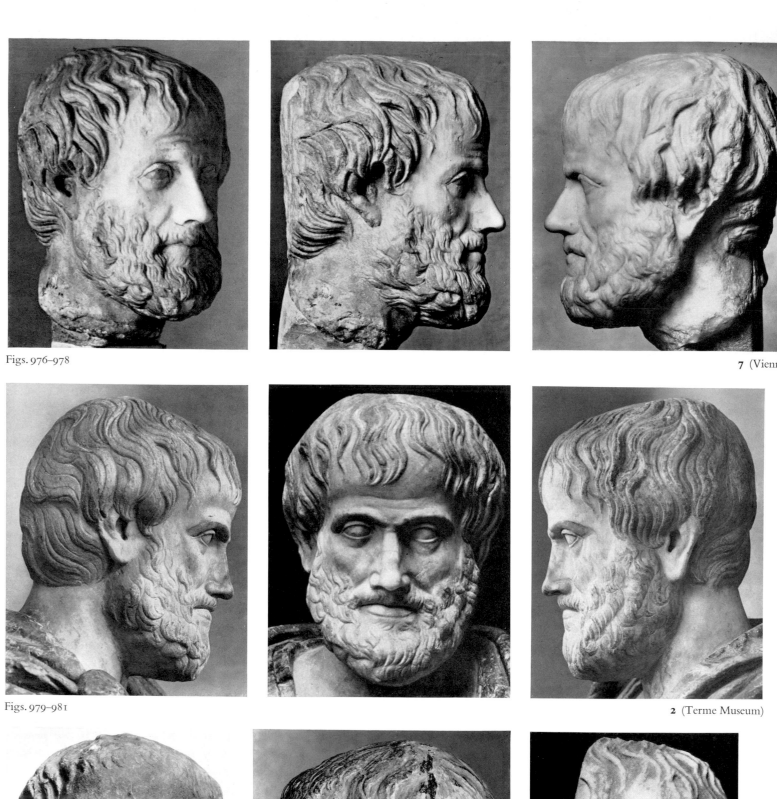

Figs. 976–978

Figs. 979–981

2 (Terme Museum)

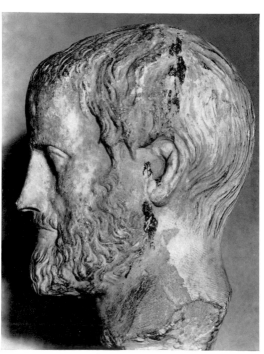

Figs. 982–983

Fig. 984

18 (lost)

1 (Terme Museum)

ARISTOTLE

Fig. 985

ARISTOTLE

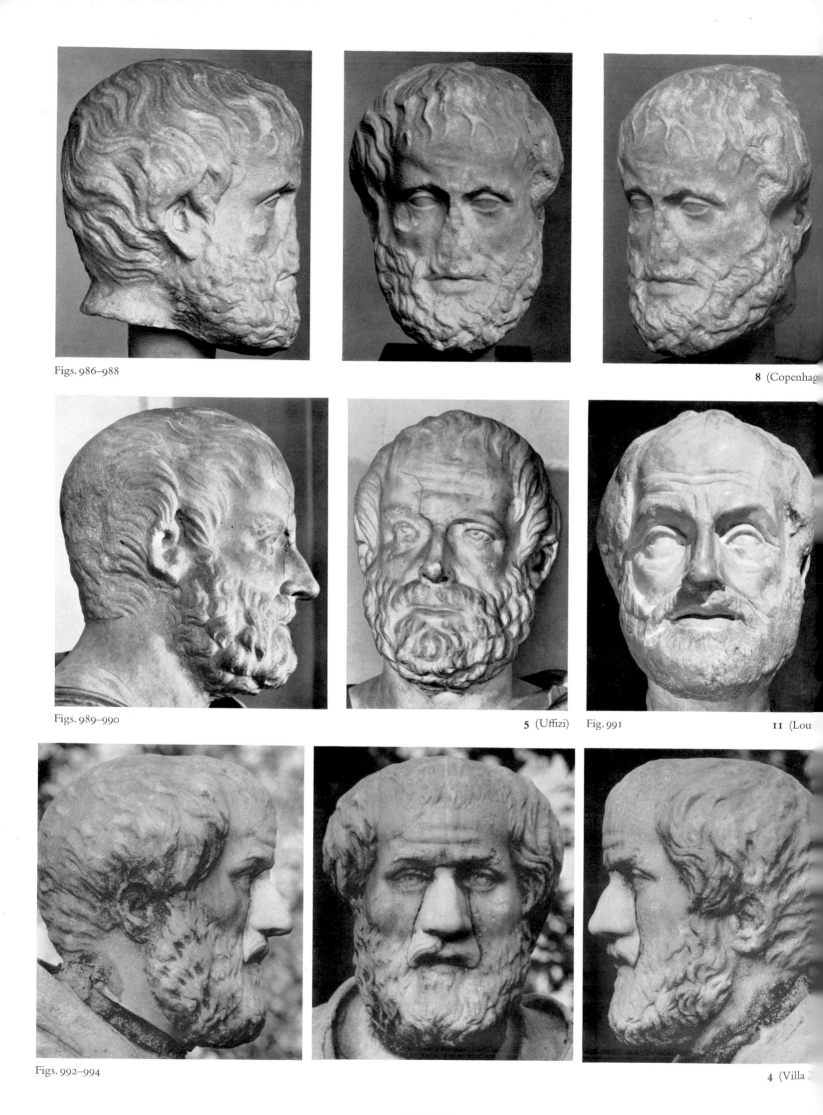

Figs. 986–988

Figs. 989–990

5 (Uffizi)   Fig. 991   II (Lou

Figs. 992–994

4 (Villa

ARISTOTLE

Figs. 995–997   **9** (Oslo)

998   **11** (Louvre)   Figs. 999–1000   **12** (Bibliothèque Mazarine)

Fig. 1001   **13** (Marseille)   Figs. 1002–1003   **6** (Palermo)

ARISTOTLE

Figs. 1004–1005

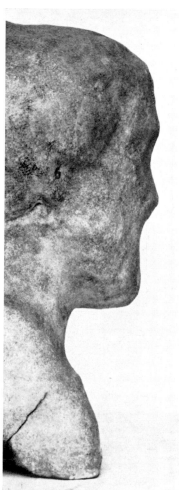
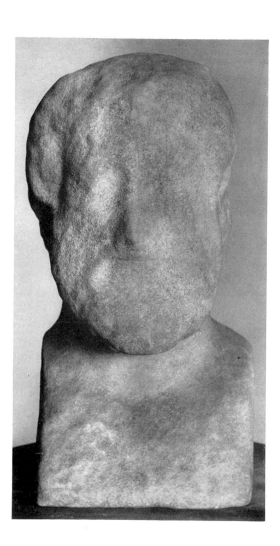
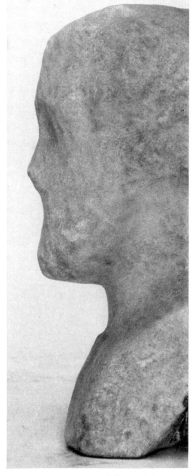

Figs. 1006–1008

ARISTOTLE

igs. 1009–1010   16–17 (Athens)   Fig. 1011   (Baalbek)

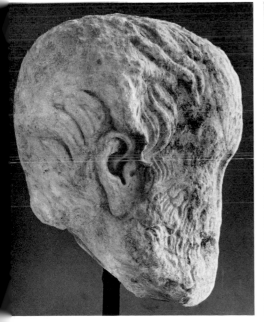

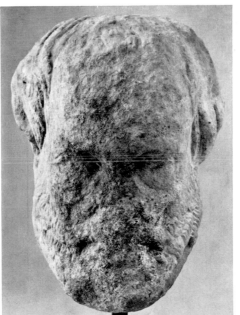

igs. 1012–1013   15 (Athens)

Fig. 1013 a   (Arndt coll.)   Fig. 1013 b   (British Museum)   Fig. 1014   (Athens)

ARISTOTLE

Figs. 1015–1017 (with Arete) (tentative identification)

(Berlin)

Fig. 1019 (modern) (British Museum)

Fig. 1020 (Palazzo Spad)

Fig. 1018 (Palazzo Spada)

Fig. 1021 (Vatican)

ARISTIPPOS (Figs. 1015–1020) · ARCHYTAS

Fig. 1023   **1** (Villa Albani)

Fig. 1022   **1** (Villa Albani)   Fig. 1024   **3** (Museo Torlonia)

s. 1025–1027   **4** (Vatican)

THEOPHRASTOS

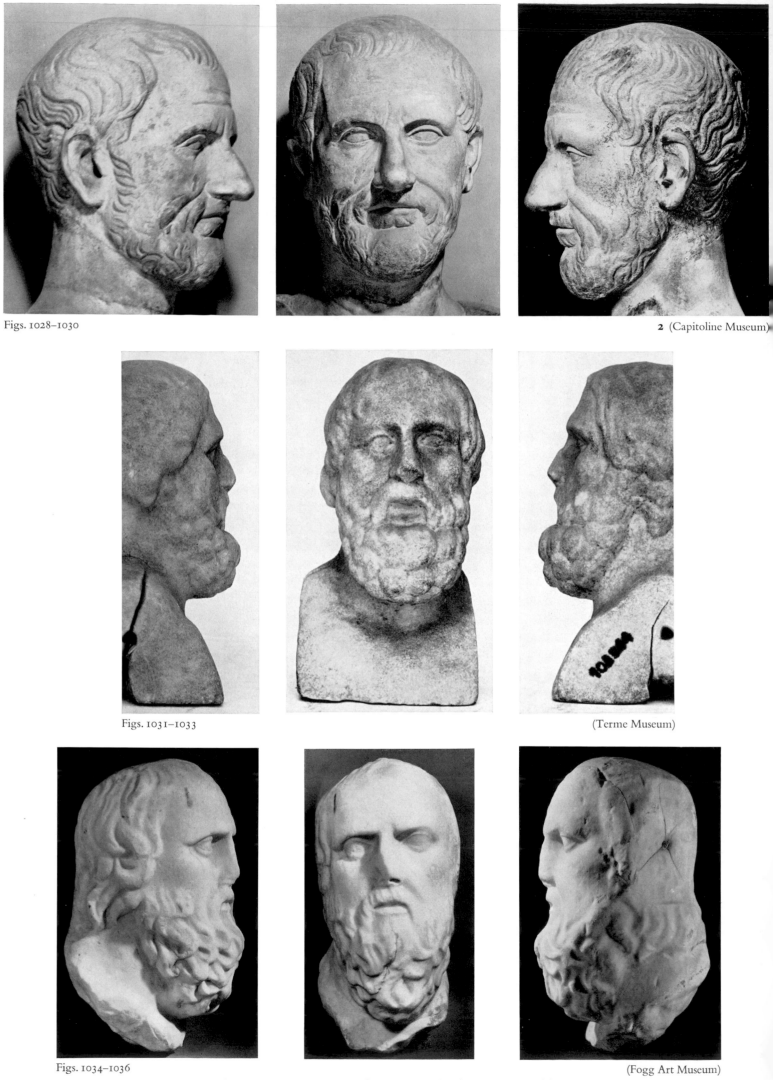

Figs. 1028–1030

2 (Capitoline Museum)

Figs. 1031–1033

(Terme Museum)

Figs. 1034–1036

(Fogg Art Museum)

THEOPHRASTOS (Figs. 1028–1030) · LYKON (?)

Figs. 1037–1039

1 (Vatican)

ANTISTHENES

Figs. 1040–1042

Figs. 1043–1045

Figs. 1046–1048

ANTISTHENES

Figs. 1049–1051

6 (British Museum)

1052   **7** (Sion House)   Fig. 1053   **4** (Villa Doria Pamphili)

1054–1055   **7** (Sion House)   Fig. 1056 (tentative identification)   (Naples)

ANTISTHENES

Fig. 1057   **2** (Villa Albani)

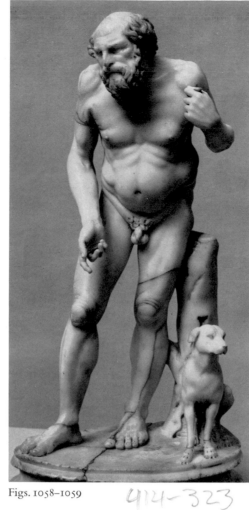

Figs. 1058–1059

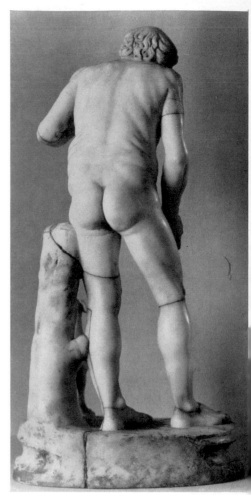

3 (New York)

414-323

Fig. 1060   **4** (Vatican)

Fig. 1061   **3** (ex Amelung)

Fig. 1062   **1** (Vatican)

Fig. 1063   **f** (Berlin)

DIOGENES

Figs. 1064–1065   **5** (Aix)   Fig. 1066   **h** (Cologne)

Fig. 1067   **a** (Villa Albani)

Fig. 1068   **d** (Thorwaldsen Museum)   Fig. 1069   **e** (Leningrad)   Fig. 1070   **f** (Berlin)

DIOGENES

Fig. 1071 (Capitoline Museum) Fig. 1072 (Fiamingo Collection) Fig. 1073 (Paris, Bibliothèque Nationale)

Fig. 1074 (Capitoline Museum) Fig. 1075 (Munich)

MENIPPOS (Figs. 1071–1072, 1074–1075) · MENEDEMOS

Figs. 1076–1078   (Vatican)

Fig. 1080   (Louvre)

Fig. 1079   (Terme Museum)

Figs. 1081–1082 (modern?)   (Cabinet des Médailles)   Fig. 1083   (Naples)

KRATES? (Figs. 1076–1080, 1083) · ANAXARCHOS

Figs. 1084–1085   **I** (Naples)

Figs. 1086–1088   **2** (Naple

ZENON

Fig. 1089   1 (Naples)

Figs. 1090–1091   4 (Louvre)

ZENON

ZENON

ZENON

Fig. 1098   **7** (Miss Martin)   Figs. 1099–1100   **6** (Aix)

Figs. 1101–1103   **9** (Athens)

Figs. 1104–1105   **5** (Musée Rodin)

ZENON

Fig. 1106   (British Museum)

Fig. 1107   I (Vatican)

Fig. 1108   4 (New York)

KLEANTHES (?)

Fig. 1109   **3** (Dresden)

Fig. 1110   **2** (Museo Barracc

KLEANTHES (?)

Figs. 1111–1112

2 (Capitoline Museum)

Figs. 1113–1114

4 (Villa Albani)

CHRYSIPPOS

Figs. 1115–1117

8 (Naples)

CHRYSIPPOS

CHRYSIPPOS

Figs. 1121–1122   1 (Vatican)   Fig. 1123   7 (U

Figs. 1124–1125   3 (Capitoline Museum)   Fig. 1126   7 (U

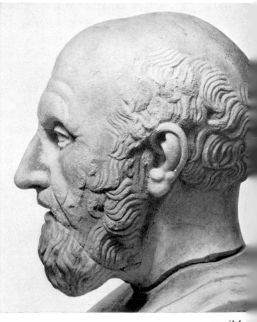

Figs. 1127–1129   12 (Mu

CHRYSIPPOS

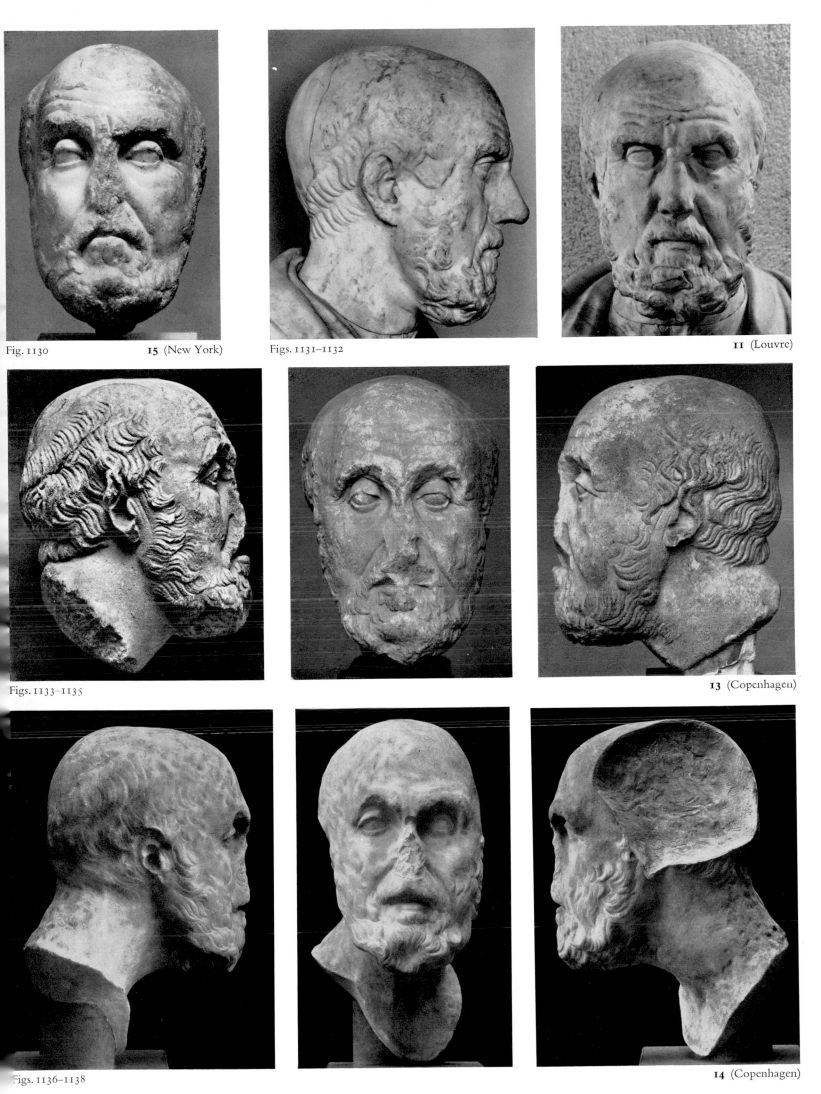

Fig. 1130   **15** (New York)   Figs. 1131–1132   **11** (Louvre)

Figs. 1133–1135   **13** (Copenhagen)

Figs. 1136–1138   **14** (Copenhagen)

CHRYSIPPOS

Figs. 1139–1141

Figs. 1142–1143

CHRYSIPPOS

Fig. 1144   **17** (Louvre)

Fig. 1145   (Athens)

Fig. 1146   **16** (Athens)

Fig. 1147   coin of Soloi

Fig. 1148   gem (Cambridge, Corpus Christi College)

CHRYSIPPOS (Figs. 1144, 1146, 1147)

Figs. 1149–1150

1 (Capitoline Museum)

Figs. 1151–1152

2 (Capitoline Museum)

EPIKOUROS

Fig. 1153   I (Capitoline Museum)

EPIKOUROS

Figs. 1154–1156

5 (Vatic

Figs. 1157–1159

4 (Vatican)

Fig. 1160   **3** (Capitoline Museum)   Fig. 1161   **6** (Villa Albani)   Figs. 1162–1163   (trade

EPIKOUROS

Fig. 1164   **7** (Museo Barracco)

Figs. 1165–1166   **13** (Ravenna)

EPIKOUROS

Figs. 1167–1168   10 (Naples)

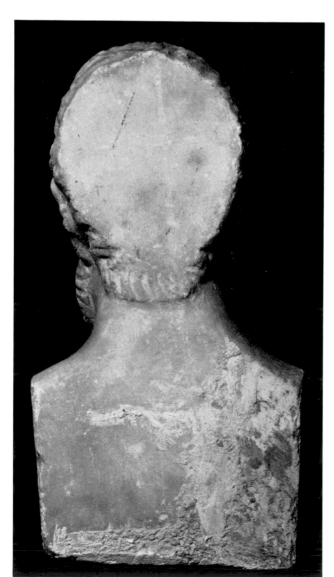

Figs. 1169–1170   11 (Naples)

EPIKOUROS

Figs. 1171–1172   **10** (Naples)

Figs. 1173–1174   **11** (Naples)

EPIKOUROS

Figs. 1175–1177

Figs. 1178–1179

EPIKOUROS

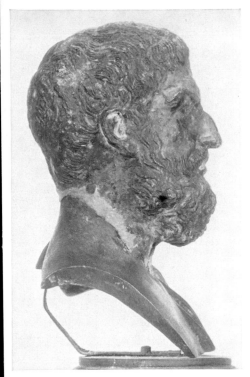

Figs. 1180–1182   **9** (Naples)

s. 1183–1185   **16** (Louvre)

EPIKOUROS

Figs. 1186–1188   17 (Louvre)

Figs. 1189–1191   18 (Louvre)

Figs. 1192–1194   19 (British Museum)

EPIKOUROS

Figs. 1195-1196

20 (British Museum)

. 1197   20 (British Museum)   Figs. 1198-1199   24 (Berlin)

EPIKOUROS

Figs. 1200–1203

28 (New York)

Figs. 1205–1206

22 (Copenhagen)

Fig. 1204

25 (Munich)

EPIKOUROS

Fig. 1207-1209   **29** (Istanbul)

Fig. 1210   **23** (Copenhagen)

Fig. 1211 (doubtful)   (Madrid)

EPIKOUROS

Figs. 1212–1213 (head alien)

1 (Rome, U.S. Embassy)

Figs. 1214–1215

2 (Florence)

EPIKOUROS

Figs. 1216–1217 (head alien)

3 (Ince Blundell collection)

Figs. 1218–1219

5 (Athens)

EPIKOUROS

Fig. 1220   (New York)
(tentative identification)

Figs. 1221–1222   **a, b** (British Museum)

Fig. 1223   (Northwick Park)
(tentative identification)

Figs. 1224–1225   **26** (Athens)

Fig. 1226   **5** (Naples)

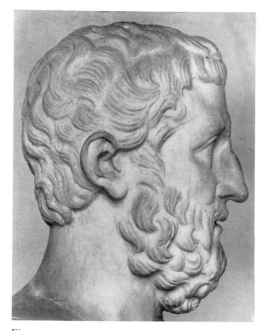

Figs. 1227–1229   **3** (Vatican)

EPIKOUROS (Figs. 1220–1225) · METRODOROS

Figs. 1230–1232   1 (Capitoline Museum)

METRODOROS

Figs. 1233–1234

2 (Capitoline Museum)

Fig. 1235

2 (Capitoline Museum)

Fig. 1236

7 (Louvre)

METRODOROS

Figs. 1237–1239

8 (British Museum)

Figs. 1240–1241

7 (Louvre)

Fig. 1242

4 (Museo Torlonia)

Fig. 1243

6 (Aranjuez)

Figs. 1244–1245

9 (Wilton House)

METRODOROS

Figs. 1246–1247   10 (Berlin)   Fig. 1248   13 (Giessen)

Figs. 1249–1250   14 (Copenhagen)   Fig. 1251   12 (Munich)

Figs. 1252–1253   11 (Castle Erbach)   Fig. 1254   12 (Munich)

METRODOROS

Figs. 1255–1256

16 (Athens)

Fig. 1257   **16** (Athens)   Fig. 1258 (with restorations)   **1** (Copenhagen)

METRODOROS

Figs. 1259–1260

Figs. 1261–1262 (head alien)

METRODOROS

Figs. 1263–1264 (head alien)

3 (Newby Hall)

ig. 1265 (head alien)   **2** (Naples)   Figs. 1266–1267 (head alien)   **3** (Newby Hall)

METRODOROS

Figs. 1268–1270

I (Vatican)

Figs. 1271–1273

3 (Capitoline Museum)

Figs. 1274–1275

4 (Terme Museum)

HERMARCHOS

Fig. 1276   2 (Vatican)

Figs. 1277–1278   5 (Villa Albani)

Fig. 1279   2 (Vatican)

Figs. 1280–1281

8 (Formerly Lateran, now Vatican)

igs. 1282–1284

11 (Naples)

HERMARCHOS

Figs. 1285–1287   6 (Palazzo Gaetani

Figs. 1288–1290   7 (Rome, American Academy

HERMARCHOS

HERMARCHOS

Figs. 1297–1299

13 (Palerm

Figs. 1300–1302

14 (Copenhagen)

Figs. 1303–1305

15 (British Museum

HERMARCHOS

Figs. 1306–1309   **16** (Budapest)

HERMARCHOS

Figs. 1310–1312   17 (Madrid)

Figs. 1313–1315   18 (Alexandria)

Figs. 1316–1318   20 (art market?)

HERMARCHOS

Fig. 1321 (Paris)
(tentative identification)

Figs. 1319–1320 (Florence)

Figs. 1322–1324 (Ostia)

HERMARCHOS

Figs. 1325–1326

1 (Capitoline Museum)

Figs. 1327–1329

3 (Venice)

KOLOTES (?)

Fig. 1330   8 (Apollonia)

Figs. 1331–1332   4 (Madrid)

KOLOTES (?)

Figs. 1333–1335   5 (Kassel)

Fig. 1336   2 (private coll.)

Figs. 1337–1338   7 (Munich)   Fig. 1339   6 (lost)

KOLOTES (?)

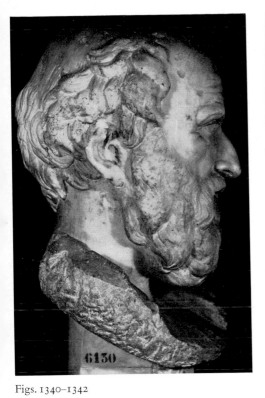

Figs. 1340–1342   **1** (Naples)

s. 1343–1345   **2** (Capitoline Museum)

LYSIAS

Figs. 1346–1347

1 (Villa Albani)

Figs. 1348–1349 (tentative identification)

2 (Berlin)

ISOKRATES

Figs. 1350–1351

Figs. 1352–1354

2 (Florence)

HYPEREIDES

Figs. 1355–1357

3 (Compiègn

Figs. 1358–1359

4 (Copenhagen)

Figs. 1360–1361

6 (Vienna)

HYPEREIDES

igs. 1362–1364 **5** (Copenhagen)

ig. 1365 (Athens)

Fig. 1367 (Louvre)
(tentative identification)

g. 1366 (Athens)

HYPEREIDES (Figs. 1362–1364) AND LYKOURGOS

Fig. 1368 Hypereides (?)   (Naples)

Fig. 1369 Aischines   **6** (Naples)

390-314

HYPEREIDES (?) AND AISCHINES

Figs. 1370–1371   6 (Naples)   Fig. 1372   I (Vatican)

Figs. 1373–1374   I (Vatican)

AISCHINES

Fig. 1376   **9** (Leningrad)

Fig. 1375   **7** (British Museum)

Fig. 1377 (probable identification)   lost emblema

Figs. 1378–1379   **7** (British Museum)

AISCHINES

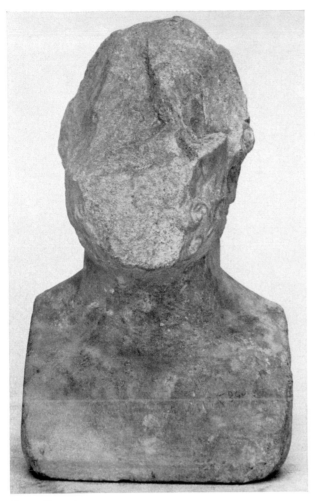

Figs. 1380–1381

3 (Terme Museum)

Fig. 1382 (tentative identification) (Villa Doria Pamphili)

Fig. 1383 (Villa Doria Pamphili)

AISCHINES

Fig. 1384   **2** (Capitoline Museum)   Fig. 1385   **8** (Copenhagen)

Figs. 1386–1387   **8** (Copenhagen)

AISCHINES

AISCHINES

Fig. 1397   **1** (Vatican)

Fig. 1398   **32** (Copenhagen)

DEMOSTHENES

DEMOSTHENES

Figs. 1401–1402   **32** (Copenhagen)   Fig. 1403   **9** (Villa Doria Pamphili)

Figs. 1404–1406   **I** (Vatican

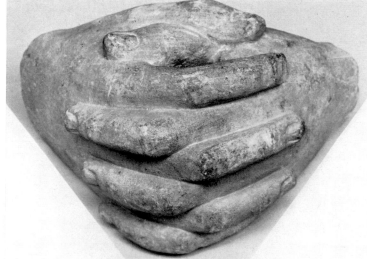

Fig. 1407   (Vatican)

Fig. 1408   (Vatican

DEMOSTHENES

Fig. 1409

9 (Villa Doria Pamphili)

DEMOSTHENES

1555

DEMOSTHENES

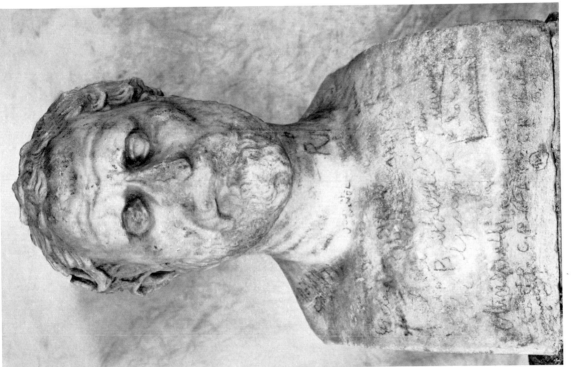

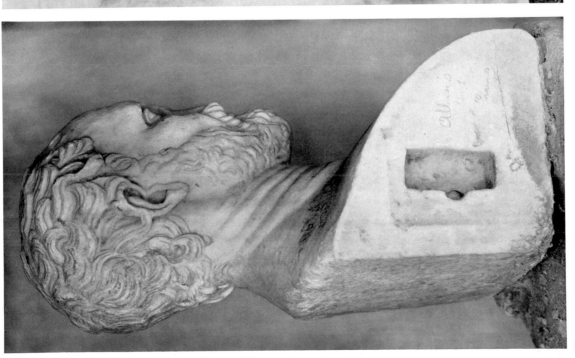

DEMOSTHENES

Figs. 1413–1415

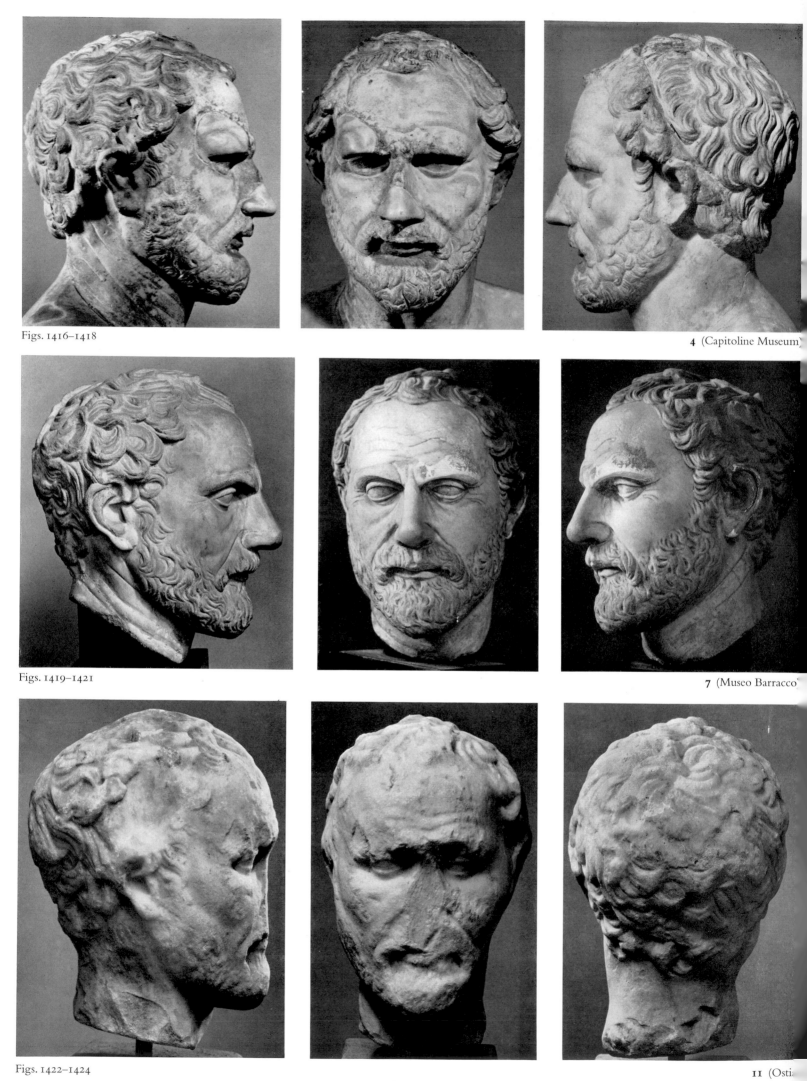

Figs. 1416–1418

4 (Capitoline Museum)

Figs. 1419–1421

7 (Museo Barracco)

Figs. 1422–1424

11 (Osti

DEMOSTHENES

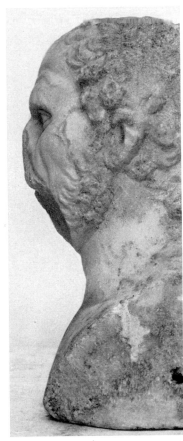

Figs. 1425–1427

6 (Terme Museum)

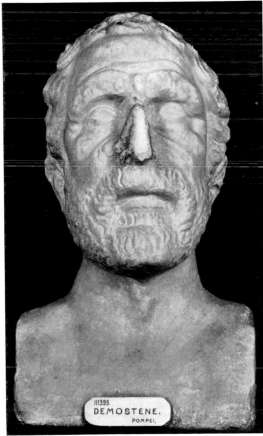

Fig. 1428

15 (Naples)

Fig. 1429

20 (Turin)

DEMOSTHENES

Fig. 1430   2 (Vatican)   Fig. 1431   5 (Terme Museum)

Fig. 1432   17 (Uffizi)   Fig. 1434   19 (Uffiz

Fig. 1433   18 (Uffizi)

Fig. 1435   21 (Louvre)   Figs. 1436–1437   25 (Tou

DEMOSTHENES

DEMOSTHENES

Figs. 1444–1446

22 (Louvre)

DEMOSTHENES

Figs. 1447–1449   **23** (Louvre)

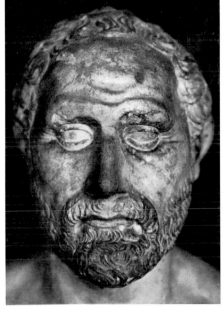

Figs. 1450–1452   **24** (Louvre)

. 1453–1455   **26** (British Museum)

DEMOSTHENES

Figs. 1456–1457   30 (Liverpool)

Figs. 1458–1460   28 (Brocklesby Park)

Figs. 1461–1463   29 (Northwick Pa

DEMOSTHENES

DEMOSTHENES

Figs. 1468–1470   **47** (Princeton)

Figs. 1471–1472   **33** (Copenhagen)

Figs. 1473–1475   **39** (Lenir

DEMOSTHENES

Figs. 1476–1477

36 (Munich)

Fig. 1478   **35** (Berlin)

Figs. 1479–1480

43 (Athens)

Fig. 1481   **36** (Munich)

DEMOSTHENES

Figs. 1482–1484

40 (Madrid)

DEMOSTHENES

Figs. 1485–1488

46 (Cyrene)

DEMOSTHENES

Figs. 1489–1490   **41** (Athens)

Figs. 1491–1493   **42** (Athens)

Fig. 1494   **b** (Agora)

Fig. 1495   **45** (Athens)

DEMOSTHENES

Figs. 1496–1497   37 (lost)

Fig. 1498   44 (Athens)

Figs. 1499–1500 (doubtful)   12★ (Geneva)

DEMOSTHENES

Figs. 1501–1502

11* (Ostia)

Fig. 1503 ringstone **d** (lost)

Fig. 1504
amethyst ringstone
c (private collection)

Fig. 1505 glass ringstone (Berlin)

Fig. 1506
amethyst ringstone
c (private collection)

Fig. 1507 sard ringstone
(British Museum)

Fig. 1508 carnelian ringstone
(Leningrad)

Fig. 1509 silver emblema
a (Berlin)

Fig. 1510 contorniate
f (Paris)

Figs. 1511–1512

(ex. Mrs. H. Straus, New York)

Fig. 1513

(Dublin)

DEMOSTHENES (Figs. 1501, 1502, 1505, 1507, 1508, 1511–1513 are problematical)

Fig. 1514   **8** (Princeton)

Fig. 1515   **7** (Pompeii)

Fig. 1516   **6** (Trier)

Fig. 1517   **10** (Mytilene)

Figs. 1519–1520   (Athens)

Fig. 1518   (Athens)   Fig. 1521   (Eretria)

MENANDER

Figs. 1522–1523   **3** (once Smyrna)

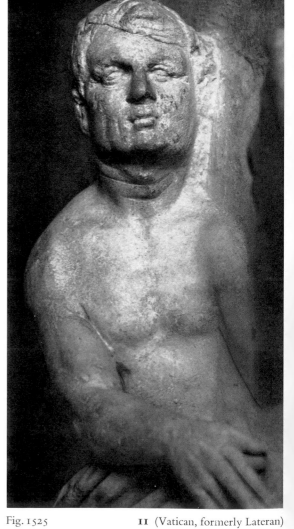

Fig. 1524   (Berlin)   Fig. 1525   **11** (Vatican, formerly Lateran)

MENANDER

Fig. 1526
12 (Princeton)

Fig. 1527
11 (Vatican, formerly Lateran)

MENANDER

Figs. 1528–1530

2 (formerly Marbury Hall)

MENANDER

Figs. 1531–1532

5 (Alexandria)

Figs. 1533–1535

1 (Vatican)

Figs. 1536–1538

2 (Vatican)

MENANDER

Figs. 1539–1540   3 (Vatican)   Fig. 1541   10 (Galleria Borghe

Figs. 1542–1544   4 (Terme Mus

Figs. 1545–1547   5 (Terme Museum)

MENANDER

Figs. 1548–1549

7 (Terme Museum)

ig. 1550   6 (Terme Museum)   Figs. 1551–1552   8 (Villa Albani)

MENANDER

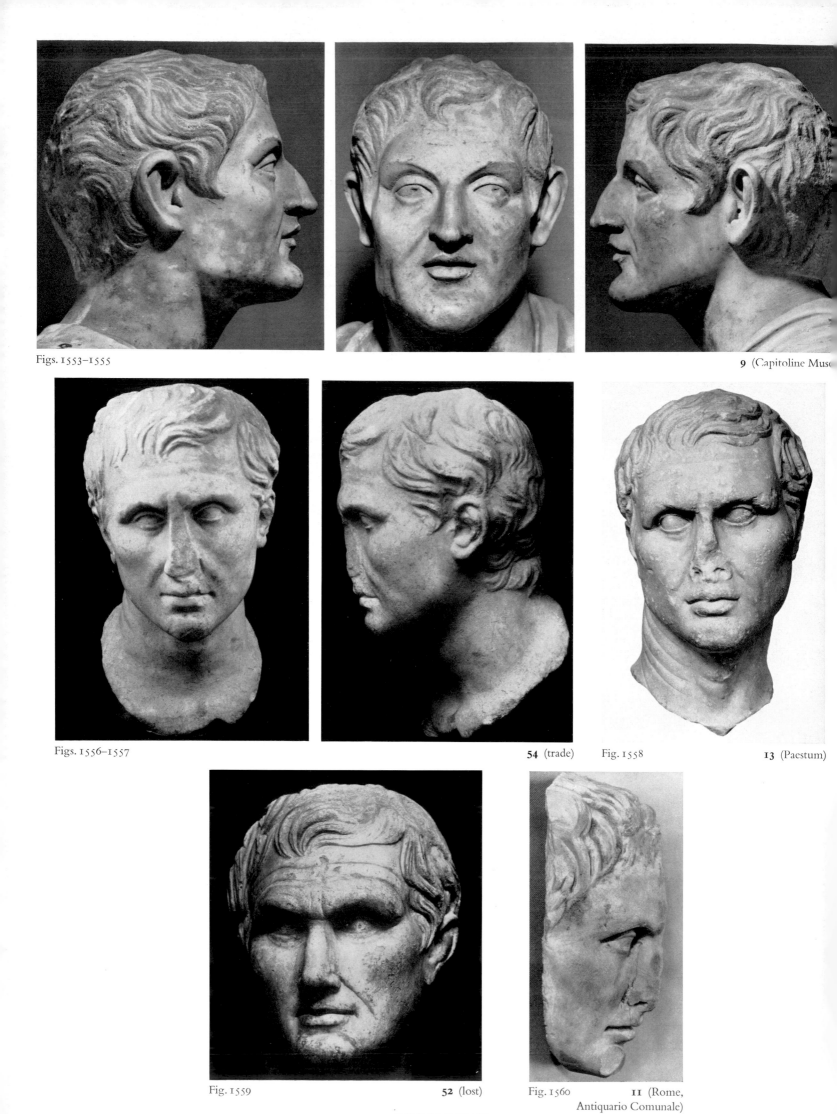

Figs. 1553–1555

9 (Capitoline Muse[um])

Figs. 1556–1557

54 (trade)

Fig. 1558

13 (Paestum)

Fig. 1559

52 (lost)

Fig. 1560

11 (Rome,
Antiquario Comunale)

MENANDER

Figs. 1562–1563   14 (Pompeii)

ig. 1561   14 (Pompeii)   Figs. 1564–1565   17 (Verona)

ig. 1566   16 (Uffizi)   Figs. 1567–1568   24 (Gerzensee)

MENANDER

MENANDER

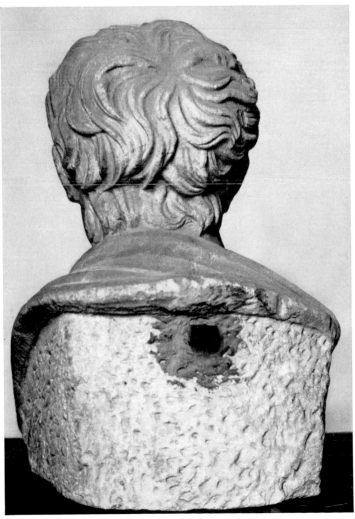

Figs. 1573–1576

MENANDER

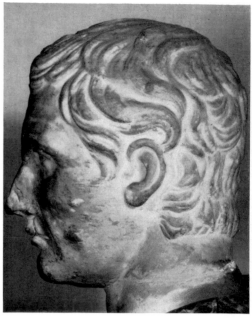

Figs. 1577–1579   **23** (Geneva)

Figs. 1580–1582   **18** (Bonn)

MENANDER

Figs. 1583–1584   19 (Dresden)   Fig. 1585   28 (Ince Blundell)

Figs. 1586–1587   20 (Castle Erbach)   Fig. 1588   27 (Ince Blundell)

Figs. 1589–1590   35 (Copenhagen)   Fig. 1591   30 (Wilton House)

MENANDER

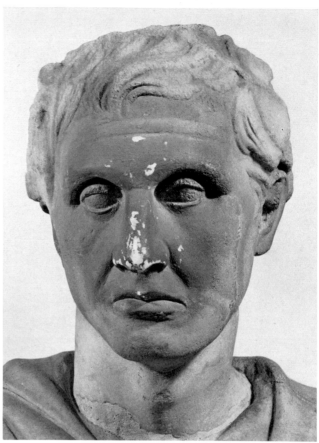

MENANDER

MENANDER

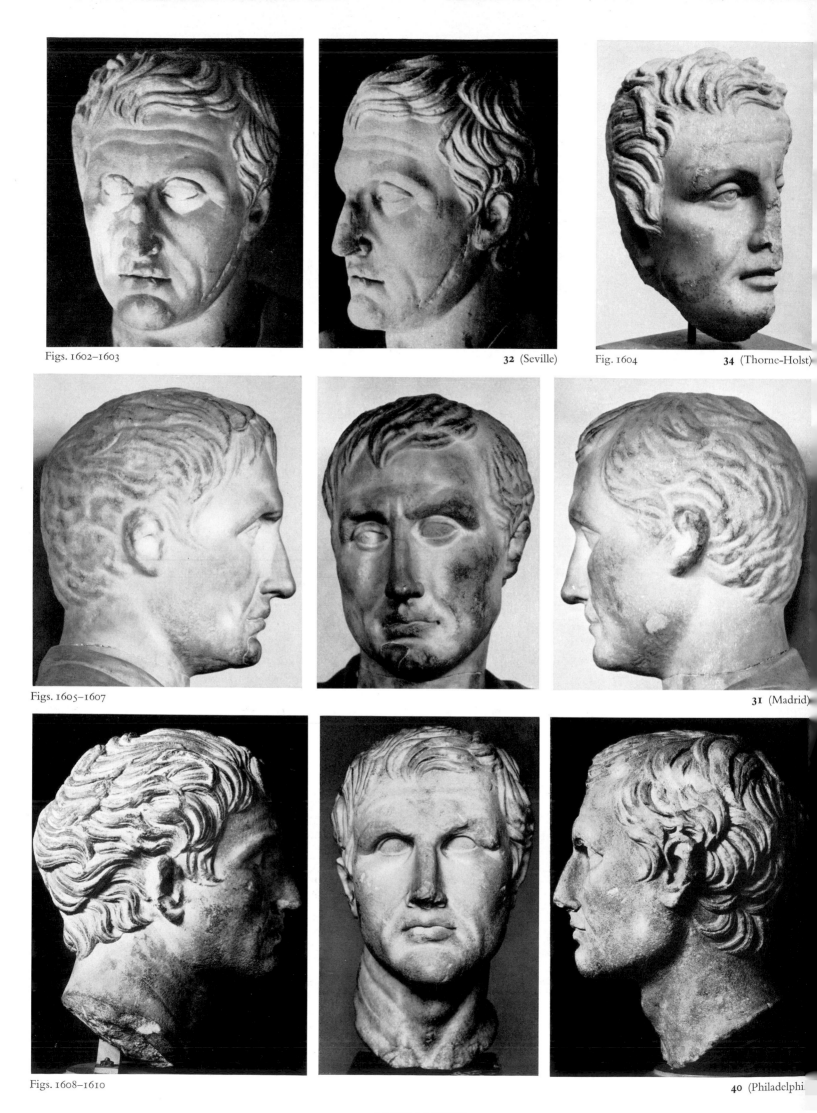

Figs. 1602–1603   **32** (Seville)   Fig. 1604   **34** (Thorne-Holst)

Figs. 1605–1607   **31** (Madrid)

Figs. 1608–1610   **40** (Philadelphi

MENANDER

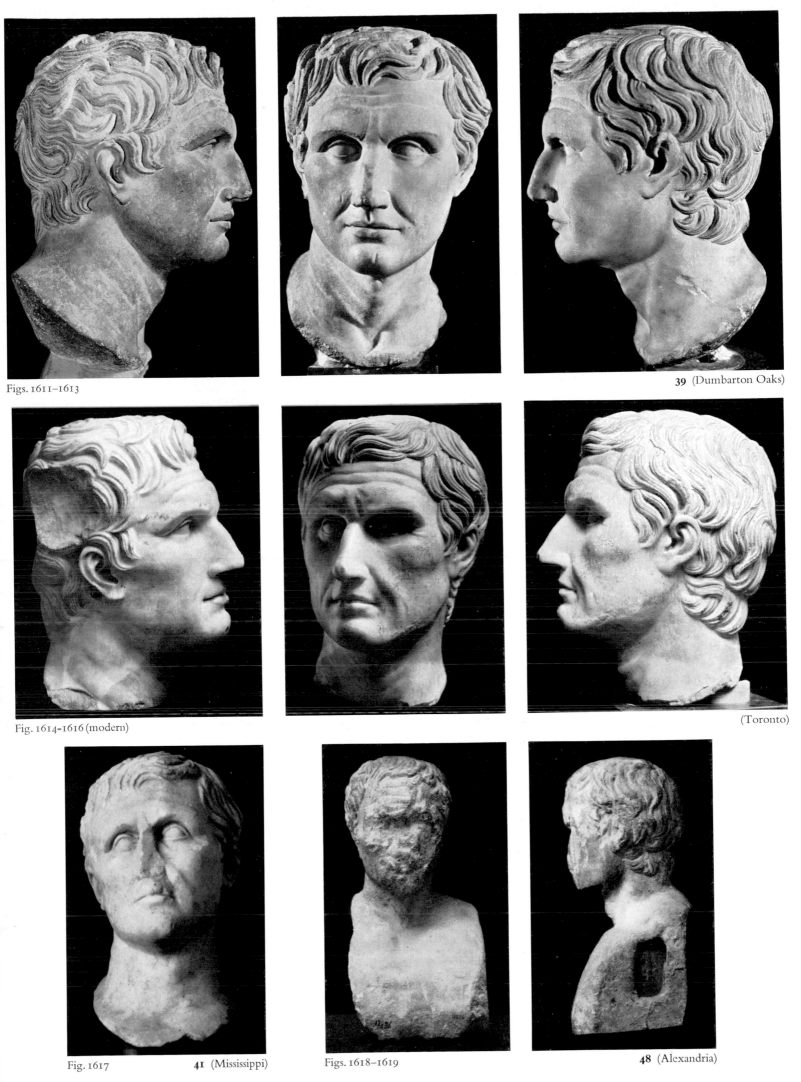

Figs. 1611–1613

39 (Dumbarton Oaks)

Fig. 1614–1616 (modern)

(Toronto)

Fig. 1617   **41** (Mississippi)   Figs. 1618–1619   **48** (Alexandria)

MENANDER

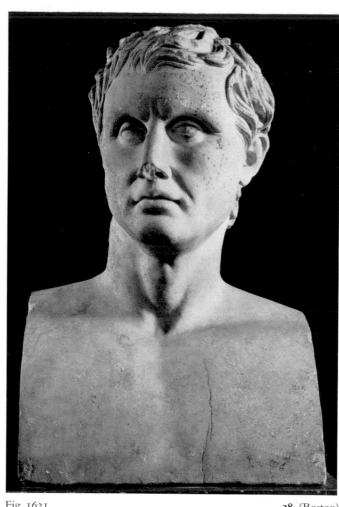

Fig. 1620   **33** (Hoff, Oslo)   Fig. 1621   **38** (Boston)

Figs. 1622–1623   **38** (Boston)

MENANDER

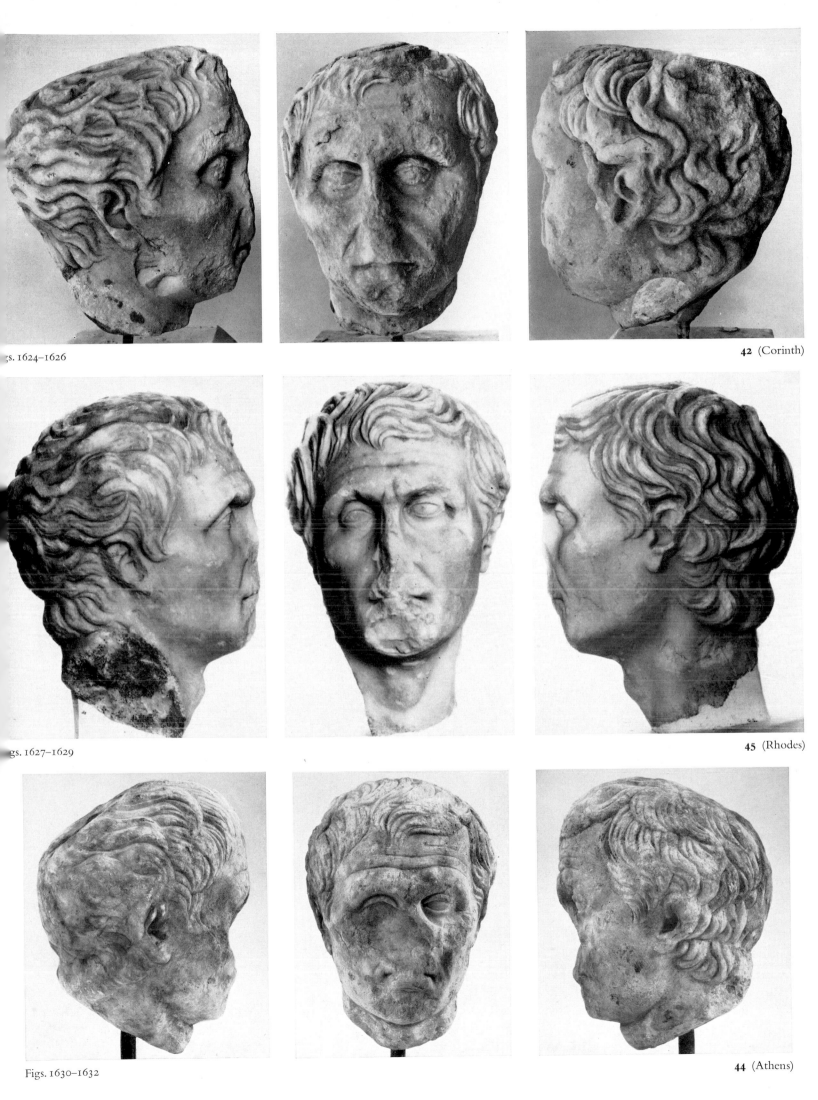

gs. 1624–1626

42 (Corinth)

gs. 1627–1629

45 (Rhodes)

Figs. 1630–1632

44 (Athens)

MENANDER

Figs. 1633–1635

Fig. 1636

Fig. 1637

MENANDER

MENANDER (?) (Figs. 1638–1643) and DIPHILOS (?) (Figs. 1644–1646)

Fig. 1647

(Vatican)

POSEIDIPPOS

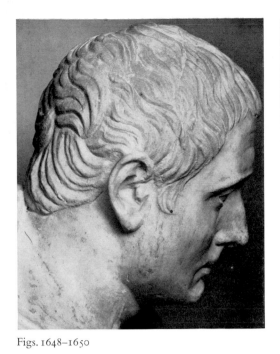

Figs. 1648–1650

(Vatican)

Fig. 1651 coin of Soloi

Fig. 1652 (hypothetical)
lapis lazuli (Cambridge)

a

b

Figs. 1653–1654   (coins of Soloi)

Fig. 1655

(Villa Albani)

POSEIDIPPOS (Figs. 1648–1650) · PHILEMON (?) (Fig. 1651) · ARATOS (Figs. 1652–1655)

Fig. 1656   **c** (Trier)

Fig. 1657   **d** (Madrid)

Figs. 1658–1659

e (Athens, Benaki)

Fig. 1660 (tentative identification)   (Bibliothèque Nationale)

Fig. 1661   (Bibliothèque Nationale)

ARATOS (Figs. 1656–1660) and THEOKRITOS (?) (Fig.1661)

Fig. 1662 (Bibliothèque Nationale)

Fig. 1663 (tentative identification)　　　　　　　　　　(Leningrad)

Figs. 1664–1665 (with Kassandra?)

(Cabinet des Médailles)

THEOKRITOS (Figs. 1662–1663) and LYKOPHRON (?) (Figs. 1664–1665)

Figs. 1666–1667 (head alien)

I (Naples)

Fig. 1668 (head alien)　　2 (Terme Museum)

Fig. 1669 (with Roman portrait head) 2 (Capitoline Museum)

MOSCHION

Figs. 1670–1672 (Florence)

Fig. 1673 (cast) (formerly Berlin)

Fig. 1674 (Mazeika)

APOLLONIOS RHODIOS (?) (Figs. 1670–1672) and POLYBIOS (?) (Figs. 1673–1674)

Fig. 1676 Aristomachos (?)
(lost)

Figs. 1677–1678 Hipparchos

coins of Nikaia

Fig. 1675 Satyros (?)   (Athens)

Fig. 1679 Eudoxos   (Budapest)

Fig. 1680 'Karneades'   (New York)

Fig. 1681 Base of statue of Karneades   (Agora Museum)

SATYROS (?) (Fig. 1675) · ARISTOMACHOS (?) (Fig. 1676) · HIPPARCHOS (Figs. 1677–1678) · EUDOXOS (Fig. 1679)
and KARNEADES (Fig. 1681)

Fig. 1682   **1 b** (cast, Ravenna)

Fig. 1683   **1 b** (cast, Ravenna)

Fig. 1684   **1 b** (cast, Ravenna)

gs. 1685–1686

6 (Aranjuez)

Fig. 1687   **2** (Holkham Hall)

Fig. 1688   **1 a** (cast, Copenhagen)

KARNEADES

Figs. 1689–1692

KARNEADES

Fig. 1693   **3** (Ravenna)

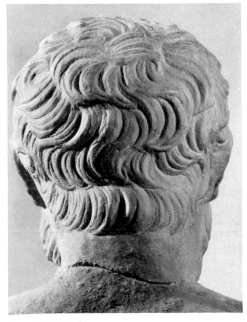  

Figs. 1694–1696   **3** (Ravenna)

KARNEADES

Fig. 1697 Moschion

Fig. 1698 Zenon and Epikouros

Fig. 1199 Anonymous

Fig. 1700 Sophokles

SILVER CUPS FROM BOSCOREALE, NOW IN THE LOUVRE

Fig. 1701 Anonymous

Fig. 1702 Menander and Archilochos

Fig. 1703 Euripides

Fig. 1704 Monimos (and Demetrios of Phaleron?)

SILVER CUPS FROM BOSCOREALE, NOW IN THE LOUVRE